SPRING-LOADED

FISH

HOOKS, TRAPS & LURES

Identification and Value Guide

William Blauser

&

Timothy Mierzwa

COLLECTOR BOOKS

A Division of Schroeder Publishing Co., Inc.

Front cover, clockwise from upper left:
Evan's Eagle Claw, $800.00, page 42.
Chicago Spinner, $150.00, page 218.
Weed Queen, $200.00+, page 238.
Trip Lure, $150.00, page 268.
Weeder Lure, $75.00, page 257.
Cat's Paw, $75.00, page 253.
E-Z Way Lure, $750.00, page 226.
Spring, Snap and Catch 'Em Hook, $65.00, page 32.

Back cover, left to right:
Sockdolager (top), $400.00, page 20.
"Old Glory" (bottom), $1,000.00+, page 67.
Hartshorn, $750.00+, page 106.
Guillotine, $400.00, page 64.
Monarch Fish Hook, $30.00, page 82.

Cover design by Beth Summers
Book design by Allan Ramsey

COLLECTOR BOOKS
P.O. Box 3009
Paducah, Kentucky 42002-3009

www.collectorbooks.com

Copyright © 2006 William Blauser & Timothy Mierzwa

The current values in this book should be used only as a guide. They are not
intended to set prices, which vary from one section of the country to another.
Auction prices as well as dealer prices vary greatly and are affected by condition as well as demand. Neither the authors nor the publisher assumes responsi-
bility for any losses that might be incurred as a result of consulting this guide.

Searching For A Publisher?

We are always looking for people knowledgeable within their fields. If you feel that there is a real need for a book
on your collectible subject and have a large comprehensive collection, contact Collector Books.

Contents

Dedication

This book is dedicated to Web Carey, who pioneered this field of collectibles, and to all of those fishermen who ever missed a bite because they were too slow to set the hook.

Acknowledgments

The authors wish to thank the following people who have contributed, in various ways, to the completion of this book. Some supplied information, others helped with the research, and many provided spring hooks, spring-loaded lures, and fish traps for our collections.

Dan Basore, Warrenville, IL; **Fred and Jeff Bendle**, Bergholz, OH; **Richard F. Blauser**, Parker, PA, for one of his Kentucky rifles; **Henry Caldwell**, Bolton Landing, NY; **Web Carey**, Sidney, OH; **Arlan Carter**, Fall Creek, WI; **Bob Cason**, Florence, KY; **Nick Catrina**, Escalon, CA; **Kerry Chatham**, Guntersville, AL; **Jeffrey Chung**, Royal Oak, MI; **James "Doc" Cirelli**, Greensburg, PA; **Sam Delavan**, Glenwood, IA; **Richard Dennison**, Jackson, MI; **Ralph Dorroh**, Buhl, AL; **Otto Duve II**, Saginaw, MI; **Rick Edmisten**, Studio City, CA; **Jim Fisher**, New Oxford, PA; **Dave Forton**, Mt. Clemons, MI; **James Fleming**, Nashville, TN; **Joseph Frankfurter**, Commerce City, CO; **Harold "Doc" Herr** (deceased), Ephrata, PA; **Walter Hickerson**, Tulsa, OK; **Larry Ignasiak**, Grand Rapids, MI; **Jeff Kieny**, Raymore, MO; **Casimir "Chad" Kotarba**, Farmington Hills, MI; **Tom Langworthy**, Vermillion, SD; **Steve Langert**, Pleasant Valley, NY; **Robert Lucal**, Traverse City, MI; **Joe Littell**, Landrum, SC; **Carl Luckey** (deceased), Killen, AL; **Lee Massey** (deceased), Seattle, WA; **Art McElhinney**, Plum Boro, PA; **Allen McNulty**, Trapper Creek, AK; **Steven Michaan**, Pound Ridge, NY; **Steve Miller**, Jackson, MI; **Tom Minarik**, Tinley Park, IL; **Bob Montgomery**, Clio, MI; **Dean Murphy**, Hartsburg, MO; **Dudley Murphy**, Springfield, MO, for his permission to use photos of the Captor, the Darby, the Cornelius Lie, and the Chautauqua Trolling Hook as appeared in the second edition of his book with co-author **Rick Edmisten**, titled *Fishing Lure Collectibles*, published in 2001 by Collector Books; **Boyd Nedry**, Comstock Park, MI; **Richard Nissley** (deceased), Beverly Hills, MI; **Henry Norris**, Gladstone, MO; **Paul Nohle**, Adams Center, NY; **Dale Nowland**, Plymouth, MI; **Chas Parker**, Tarentum, PA; **Tom & Jane Parr**, Galloway, OH; **Larry Pennell**, Osceola, WI; **Terry Perrigo**, Tupper Lake, NY; **George Richey** (deceased), Honor, MI; **Thomas Richmond**, Jackson, MI; **Roger & Laura Ruginis**, Kalkaska, MI; **Elmer Scherder**, Parker, PA; **John Shoffner**, Fife Lake, MI; **Larry Simpson**, Niles, MI; **Robert Slade**, Muskego, WI; **Tony Smith**, Holland, MI; **Joup Staps**, Tilburg, Holland; **Jim Stewart**, San Ramon, CA; **Don Stone**, Allegan, MI; **Dick Streater**, Mercer Island, WA; **Karl White**, Luther, OK; **Greg Wilcox**, Great Lakes Trader, Williamston, MI; **Clarence Zahn**, Traverse City, MI.

A special thanks to **Jeff Kieny** for all his help with hook and patent research through the years and his constant encouragement and enthusiasm towards this book project.

A special thanks to **Paula Kepich** of the Carnegie Library in Pittsburgh, PA, for all the time and effort she spent helping us with patent research.

Thanks also go to our excellent typist, **Gerry McLean**, Pittsburgh, PA.

Last but not least, I would like to thank my daughter, **Sarah Blauser**, whom I love very much, for being who she is.

Additional signed copies of this book may be ordered from:

Timothy Mierzwa
P.O. Box 1571
Jackson, MI 49201

Please visit our website, www.Springhook.com, for items and information in regards to springhooks. This website will be operational in the near future, until which time books may be ordered only through the mail.

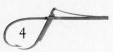

Foreword

Most readers of this book will probably agree that the collection and preservation of historical artifacts is one of the most pleasurable activities an individual can undertake in his or her life. To true collectors and historians, it is the aura and mystique of acquiring past objects and somehow experiencing or sensing their place in history that drives them to collect, not the economic value or investment potential of the pieces. As collectors advance, specialization often occurs. Suddenly, researching and documenting inventors and inventions with a sensitivity towards the historical context in which the objects were used becomes far more important than accumulation. Knowledge expands, networks are created, and relationships are forged, and at some point certain collectors are viewed as experts in their chosen fields.

The vast majority of collectors follow the lead of others and collect what others collect. Some have the financial resources to collect only the rarest and/or highest-condition specimens available in a collecting area using the knowledge shared and documented by the pioneers of their chosen area to guide them. While these collections may evolve to become recognized as the finest in existence, they do not make or advance collecting history — rather, it is the true pioneers, the risk-takers who unearth and mine important areas of a collecting field and tell their stories, that deserve the most credit.

Tim Mierzwa and Bill Blauser are pioneers, historians, and recognized experts in the area of spring-loaded fishhooks, traps, and lures. Through diligence, exhaustive research, inquisitive minds, "good eyes," and a penchant for detail, the authors have built world-class collections of mechanical and spring-loaded fishing-related artifacts. While the fertile collecting area of spring-loaded fishhooks, traps, and lures has obtained some well-deserved attention from the collecting community over the past few years, by and large it remains an obscure area to most collectors of fishing tackle. This book is about to change all of that....

I've had the pleasure of befriending, interacting with, and corresponding with Tim Mierzwa for over 12 years and Bill Blauser for over 8 years.

Tim was a man on a mission! With 20 years experience in the field, his specialized knowledge of all things mechanical related to fishing tackle was awe inspiring. Tim quickly became and remains my "hook mentor." Through the years, he has readily and openly shared his knowledge not just with me but with scores of other collectors. In turn, this honesty and openness has motivated others to help Tim with his collection and, over the past several years, his research. The circle thus forming, this involvement and connection with others, particularly in researching a historically significant and previously undocumented area of the hobby, has energized everyone involved.

Tim did not come by these research and collecting skills by accident. He has been a collector nearly his entire life. Through the years he has actively collected coins, early American tools (with a focus on early axes and Indian relics), and old store and company catalogs. Tim is also a noted author, having written over 100 articles as a feature writer for the *Great Lakes Trader*, based in Williamston, Michigan. Topics covered have been wide ranging, from Michigan pioneer life to various collectibles. He has also written for the *National Fishing Lure Collectors Club Quarterly Gazette*. Tim has two sons, James and Adam.

By day, Tim can be found working at the Vacuum Hospital, which he co-owns, in downtown Jackson, Michigan. At night and on weekends he prowls for spring-loaded hooks, gaffs, and lures, or fishes or enjoys quiet time and hunting on his rural property along the Kalamazoo River just 15 minutes from his home in Jackson. In the winter Tim enjoys spear and ice fishing.

Bill Blauser, born and raised outside Pittsburgh, Pennsylvania, is also a lifelong fisherman, outdoorsman, and collector. A geologist by training, Bill received his undergraduate degree at the University of Pittsburgh and his masters at the University of Texas at Arlington.

Bill did his geological fieldwork in the Beartooth Mountains of Montana and in northern Mexico. Later he was employed as a petroleum geologist in the Gulf of Mexico, first working with the Union Oil Company of California (that big "76" you see). Bill is also a Certified Tree Farmer with the American Tree Farm System, specializing in deciduous trees. A member of the

Masonic fraternity, Bill has held a lifelong interest in antiques and previously collected antique toys, pottery, and folk art. Today, though, his passion is spring-loaded hooks and fish traps. As evidence, he once traded a superb and original example of a Kentucky long rifle to acquire an early fish trap.

Trapping muskrats and raccoons in western Pennsylvania as a boy spawned Bill's interest in traps. He was fortunate to be able to hone his fishing skills working as a guide in Alaska during summers in the mid-1980s. Bill returned to the Pittsburgh area in 1987 as a consulting geologist; this is where he lives with his daughter Sarah, 12. When he's not hunting spring hooks and spring lures, Bill enjoys fly fishing for trout and salmon.

Both authors reside in the heart of an area stretching from upstate New York through the Great Lakes region to Minnesota that is rich in fishing history and renowned as the center of the universe for all manner of hooks, gaffs, spears, harnesses, fish decoys, and lures. They are both active members of the National Fishing Lure Collectors Club and the North American Trap Collectors Association.

Times were different in this vast region in the 1800s and early 1900s. While sport fishing and catch-and-release fishing did exist, the common man was more concerned with survival and putting food on the table. Once his prey was hooked, the priority was keeping it hooked and landing it. His weapons of choice were elemental and basic — hooks, harnesses, spears, and gaffs. Yet, while seemingly utilitarian implements, their diversity and the individual creativity of their makers were vast. It is this endless diversity, coupled with the primal appeal of these historical fishing objects and the importance of their position in our sporting past, that led the authors to publishing this extensively researched major work.

Welcome! Join Tim and Bill as they celebrate times past and share with you their invaluable research concerning the people, places, and inventions of our fishing past.

Jeff Kieny
Raymore, Missouri
December 2004

Bill Blauser

Tim Mierzwa

About This Book

This book is divided into two sections. The first section deals with spring-loaded and mechanical fishhooks and metal killer fish traps. The second section deals with spring-loaded and mechanical fishing lures and spoons. Each section is arranged chronologically when dates are known, with the oldest items appearing first.

The majority of the items in this book were granted letters of patent from the United States government, which means that each item was unique and had something about it that was substantially different than anything that had been invented before. Since it was patented, one can be assured as to not only where an item is from, but when it was made, by whom it was made, and why it was different than anything that had preceded it.

In some instances the items in this book are best represented by use of a computer scan. When noted, these scans are exactly to scale. This is important because many spring-loaded hooks came in different sizes, and when a scan is to scale, a hook may be laid directly on the page to match the size exactly. In other instances, color photographs are used, and in others a combination of the two.

Unless otherwise noted, the items that appear in this book are in the collections of and belong to one of the authors.

Historical Perspective

The first seven patents in the United States of America that pertained to catching a fish, the first being granted in the summer of 1846, were for mechanical fishhooks that were spring activated. These spring-loaded fishhooks were designed to set in the manner of a trap, and to grasp and hold the fish by means of one or more striking hooks when it took the bait, which sometimes resulted in death.

These types of fishhooks were, in theory, more practical and productive than conventional fishhooks for many reasons. They could be used unattended, so that they could be set in the morning and checked at the end of the day, thus freeing up the time of the person using them, or they could be set in the evening and checked in the morning, thus possibly providing the next day's food for the fisherman's family.

Also, since these fishhooks did not require the fisherman to jerk on the line to set the hook, more than one could be used at a time, as in the manner of a trotline, where any number of these could be hung from a line stretching across a lake, river, or other body of water. Another advantage would have been that once a fish pulled on the bait and sprung the trap, it would have been held much more securely than if it had but one hook engaged in it.

Literally hundreds of different spring-loaded hooks have been invented and patented in the United States since 1846, in a range of sizes from only a couple of inches to as big as a basketball, and with from one to more than a dozen additional striking hooks being employed. The materials used in the hooks' constructions were as varied as the mechanisms themselves and included steel, brass, iron, copper, zinc, aluminum, lead, nickel, or any combination thereof. Some of these devices were designed not necessarily to kill the fish instantaneously, but rather to get multiple holds upon it and thus greatly increase the chances of landing it.

As pertains particularly to pre-Civil War spring-loaded fishhooks, which were generally hand-forged, relatively large, and probably expensive at the time, it is debatable as to who would have used them the most, the commercial fisherman, whose intent was to put money in his pocket, or the subsistence farmer, whose family's existence depended upon him putting food on the table day in and day out. What must also be factored into this debate, however, is that the hooks were obviously not used to any great extent by anyone, which is attested to by the fact of their scarcity today.

In regard to spring-loaded fishhooks made after the Civil War, many were mass produced, came in various sizes, and were marketed and sold to the ever-increasing number of recreational fishermen through advertisements in outdoor magazines of the time and also through catalogs of large retail companies, such as Sears, Roebuck and Company.

With the passage of time and the advent of fishing regulations that contained size limitations with regards to fish that could be killed and kept, the production and use of spring-loaded hooks and metal killer fish traps diminished, to the point of now being nearly non-existent; in fact, these hooks and traps are illegal to use in most, if not all, of the United States.

The first appearance of a spring-loaded hook in literature was in a 1760 edition of Isaak Walton's *The Complete Angler*, where the hook was pictured and referred to as a "Pickerell Spring Snap Hook." This information places spring-loaded hooks in use since before the Revolutionary War. Spring hooks would have to be considered important if for no other reason than their longevity.

The first spring-loaded fishing lure patented in the United States was patented in 1874. Since that time more than 200 others, consisting of both wood and/or metal, have been invented and patented. The primary objective of the vast majority of these devices was to essentially be weedless, with the hook or hooks only being exposed after having been struck by a fish.

Less than one-half of the more than 200 patented spring-loaded lures are known to exist in the hands of collectors, with many of these patented items having never been produced on a large scale.

From personal experience, it has been found that with some detective work, and some luck, the families of many of the inventors may be located, in the hope that some of the lures are still held by the family and may be obtained from them. This also holds true for the more than 100 patented spring-loaded fishhooks that are not known to exist in the hands of collectors.

Condition

Spring-loaded fishhooks and metal fish traps should be 100% complete and capable of being set in order to realize the values assigned to them in this book. If they are broken or incomplete and cannot be set, then their value is negligible and they are not desired by collectors.

The guidelines best used for grading the condition of metal spring-loaded hooks and traps are those of The North American Trap Collectors Association (N.A.T.C.A.) and are as follows:

Fine (FN) – The trap is 100% complete and original with a patina surface. There is absolutely no rust pitting and the lettering is very sharp and readable.

Very Good (VG) – The trap is 100% complete and original with light to moderate rust pitting. Lettering on this will be light but still 90% to 100% readable.

Good (G) – The trap has moderate to heavy rust pitting, with at least 50% of the lettering visible.

Fair (F) – The trap has heavy rust pitting such that no lettering is shown, but is still complete with no missing parts.

Poor (P) – Junk parts. The trap is missing major parts or extremely damaged regardless of condition.

Plus (+) and Minus (-) – May be used on grades to show an in between state.

The guidelines best used for grading the condition of spring-loaded lures are those of The National Fishing Lure Collectors Club (N.F.L.C.C.) and are as follows:

10 (NIB) New-In-Box – Unused with original box

9 M (Mint) – Unused without box

8 (EXC) Excellent – Very little or no age cracks; very minor defects

7 (VG) Very Good – Little age cracks; some minor defects

5-6 (G) Good – Some age cracks; starting to chip; small defects

3-4 (AVG) Average – Some paint loss and/or chipping, showing age

2 (F) Fair – Major paint loss and/or defects, much chipping

1 (P) Poor – Parts missing, poor color and/or major chipping

0 (R) Repaint – Original paint covered over in part or all

Plus (+) or Minus (-) – May be used on grades to show an in between state or add ½ to the rating number

Values

The value of any antique is subjective. Antiques often serve no functional purpose and are not essential in the day-to-day lives of mankind. Rather, it is for intangible reasons that antiques are sought after in so many fields and by so many people.

For example, it is not uncommon for highly sought-after carved wooden duck decoys to bring in excess of $250,000.00 each. Is this their real value? What value do they serve? While many people would consider a price such as this outlandish, some collectors of wooden duck decoys might consider this price a bargain on certain pieces.

In contrast to wooden duck decoys or wooden fish spearing decoys, which could be carved and painted in perhaps a day, with whittling being probably one of the oldest hobbies in the United States, spring-loaded fishhooks and metal fish traps were invented and made by men who were not only adept with their hands, but were also mechanically skilled, with some spending their entire adult lives trying to improve and perfect their devices.

An empty shotgun shell box recently sold for over $25,000.00, while certain empty boxes for rare fishing lures commonly command prices of $5,000.00 each. Is this the real value for these boxes? Not to the general public it isn't, but to collectors of such items, it is.

It is not uncommon for certain rare, desirable fishing lures to be bought and sold for in excess of $10,000.00 each, with one lure recently going at auction for over $100,000.00, even though its book value was listed as merely $2,500.00+. Is the higher figure its value? It is to certain collectors of such items.

It may then be said in conclusion that the value of any antique is relative, and that the value is the price that a willing buyer is willing to pay and that a willing seller is willing to accept.

The prices in this book are based on items' ages, rarity, desirability, and the knowledge of what prices have been paid for them, and also the knowledge of what prices have been refused for them. Each price is generally for the exact item shown.

Chapter XII Spring Snap Books

"A weak invention of the enemy." Why the humble and gentle piscator should be called the enemy of the finny race, or why anglers, in speaking of their exploits should call their finny friends their enemies, is a mystery yet to be explained. Such cannot certainly pursue their sport with a true Waltonian spirit; for the father of anglers never used the word enemy, and always spoke in the most mild and pleasant manner of the finny race. "Handle him as though you love him," says he, when speaking of preparing a line bait for the hook. This piscatorial world was for generations without any invention for taking their game other than the ordinary kerbed steel unit about fifty years ago, when the spring snap hook was invented. This was in general use until a few years since, when a boy by the name of Griswold, about sixteen years of age, living in the vicinity of Schroon Lake, conceived the idea of inventing a spring snap that would hold the fish after he was hooked. He succeeded in making the hook, which is called the Griswold — see plate 1. It is arranged with a spring, a lever, and striking hook. The striking hook is so adjusted that when set it lies alongside of the main hook, and is retained by a slide at the top; when the fish nibbles the striking hook descends and takes him on the outside of the head — see plate 2. By an improvement patented by Mr. Ellis, of Naugatuck, Conn., the striking hook is relieved from the lever instead of the upper part of the hook.

It was much approved of at the time, and considered an aid to the angler. Immediately, the mechanical genius of the country was put in motion, and presto! at least a dozen inventions of striking hooks of various descriptions were made to facilitate the taking of our scaly friends. They all have their merits or demerits, a diversity of opinion existing among the fraternity. Some consider them "a weak invention of the enemy," very cruel, and those unworthy of a sportsman's name who use them; others highly approve of them. They are not well adapted for salt-water fishing where there is a strong tide, as they are apt to spring before the fish bites. They are better suited to lake fishing for pike, black basse, and lake trout. The are preferred and recommended by some for that purpose, and for fish, such as often slip the hook, will always be used to a certain extent. Many improvements and suggestions have been made, but none to alter materially the character of the device.

From the 1857 edition of *American Anglers Guide Book*

Spring-loaded Fishhooks and Metal Killer Fish Traps

Name:	Engelbrecht & Skiff Fish Hook
Patented:	July 28, 1846, patent #4,670 by Theodore F. Engelbrecht and George F. Skiff
Origin:	New York, New York
Size:	6½" overall length
Material:	Hand-forged steel
Value:	$10,000.00+

The Engelbrecht & Skiff Fish Hook is the first invention ever patented in the United States of America that had to do with catching a fish, and therefore, its historical significance is profound.

This style of fish trap employs a "flat spring." Only a few other fish traps ever employed this type of spring, the most recent having been patented and made in 1875.

The Engelbrecht and Skiff Fish Hook is set as thus: the striking hook, which is attached to the flat spring, is moved into a vertical position, which thus compresses and puts tension on the spring. The line-tie on top of the hook is a sliding bar of hand-forged steel and is inserted into a slot cut into the striking hook, thus setting the fish trap. The trap is sprung by either a downward movement of the bait hook (a fish biting the hook) or by an upward movement of the line; either of which action would disengage the sliding bar to which the line is tied from the striking hook, with the flat spring now forcibly sending the striking hook into the top of the fish's head.

The mechanism itself for this fishhook is gen- erally attributed to George W. Griswold of Pottersville, NY, "in the vicinity of Schroon Lake."

This spring-loaded fishhook, like other fish traps to follow, had the great advantage over conventional one-piece fishhooks in that it could be left unattended by the fisherman and still catch fish. Therefore, one can see that this could have been used either singularly on a fishing rod or by leaving it unattended, as long as the line was anchored to a boat or some other point on the surface. A multitude of these traps could also be hung from a trotline, a line that would have been stretched across a stream, river, or lake, and which would only have to be checked from time to time, as one might now check a conventional trapline set for furbearers.

The example shown here, one of only two known to exist in collectors' hands, still retains an original horsehair leader.

From patent text: "the invention of a hook for catching fish, operated by a (flat) spring, a lever, and a slide, whether working as described above or in any other way."

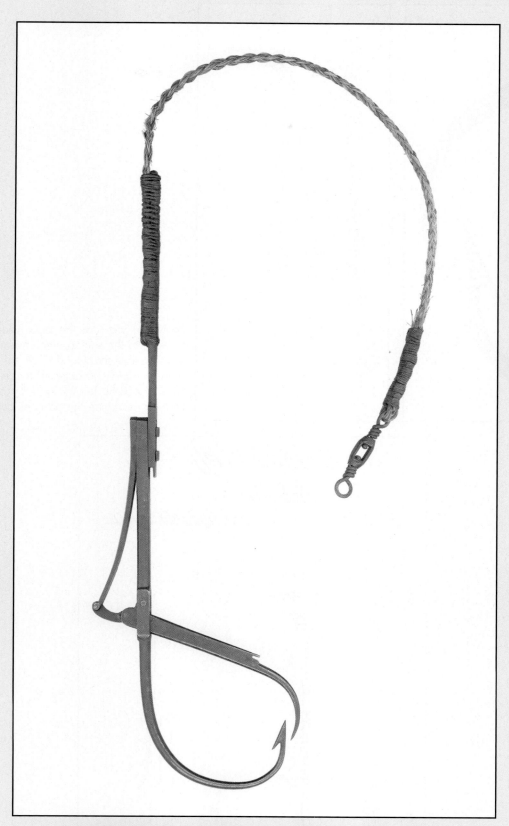

Engelbrecht & Skiff, shown actual size, in the sprung position.

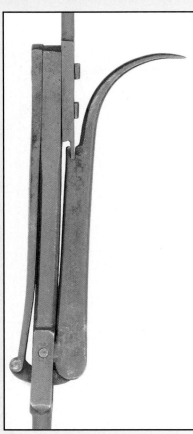

Enlarged view of the bait hook, the striking hook, and the setting mechanism. Every part of this Engelbrecht & Skiff hook exhibits fine workmanship and character. The striking hook mimics the deadly talons used by a bird of prey. Did talons inspire the graceful curve, perhaps?

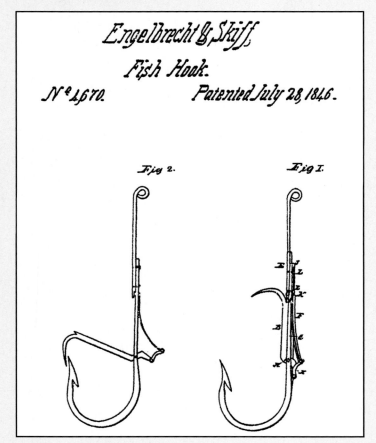

Engelbrecht & Skiff,

Fish Hook.

Nº 4,670.   Patented July 28, 1846.

Fig 2.   Fig 1.

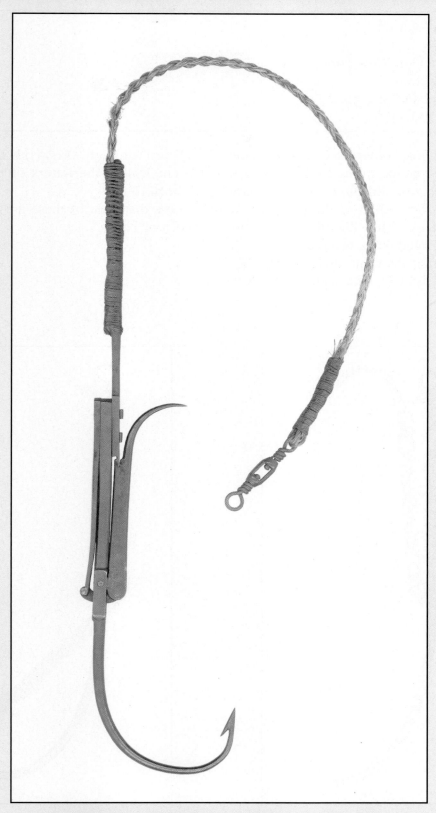

Engelbrecht & Skiff, shown actual size, in the set position.

Name:	Job Johnson
Patented:	1846
Origin:	Brooklyn, New York
Size:	4⅝" long
Material:	Steel and spring-steel
Value:	$3,500.00+

This striking hook is stamped "Job Johnson No. 1," suggesting that the spring-loaded fishhook came in various sizes, although no others are known. One side of the shaft of the bait hook is stamped "Patent 1846," while the other side of the shaft is stamped "Engelbrecht, Hale & Co."

Job Johnson, originally from England, described himself as being a "fishhook manufacturer."

Even though this fish trap is stamped "Patent 1846," the letters of patent for it have not been found.

Less than five of these are known to exist in collectors' hands.

Set position, actual size.

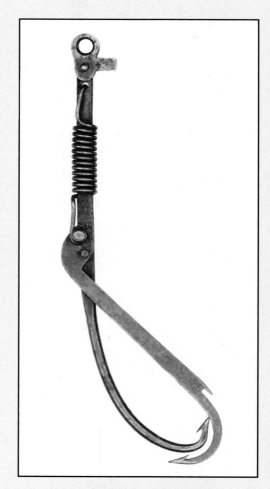

Sprung position, actual size.

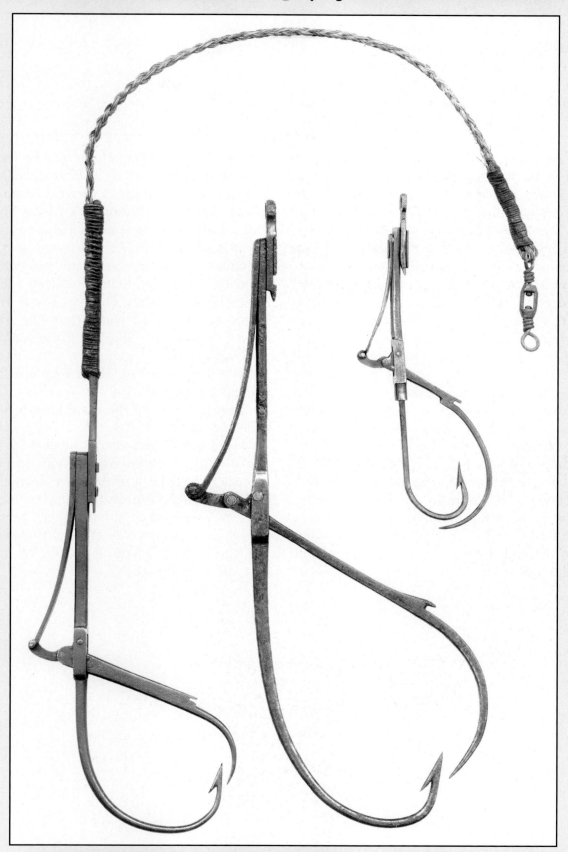

These three hooks all exhibit the Engelbrecht & Skiff mechanism patented in 1846.

Name:	Pendleton Fish Hook
Patented:	August 21, 1847, patent #5,255 by Stanton Pendleton
Origin:	New Haven, Connecticut
Size:	3½" – 6" in length
Material:	Brass, steel, and spring-steel
Value:	$7,500.00+

The Pendleton Fish Hook was the third patent granted in the United States of America for a device whose sole purpose was to catch a fish. This spring-loaded fishhook employs a flat spring, as does the Engelbrecht and Skiff, which was patented a year earlier, and in fact, these two fish traps employ exactly the same mechanism.

What differentiates the Pendleton from an Engelbrecht and Skiff, and what allowed it to be patented, is that the Pendleton has a bait hook that can be replaced in the event it is ever broken. This was a vast improvement over earlier spring-loaded fish traps, the reason being that once the hook of one of these was broken, the entire trap was useless. The change also allowed for different sizes of fishhooks to be interchanged at an angler's pleasure.

Stanton Pendleton accomplished this novel improvement by manufacturing the main shaft of his bait hook with a "female" threaded end rather than a curved fishhook. Onto this threaded end, he then screwed a steel "fishhook with a male screw cut onto the end of the shank," which could be easily replaced.

The Pendleton Fish Hook may be found with a stamping that reads "J. J. Brown, NY." This is an extremely significant historical feature in that John J. Brown and Company of New York, New York, was one of the earliest fishing tackle dealers in America. John J. Brown was also, in fact, the author of the first complete book written and printed in the United States that dealt with fishing in the United States. This book was first published in 1845 and was titled *The American Angler's Guide; or, Complete Fisher's Manual for the United States.*

The Pendleton Fish Hook may also be found with no stampings.

Less than five of these are known to exist in collectors' hands.

From patent text: "have invented a new and useful improvement in the spring fishhook claimed to have been invented by George W. Griswold of Pottersville, in the state of New York, some two years since, it being the same invention for which a patent was granted to Theodore F. Englebrecht and George F. Skiff….by patent letters dated July 28, 1846."

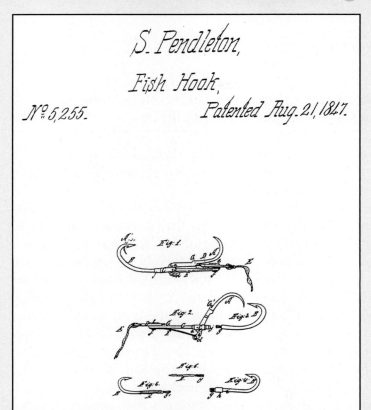

S. Pendleton,
Fish Hook,
Nº 5,255. Patented Aug. 21, 1847.

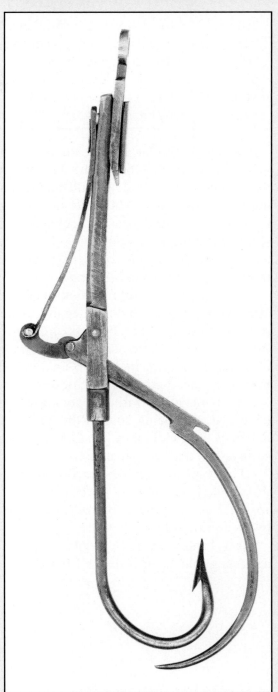

Enlarged to show detail.

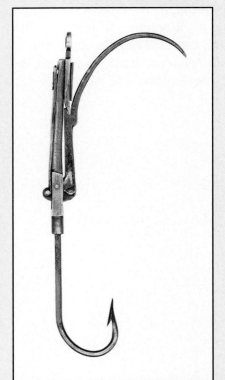

Set position, actual size.

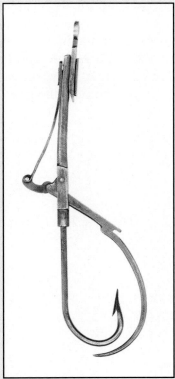

Sprung position, actual size.

Name:	Job Johnson "Sockdolager"
Patented:	August 21, 1847, patent #5,256 by Job Johnson
Origin:	Brooklyn, New York
Size:	3" – 6" in length
Material:	Japanned steel and spring-steel wire; may have brass rivets, brass spring is rare
Value:	$400.00 – 2,000.00. The earliest and largest versions are worth the most.

Although similar in appearance, to the casual observer, to his 1846 patent, the mechanism of this fishhook is completely different, thus allowing it to be patented. This style of a spring-loaded fishhook is referred to as a "sockdolager," a word whose meaning is: a) something that settles a matter, b) a decisive blow or answer, and (c) something outstanding or exceptional.

The patent for this fishhook expired in 1861, after which time it could be legally made without patent infringement by anyone, and it was. Because of this, there occur many variations from blacksmiths to gun makers to anyone "skilled in the art of construction of such devices."

A spring hook with the sockdolager mechanism was still being sold in the 1900 Fall Sears, Roebuck and Company catalog; it was made of spring-steel and was japanned.

The type of spring employed by a Sockdolager is known as a "contractile helical spring," as the power of the spring is generated by its contracting.

A 6" hand-wrought Sockdolager with 90% original bluing sold on eBay for $1,401.89 five years ago.

The sockdalager-style fishhook was also known and marketed at one time as a "Yankee Doodle" fishhook.

After reaching England, it was pictured and described in the 1886 British book entitled *Fishing Tackle, Its Material and Manufacture. A Practical Guide for the Angler and Fly-Fisher* by J. H. Keene. Under a chapter entitled Hooks of Various Kinds, he describes the Yankee Doodle in Figure 30, on page 31, thus: "Figure 30 shows another spring tackle which, as an infernal machine of torture, has not its equal. Get it in your hand, as I did some time since, and you will find it so. The drawings explain themselves."

Authors' note: We have both drawn our own blood while handling, setting, and unsetting some of the items in this book.

From patent text: "Whereby the bite of a fish at the bait on a hook causes a crooked barb dart to strike into and hold the nose, head, or gills of the fish, independently both of the line and the person holding the line.'

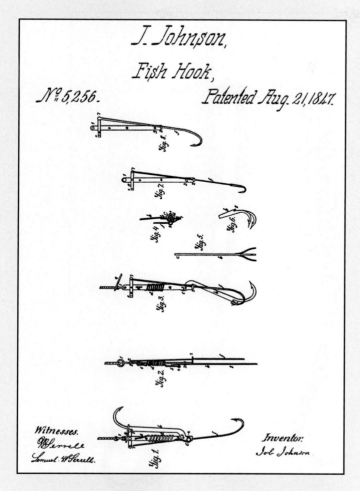

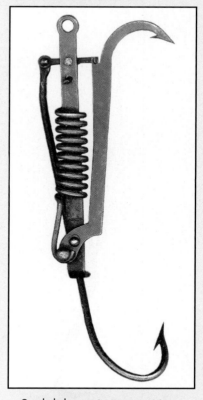

Sockdolager in set position.

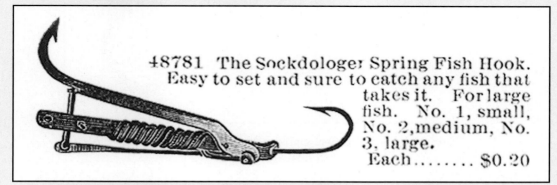

Ad from 1895 Montgomery Ward & Co. catalog.

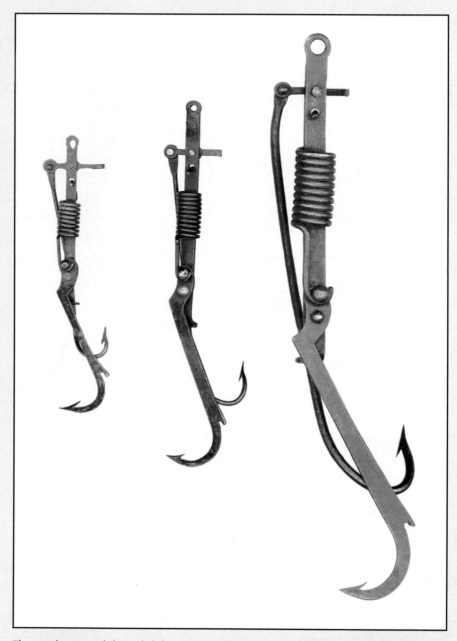

The earliest model Sockdolagers employed rectangular bars as their "dogs." All three hooks are shown actual size.

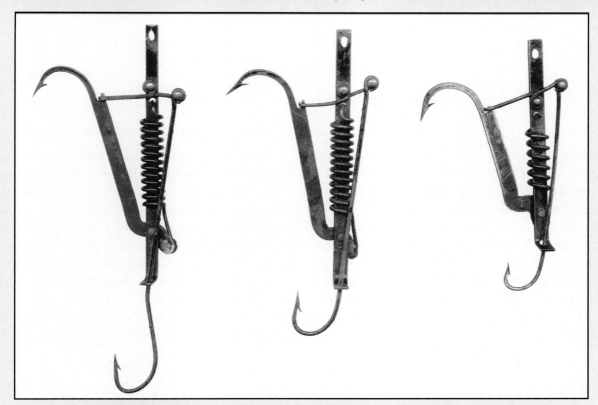

Later versions of the Sockdolager employed wire bars as their dogs. All three hooks shown actual size.

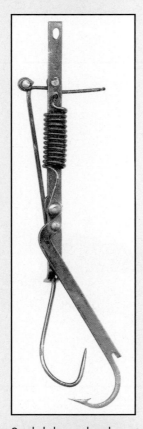

Barbless Sockdolager hook, actual size.

The Sockdolager would have been an effective fish hook for commercial fishermen using a hand line for cod or other fish.

Name:	Babcock Spring Hook
Patented:	1847, Job Johnson
Origin:	Made by Zeby Babcock in the Saginaw Bay area of Michigan
Size:	6" – 9" in length
Material:	Hand-forged steel and spring-steel
Value:	$2,000.00+

The Babcock Spring Hook is a sockdolager by design, and so is thus empowered by a contractile helical spring, which in this case is massive as compared to other sockdolagers.

Zeby Babcock was born in June 1817 in Watertown, New York, and died in August 1889 in Ellington Township, Caro, Michigan, at the age of 72. He was a farmer and a blacksmith by trade, but is best remembered by his seasonal occupation as that of a commercial sturgeon fisherman in Saginaw Bay and its tributaries.

The hand-forged spring hooks made by Zeby Babcock were specifically for sturgeon, which he would sometimes take by the wagonload. If one can assume that he did not make these hooks on his deathbed, and that they were inspired by the 1847 patent, then the period of their production would have been from the 1850s to the 1870s.

The striking hook on these traps may exhibit a barb or may be barbless.

Less than a dozen of these very desirable fish traps are known to exist in the hands of collectors.

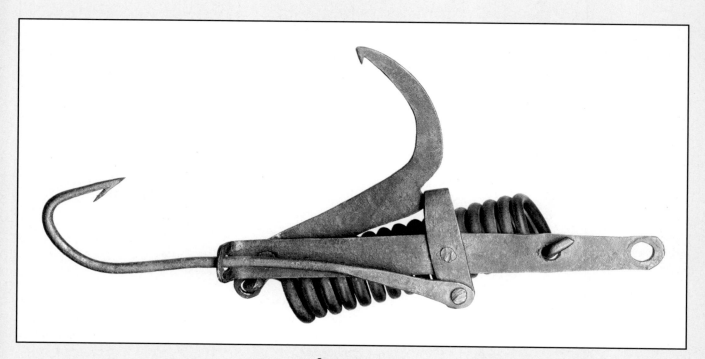

Set position.

Picture of Zeby Babcock procured from his descendants
when they were interviewed.

Sprung position.

Name:	Ellis and Grilley Spring Fish Hook
Patented:	August 15, 1848, patent #5,709 by Darwin Ellis and Charles Grilley
Origin:	Naugatuck, Connecticut
Size:	11"
Material:	Brass and steel
Value:	$15,000.00+

The Ellis and Grilley is the largest of all flat spring fishhooks and employs a unique three-hook mechanism. This mechanism is not line actuated, nor is it actuated by a pull on the bait hook. Rather, the Ellis and Grilley relies on the fish being lured to it by the bait on the stationary bait hook, and the trap is only sprung when the fish's head bumps the second hook, which is essentially a trigger, thus releasing and propelling the third, striking hook downward into the head of the unsuspecting member of the finny race. This mechanism is therefore completely independent of the line and/or the bait hook; this was an ingenious idea that had never been used before. The one example of the Ellis and Grilley known to exist in the hands of collectors is unmarked.

From patent text: "The advantage of our improvement over all others heretofore used consists in using a catch or dog attached to the main bar of the hook in such a manner as to secure the striking-hook or gaff firmly in its position when set for use. This catch or dog, having no connection with the line or cord, will not allow the hook to be sprung by the weight of the hook and bait when casting it into the water, nor by the movement of a live bait, nor by the point of the baited hook catching against a hard substance at the bottom, and therefore will only be sprung by the action of the fish's mouth, and then only when the fish is within the reach of the striking-hook or gaff.

All hooks now in use may be accidentally sprung by their own weight while casting them into the water, and this may happen without the knowledge of the fisherman, so that the bait may be taken off by a nibble, and there will be no possibility of catching the fish, and should the baited hook get fast at the bottom by any means a slight strain on the line or cord would spring the hook, and probably render it impossible ever to extract it. To guard against such accidents we have invented our own improvement.

By our improvement we also dispense with the slide as used in Engelbrecht and Skiff's patent, and also the lever used in Johnson's patent, while we make a much neater, safer, more useful, and economical article than either of them."

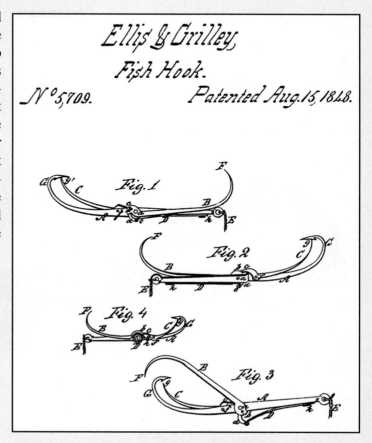

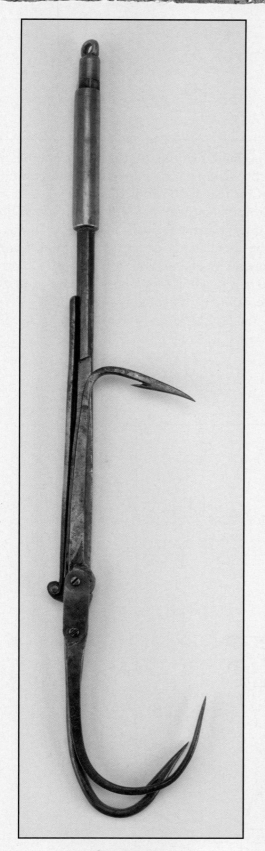

Set position.

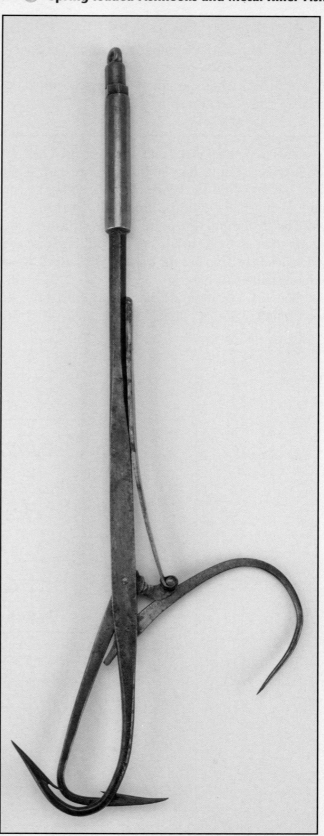

Sprung position.

Name:	Davies Fish Trap
Patented:	June 5, 1849, patent #6,495 by Thomas A. Davies
Origin:	New York, New York
Size:	2½" when closed, 4½" in set position
Material:	Steel and brass
Value:	$5,000.00+

To use this trap, the pointed end would be driven into a log, which would thus hold the base shaft and spring bar up in the air. When tripped, the base shaft and spring bar would be forcefully driven downward with the curved pointed jaw striking and pinning the fish by its head, and thus killing it.

The Davies Fish Trap has the date 1849 stamped into the base shaft.

Less than five of these are known to exist in collector's hands.

The model of this trap used for animals has a straight striking jaw, rather than the curved jaw meant for fish as shown here.

From patent text: "…will in all probability act best in a horizontal position, as in that way you will be most likely to spring the hook upon the fish in one given position. A fish mostly approaches the bait in a horizontal position and a horizontal stroke would be most likely to hit him."

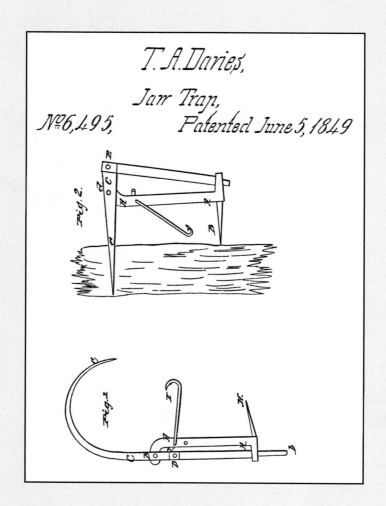

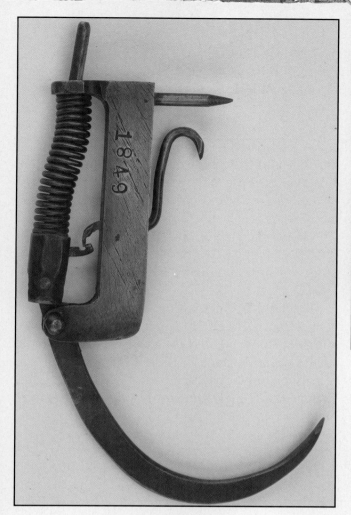

Set position.

Sprung position.

Enlarged to show date stamped in brass body.

Name:	Sigler Fish Hook
Patented:	April 11, 1854, patent #10,761 by Henry Sigler, Houston, Texas
Origin:	Invented in Houston, Texas. Manufactured by Job Johnson, New York.
Size:	One size known so far, 6⅝" long in the sprung position
Material:	Steel and spring-steel
Value:	$5,000.00+

The Sigler Fish Hook, according to the patent text, "consists in making the top portion of the main hooks elastic, and so attaching them to the vertical guide pieces that they will be made to serve as springs for giving action and forcing them together, and with two levers or toggle-arms, form a toggle-joint for forcing said hooks apart and retaining them set for a given time; and in combination with the above, employing a common bait hook, which is attached to the lower extremity of a regulating slide and so situated that its end will be some distance above the ends of the spring-hooks, and consequently the fish or animal will have to pass his head between the spring-hooks to reach the bait, in drawing upon which he will instantly draw the toggle-arms out of a horizontal position, and simultaneous therewith operate the spring-hooks, which are caused to take into the body of the fish and hold him perfectly secure, without any chance of escape, owing to the peculiar action of the hook, it biting harder upon its object when the strain is greatest."

On the flat side of one spring is stamped "JOB JOHNSON, MAKER, NY." On the flat side of the other spring is stamped "H. SIGLER PATENT, 1854."

It would be interesting to discover how the connection between H. Sigler of Houston, Texas, and Job Johnson of New York was achieved at such a great distance back in 1854 and what sort of partnership they worked out. There are less than five of the Sigler/Johnson hooks in collectors' hands.

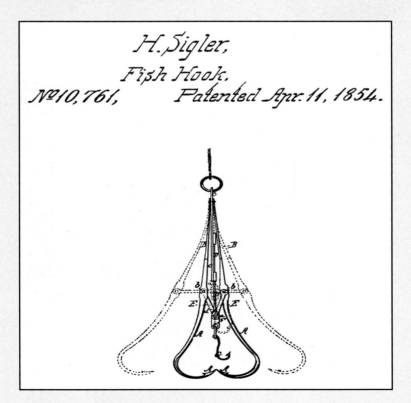

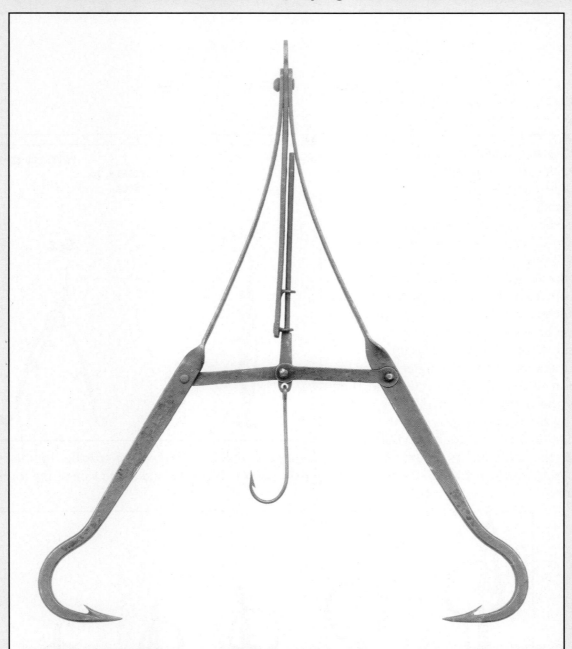

Above: The Sigler Fish Hook, actual size, is shown in the set position.
Below: The Sigler Fish Hook, actual size, is shown in the sprung position.

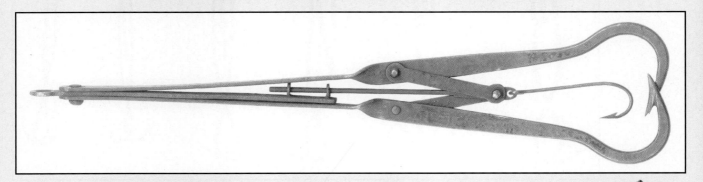

Name:	Spring, Snap and Catch 'Em Hook
Patented:	September 20,1864, patent # 44,368 by Nathan A. Gardiner, Jr.
Origin:	Willett, New York
Size:	Six sizes from 2"-3¾" closed
Material:	Japanned spring-steel wire
Value:	$65.00 – 125.00

The Spring, Snap, and Catch 'Em came in six sizes, with the largest one uncommon and smallest size scarce. The smallest one is very small.

These hooks were mass produced and distributed by different companies over the years, the first being the Thomas H. Bate & Co., New York, New York, followed by the Wilkinson Co. of Chicago, Illinois and finally by The Sears, Roebuck and Co. of Chicago, Illinois.

These hooks are found in varying conditions, and should be priced accordingly.

From patent text: "The angler places the bait upon either or both hooks and then presses them together until the spindle, guided by the eye, will pass into the eye of the opposite fork and lock the hook. The

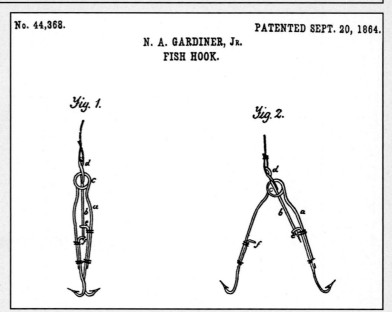

No. 44,368.   PATENTED SEPT. 20, 1864.

N. A. GARDINER, Jr.
FISH HOOK.

Fig. 1.   *Fig. 2.*

fish takes the hook into its mouth and gives a slight pull, which withdraws the spindle from the eye, and the spring drives the hook into the mouth of the fish, holding it firmly, and at the same time forcing open the mouth."

Hooks are shown actual size.

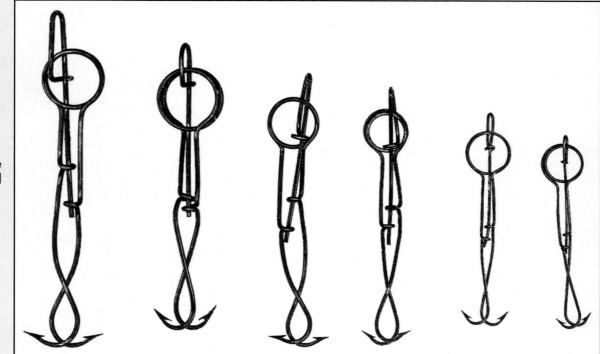

Name:	"Lincoln Trout Hook"
Patented:	December 19, 1865, patent #51,651 by William Davis and Job Johnson
Origin:	Brooklyn, New York
Size:	3⅜" closed
Material:	Japanned spring-steel wire
Value	$500.00 – 750.00

Note: The "Lincoln Trout Hook" is known only to have been manufactured in one size, and is very scarce. The name would obviously be derived from the recently assassinated President Abraham Lincoln. One can only wonder if the name was given as a purely patriotic gesture, or if it was a more calloused marketing ploy to appeal to the patriotic fisherman of the time and thus sell more hooks, with the famous spring-hook maker

Job Johnson having by now a great deal of experience in the marketplace.

From patent text: "The nature of our said invention consists in a fishhook shank having an eye sliding on one of the shanks of the hook and a point or bolt entering an eye turned in the shank of the other hook, so as to hold said hooks together when baited, said sliding shank passing through an eye at the junction of the hook."

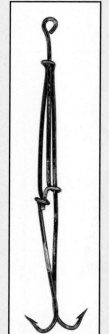

Set position.

Sprung position, actual size.

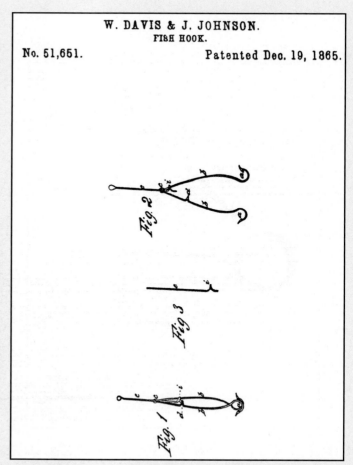

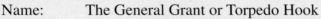

Name:	The General Grant or Torpedo Hook
Patented:	April 24, 1866, patent #54,251 by Job Johnson and Hezekiah Howarth
Origin:	Brooklyn, New York
Size:	2⅜" by 1¾"
Material:	Japanned spring-steel wire
Value:	$500.00 – 750.00

This spring hook is the last device for catching fish that Job Johnson, the most prolific fish trap maker and inventor in American history, is known to have been involved with. It is formed from a single piece of spring-steel wire and designed so that when a fish pulled on the bait hook, a spear point would be thrust into the fish.

Having the previous year named a spring hook for the just-assassinated President Abraham Lincoln, it seems fitting that Job Johnson would name his next invention after Civil War hero Ulysses S. Grant, Lincoln's successor. Whether this was from a sense of patriotism or was a marketing ploy is unknown.

This is a rare hook, with less than a dozen known to exist in collectors' hands, and being so small is literally worth its weight in gold.

From patent text: "...a pull of the fish upon the hook disconnects the spear and causes that and the hook to come toward each other, drawing the hook more firmly into the fish's or animal's mouth and causing the spear to stick into the fish or animal in the opposite direction."

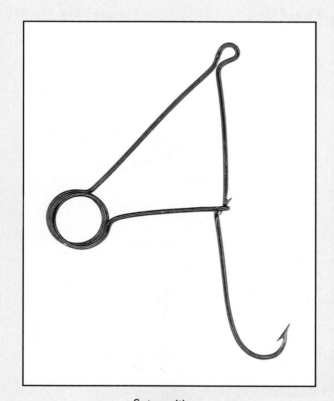

Set position.

Sprung position.

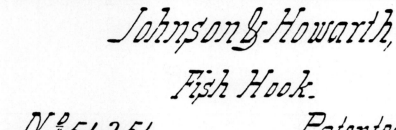

Johnson & Howarth,

Fish Hook.

N⁰ 54,251.   Patented Apr. 24, 1866.

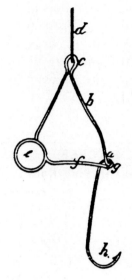

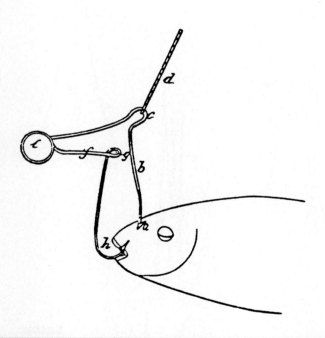

Johnson & Howarth patent showing the hook impaling the fish.

Name:	Pitcher Fish Hook
Patented:	July 16, 1872, patent #129,053 by Edward Pitcher
Origin:	Brooklyn, New York
Size:	7½" closed, 10½" extended
Material:	Japanned spring-steel
Value	$1,000.00+

The fishhook invented by Edward Pitcher is of the type that relies upon the configuration of the fishing line and the way that it is attached to the fishhook to operate the mechanism. This fishhook is designed so that as the fish pulls on the central bait hook, and thus exerts pressure on the fishing line, two barbed spears are drawn downward and expand slightly, impaling the fish and holding it fast, thus preventing its escape.

From patent text: "As the fish, in taking the hook, draws upon it, the spear is drawn down, piercing him and rendering it impossible for him to get away from the hook."

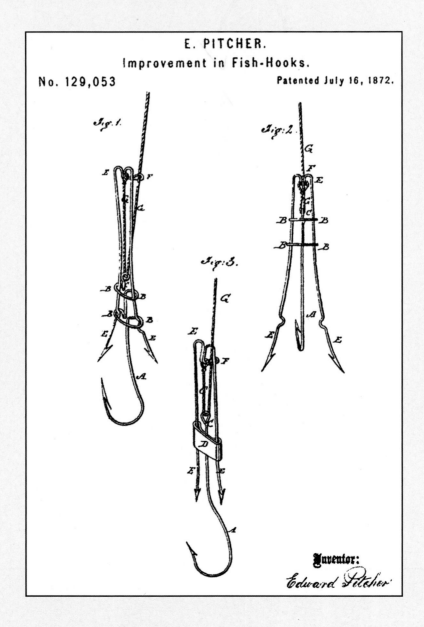

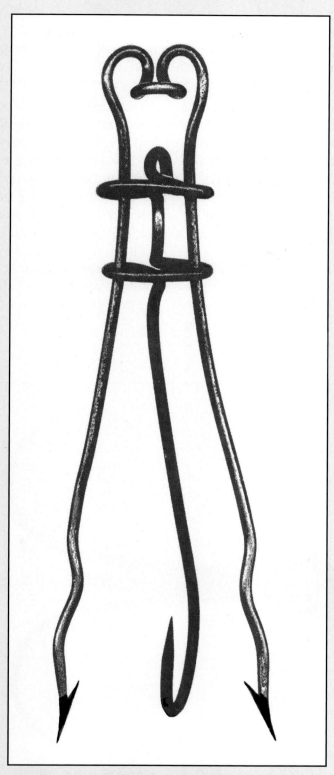

Pitcher hook in the sprung position, shown actual size.

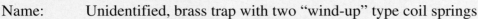

Name:	Unidentified, brass trap with two "wind-up" type coil springs
Patented:	Unknown, but probably. Circa 1875?
Origin:	Unidentified
Size:	8½" long relaxed, 6" long set
Material:	Brass with two hand-wrought steel striking hooks retaining original bluing
Value:	$10,000.00+. Value doubled if patent found

This fish trap employs two opposing wind-up type coil springs to drive the mechanism. To set the trap, the striking jaws are simultaneously raised to the vertical position, which "winds up" the centrally located opposing coil springs. A central, slidable flat brass bar acts as both the holder for the bait hook and acts as the "dog" of this trap and slides into the catches integrated into the striking jaws, thus setting the trap.

The release of this trap is simply done by exerting minimal pressure on the bait hook in a direction away from the line-tie, which slides the bait-hook holding dog away from the two catches on the striking hooks, which then simultaneously come crashing down onto the head of the fish, thus impaling him from both sides at once.

The line-tie on this trap is simply a hole on the upper end of the main brass frame, and as a result, no amount of jerking on the fishing line has any effect on whether the trap is set or not.

This obviously manufactured metal killer fish trap is such a finely-crafted piece of early mechanical genius that the authors give the one known example this value, even though it is as of yet unidentified.

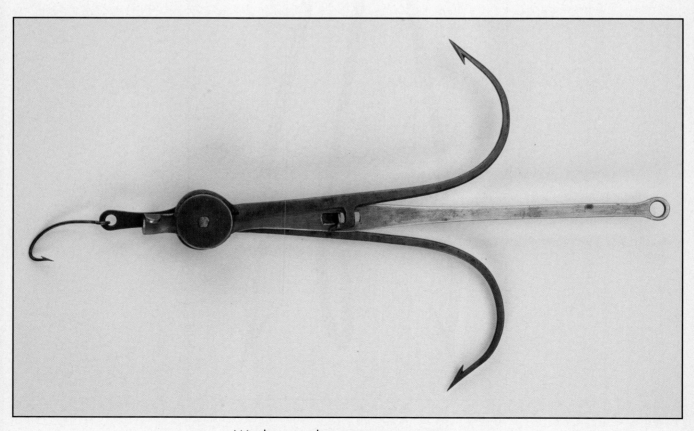

Wind-up type brass trap in set position.

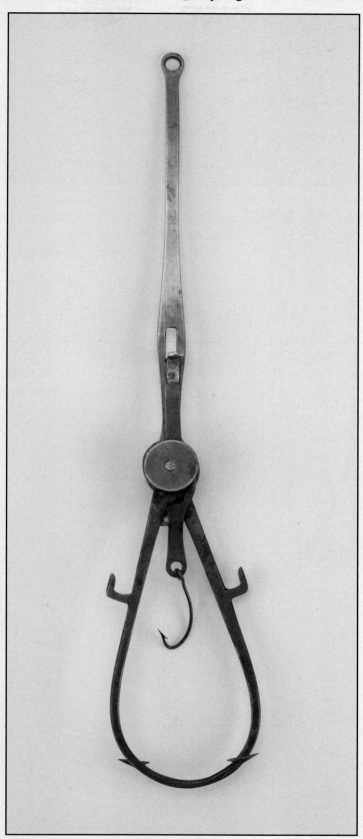

Wind-up type brass trap shown in the sprung position.

Name:	Dunlap Fish-Hook
Patented:	June 1, 1875, patent #163,980, by Ephraim L. Dunlap
Origin:	Eustis, Maine
Size:	3½"
Material:	Steel with brass rivets and line-tie
Value	$1,500.00+

Note: The Dunlap Fish-Hook is small, and is the last of the spring hooks and metal fish traps to employ a flat spring to power the mechanism. This fishhook is stamped "PAT. JUNE. '75" on the shaft of the main bait hook. This is a very desirable fish trap.

From patent text: "The bait is placed upon the hook, and the effort of the fish to get away, after swallowing the bait, jerks the lever from under the catch, when propelled by the spring, the lever is rapidly brought down, its hook striking into the head of the fish, while the hook fastens within the mouth."

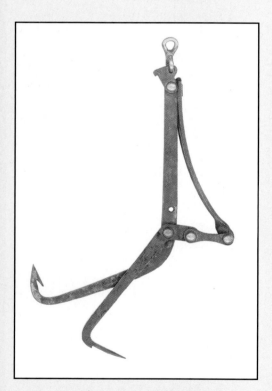

Actual size, sprung position.

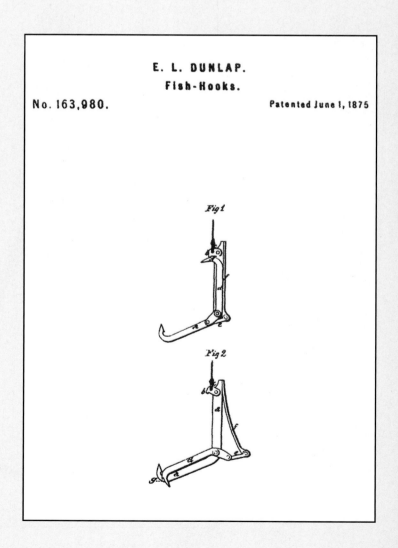

E. L. DUNLAP.
Fish-Hooks.

No. 163,980.   Patented June 1, 1875

Fig 1

Fig 2

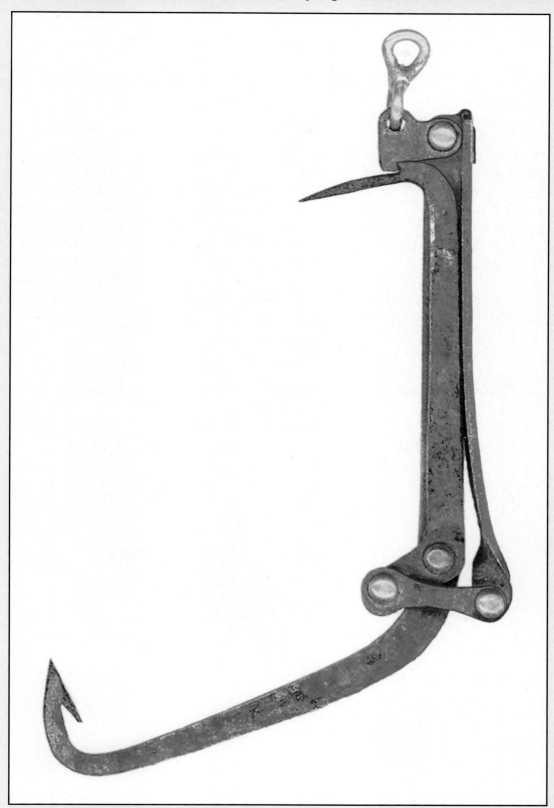

Dunlap Fish-Hook, enlarged to show details, in the set position.

Name:	Evan's Eagle Claw
Patented:	April 17, 1877, patent #189,805 by Benjamin F. Smith
Origin:	Frankfort, Pennsylvania
Size:	Produced in two known sizes, 3" high and 4" high not measuring the line-tie rings
Material:	All brass
Value:	3", $800.00 – 1,200.00; 4", $1,750.00+

These may have no stamping, may have a partial stamping, or may have a complete stamp, which reads:

PAT Apl 17, 77
S. W. Evans and Son
Frankfort, PA

S. W. Evans and Son was outside of Philadelphia, PA, and was primarily a manufacturer of umbrellas.

An advertisement for the Eagle Claw, taken from the May 17, 1877, edition of *Fish and Stream Magazine*, shows three sizes. The No. 3 size, big enough for bears, wolves, panthers, etc., is not known to exist and was probably never manufactured.

From patent text: "...certain new and useful improvements in devices for catching fish and game....with the pivoted hooks connected to a snapping spring of a suitable bait holder, latch, and dog, which will retain said spring and hooks when the trap is set."

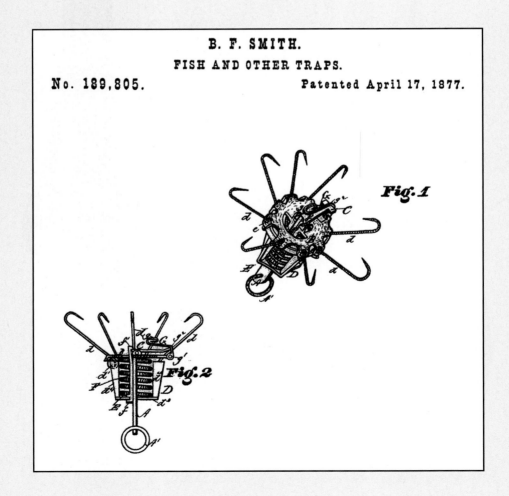

Two different styles of Evan's Eagle Claw Fish Trap, in the small and large sizes.

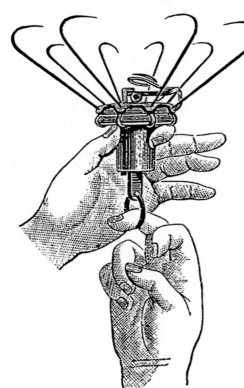

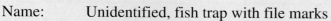

Name:	Unidentified, fish trap with file marks
Patented:	Unknown. Circa 1870s.
Origin:	Unidentified
Size:	7" long, 6" jaw spread when set
Material:	Steel and spring-steel
Value:	$850.00+

This metal killer fish trap is empowered by a spring-steel rod, which is coiled at its center so as to produce an eye, which serves as the line-tie. The mechanism itself for this trap is nearly identical to that employed by the 1899 Guillotine, which is discussed later in this book.

Both arms of this trap exhibit the original file marks of the maker, with each of the six teeth still being sharp enough to scratch your fingernails.

This is a very desirable fish trap.

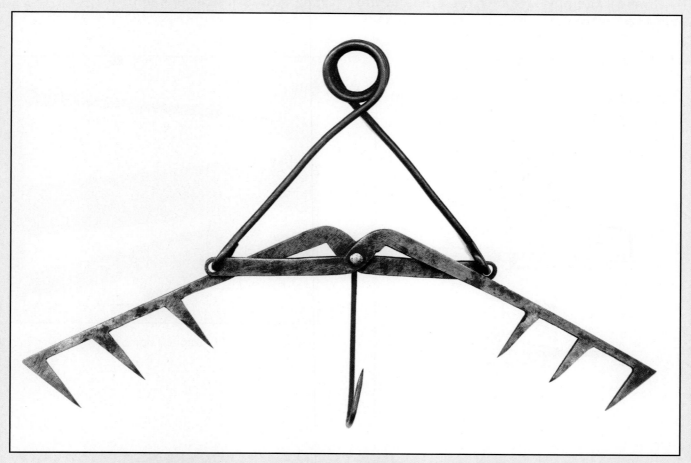

Fish trap is shown in the set position. This trap has a very powerful spring.

Name:	King's Patent "Never-Fail" Fish Hook
Patented:	May 1, 1877, patent #190,222 by John O. King
Origin:	Altamont, Kansas
Size:	4¼" long, 2" wide, 2½" high, excluding the 2½" rod, which serves as the line-tie
Material:	Steel and spring-steel
Value:	$6,000.00 – $7,500.00+

Note: The King's Patent "Never-Fail" Fish hook is one of the most finely made metal killer fish traps in American history and thus one of the most desirable. Because of its unique shape and design, it cannot be confused with any other fish trap or fishhook.

When set, the King's Patent, including its integral bait hook, is in a horizontal position, and employs two "fulcrum grab-hooks having outer claws and u-shaped ends back of the fulcrum." An old advertisement guarantees that it "Will Catch Every Fish That Bites."

Some examples of the King's Patent are unmarked, while others have the word "LATANE" stamped into one side of the main horizontal frame. The meaning of this word has yet to be determined.

Also unique to this trap is a small clip that can be slid along a notched vertical rod, allowing the amount of vertical play in the 2⅝" long bait hook to be adjusted.

From patent text: "This invention relates to that class of fish-hooks which are sprung when the fish tampers with the bait, so as to close and catch the same. The forward pulling of the bait hook releases instantly the trip-lever, and closes the grab-hooks by the action of the loop of the spiral spring, so as to take hold of the fish."

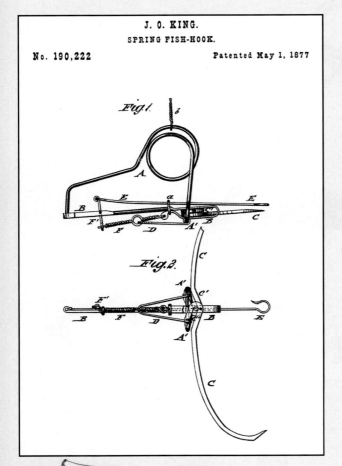

"Latane" stamp.

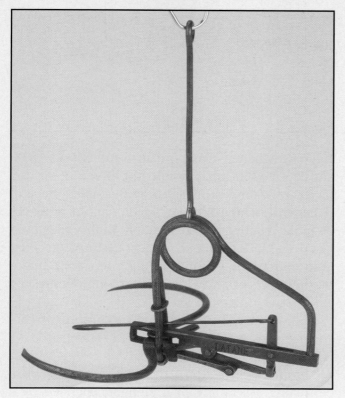

King's Patent, set position.

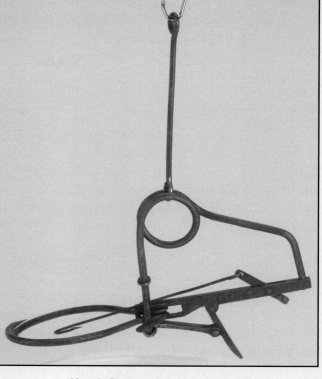

King's Patent, sprung position.

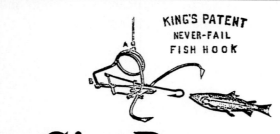

KING'S PATENT
NEVER-FAIL
FISH HOOK

Six Reasons

❧ ❧ Why it is The Best on The Market ❧ ❧

1. Bright metal attracts the fish.
2. There is no stealing of bait.
3. Easy to release from fish; no swallowing of hook.
4. Impossible to release spring when coming in contact with obstructions.
5. Can be used with or without cork.
6. Will catch any size fish and can be used successfully with all kinds of bait.

Will Catch Every Fish That Bites.

For prices and full particulars, address

W. E. King, General Agent.

Carlisle, ❧ Kentucky.

Advertisement from 1898.

Name:	John A. Mitchell "Throat Trap"
Patented:	February 5, 1878, patent #199,926 by John A. Mitchell
Origin:	Maysville, Kentucky
Size:	7" overall, 5" when set
Material:	95% brass, 5% steel
Value:	$15,000.00+

The "device for catching fish" invented by John A. Mitchell, which he also refered to as "a fishing-gun," was designed so that when a fish pulled on the bait, a plunger with two spring-activated, exquisitely barbed hooks was forced downward into the fish's mouth, where the opposing hooks were thrown outward and became lodged in the fish's throat "and utterly precluded the possibility of his escape."

The collar, which acts to retain the plunger and hooks when in the set position, is attached by a single brass chain to prevent it from becoming separated from the trap. This collar also serves as the bait holder and has around its circumference, both top and bottom, a series of small holes to which the bait is attached in "any suitable manner."

Archival records from the *Atlas of Mason County, Kentucky*, published in 1876, states that John A. Mitchell was born in Kentucky in 1838, and it gives an insight into the inventor of this incredibly complex, beautifully machined piece of American fishing history, which should probably be in the Smithsonian Institution. In this atlas he is listed as "J. A. Mitchell — Dental Surgeon. Pure gold and silver fillings. Embalming done under the new process. Seeing is believing. Come and see."

There is only one known example of this "device for catching fish," and it is stamped "PAT APLD FOR" near the line-tie.

From patent text: "A device for catching fish, consisting essentially of a plunger, operated by a driving-spring and carrying two or more hooks, thrown outward by springs, and parts being so arranged that the butt ends of the hooks will enter the mouth first."

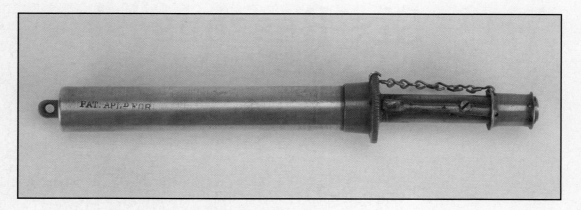

Mitchell trap in the set position.

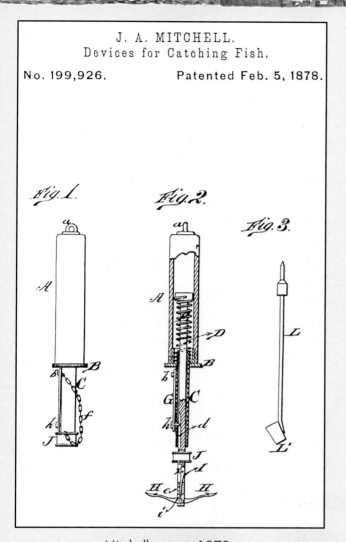

J. A. MITCHELL.
Devices for Catching Fish.

No. 199,926.   Patented Feb. 5, 1878.

Fig. 1.   *Fig. 2.*   *Fig. 3.*

Mitchell patent, 1878.

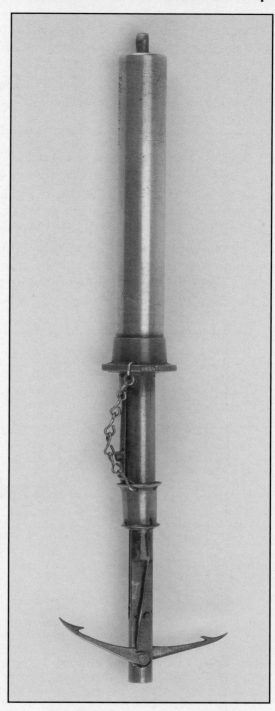

Mitchell trap in the sprung position, actual size.

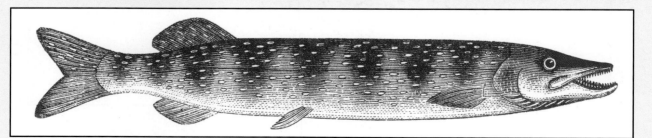

Name:	Unidentified, but referred to as "the Batwing Hook"
Patented:	Unknown, but probably. Circa 1880s.
Origin:	Unidentified
Size:	8½" long
Material:	Steel and spring-steel
Value:	$3,000.00+

The Batwing Hook is a relatively simple device in design. Each striking jaw is empowered by a separate contractile helical spring. When the jaws are drawn into a vertical position, the two dogs that are attached to the line-tie are pivotally lowered into the lugs on the outside of each striking jaw, thus setting the trap, at which point it may be said to resemble a bat in flight, thus its nickname.

The trap is sprung when pressure is exerted either on the bait hook or on the line-tie, with either action disengaging the dogs from the lugs on the striking hooks.

The two springs then contract and bring the two striking jaws forcibly into both sides of the fish's head.

Less than five of these fish traps are known to exist in the hands of collectors.

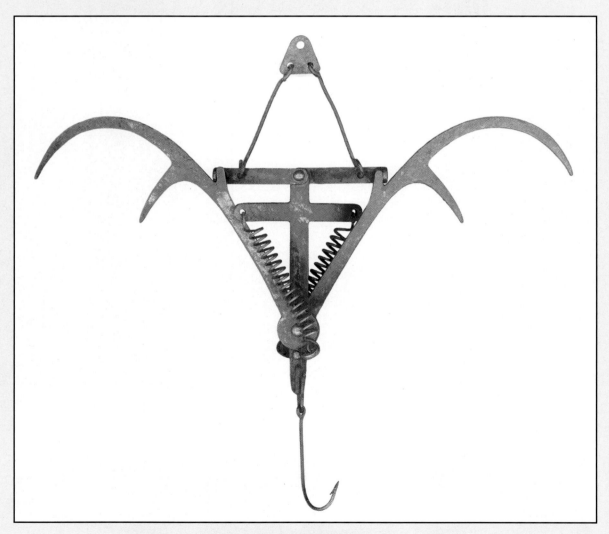

"Batwing Hook" in the set position.

Name:	Unidentified, has five striking hooks
Patented:	Unknown, but probably. Circa 1880s.
Origin:	Unidentified
Size:	5¾" when relaxed, 7½" jaw spread when set
Material:	Brass, steel, and spring-steel
Value:	$3,500.00+. Value doubled if patent found.

This finely made fish trap is of the type whose actuation is controlled by the manner in which the line to it is attached. The line must be strung through the dog of the trap and thence down through the two hollow brass shafts, at which point a bait hook is attached. When the trap is strung in such a manner, when a fish pulls on the bait hooks, the dog, near the top of the trap, is pulled from its retaining hole, allowing the expansive helical spring to expand and thus forcibly swinging down five striking hooks.

This trap is so constructed that the lower hollow brass shaft around which the spring is coiled slides into the slightly larger upper hollow brass shaft. As it slides in, the five striking hooks are drawn into a horizontal configuration by means of a five-armed bracket. When the smallest shaft is completely inserted, against spring pressure, a hole in it aligns with a hole in the larger shaft, such that the externally mounted dog on the upper shaft passes through both holes, thus setting the trap.

The one known example of this fish trap is unmarked.

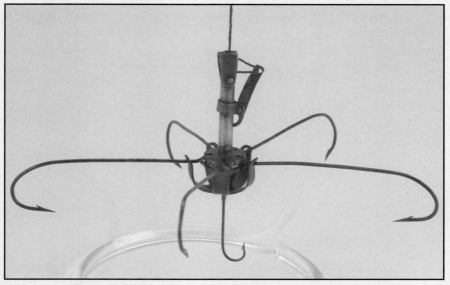

Set position.

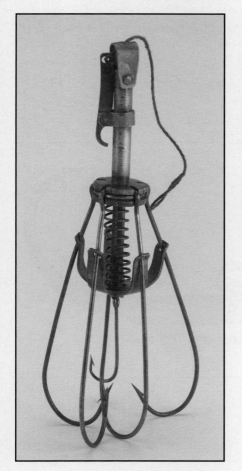

Sprung position.

Name:	Adirondack Fish Trap
Patented:	Unknown
Origin:	Adirondack Mountains, New York
Age:	Circa 1880s – 1900, may be older.
Size:	4" – 8" long
Material:	Steel and spring-steel, hand-forged
Value:	$850.00 – 1,250.00

The name of this trap derives from the fact that all known examples of this uncommon trap have come from the Adirondack Mountains.

The mechanism of this trap employs a flat spring and is designed in such a way that it is sprung by either pulling on the line-tie or by pulling on the bait hook. The obvious disadvantage to this style of mechanism is that it would be almost impossible to cast, as the line tension would undoubtedly spring the trap. Rather, this trap would be much more effective when used on a trotline.

This trap would have been a preferred tool of the commercial fisherman who plied the rivers and lakes of upstate New York and who supplied the multitude of resorts and lodges with fish for their advertised "fresh fish and game dinners" for their guests.

The exact construction and dimensions of this trap varied from blacksmith to blacksmith, but the mechanism remained the same. This trap may be found with a blacksmith's mark (such as two or three punches in the metal) or, as is more common, unmarked.

When found in the field, it is not uncommon for there to be more than one.

This trap may also have been effective for mink and foxes when suspended from a tree.

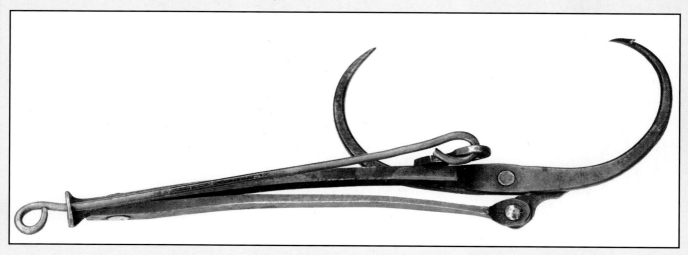

Adirondack Fish Trap in the set position.

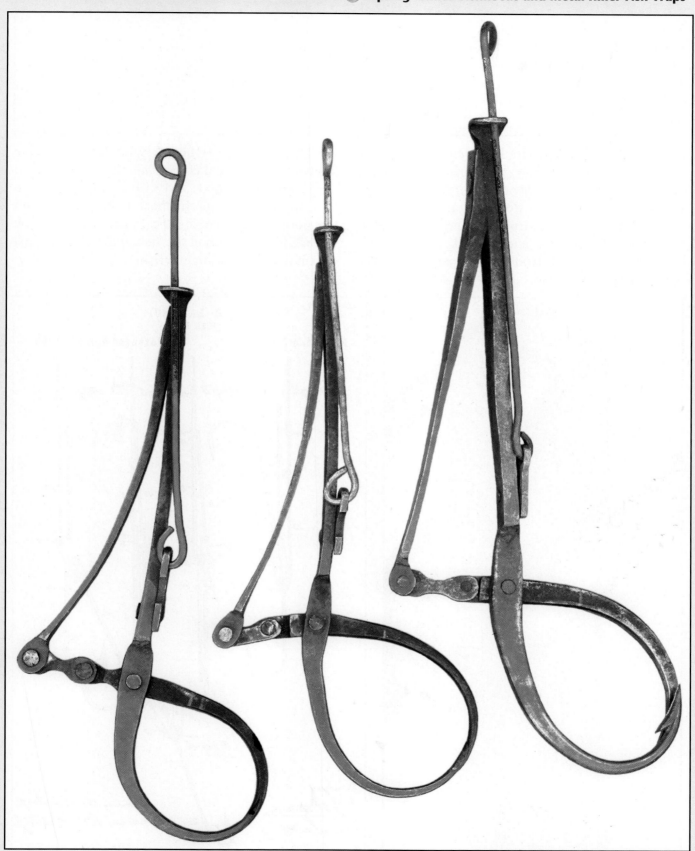

Three Adirondack hooks shown slightly smaller than actual size.

Name:	Lathrop Fish Hook
Patented:	April 22, 1890, patent #426,027 by Junia H. Lathrop
Origin:	Northfield, Minnesota
Size:	4½" set, 6" closed
Material:	Brass with japanned steel hooks
Value:	$750.00+

The Lathrop Fish Hook is designed so that when a fish pulls on the stationary bait hook, a second, "grip hook" is drawn down into the top of the fish's head. This device has no springs involved with its construction and is therefore more aptly described as a lever hook.

The Lathrop Fish Hook is stamped PAT. APR-22-90 on its pivot-plate.

This is a rare fishhook with less than five known to exist in collector's hands.

From patent text: "My invention relates to …'trap-hooks,' wherein there is combined with the hook which carries the bait a second hook intended to close upon the fish and assist the first or bait hook in holding the fish."

Mechanism enlarged to show patent date stamp.

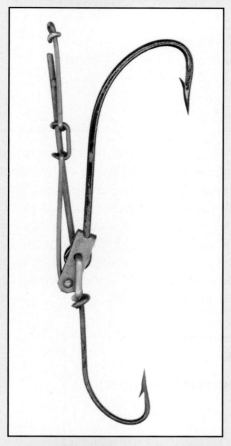

Lathrop Fish Hook in the set position. above, and the sprung position, right. Both are shown actual size.

Name:	Mack Automatic Weed-Deflecting Bait
Patented:	June 23, 1891, patent #454,580 by Albert G. Mack
Origin:	Invented in Rochester, New York; manufactured in Chicago, Illinois
Size:	Six sizes, 5" – 8" long
Material:	Steel and spring-steel
Value:	Lures, $150.00 – 250.00; loose hooks, $75.00 – 100.00

The Mack fishhook is so designed as to be made by connecting two sets of opposing fishhooks in such a way that they have a common eye and that their planes are perpendicular to each other. In this manner, the Mack hook is essentially weedless, with the points not becoming exposed until the Mack is compressed by the bite of a fish. The spinner blade on a Mack Lure is marked "The Mack Hook," along with the patent date and the size of the hook.

From patent text: "A cluster or group of two, or of any desired multiple of two hooks, arranged accordingly in one or more pairs, the members of each pair being rigidly fastened together near the upper ends of their shanks to cause their curved hook ends to coincide inversely and be maintained normally in their mutually-shielding positions and tend to resume the same when separated by the elasticity of the hooks."

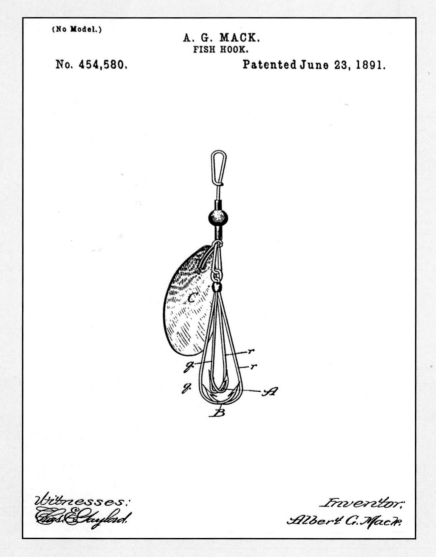

(No Model.)

A. G. MACK.
FISH HOOK.

No. 454,580.   Patented June 23, 1891.

Witnesses:

Inventor:
Albert G. Mack.

Left to right: Mack Automatic Hooks No. 3, No. 5, and No. 7. The Mack Hook at the bottom is a No. 5 with a different hook arrangement. Loose hooks are at the top of the page.

Left to right: Mack Automatic Hooks No. 9 and No. 11. The hook on the far right is a No. 9 with an unusual hook setup and a brass spinner blade that is not plated like the others.

Name:	Unidentified, early ice-tong trap
Patented:	Probably. Stamped "PAT. APPL'D FOR," but letters of patent have not been found as of yet. Circa 1890s.
Origin:	Unidentified
Size:	6" long relaxed, 7½" jaw spread when set
Material:	Nickel-plated steel and spring-steel with brass bait-hook attachment
Value:	$3,500.00+

This fish trap has two striking jaws, each of which is powered by a separate contractile helical spring, and it appears to be from the 1800s. It has a replaceable bait hook at its center and retains some of its original nickel plating.

Attached at the line-tie is an early brass barrel swivel.

This trap is not line actuated, but rather can only be sprung by applying pressure to the bait hook, as would happen when a fish would pull on the bait.

This trap is considered dogless, as there are no parts of it that need to be disengaged for it to be sprung.

This fish trap is stamped "PAT. APPL'D FOR." on the central post near the line-tie.

Less than five examples of this fish trap are known to exist in collectors' hands.

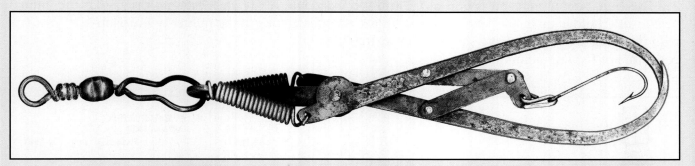

Unidentified early ice-tong trap in sprung position. Reduced in size.

This trap would have been the right size for musky or northern pike.

Name:	"The Tarantula" or McWhirter's
Patented:	July 23, 1895, patent #543,263; August 17, 1897, patent #588,167; and December 28, 1897, patent #596,334 by William Henry McWhirter
Origin:	Pontotoc County, Mississippi
Size:	16" long, jaws 8" wide when set
Material:	Steel, spring-steel, and cast iron
Value:	$2,000.00+, when complete and in good condition

William McWhirter's "Tarantula" trap is large and is or was rarely found in a fishing tackle box. Because of its unique shape, size, and design, it is difficult for it to be mistaken for another trap of any kind.

There are three patents covering the "Tarantula," all being basically the same. This trap is usually dated, with either the date 1895 being cast into the ring holding the twelve jaws, or more commonly, it is seen with "PAT. 1895" stamped into the safety dog.

The bait holder may be found as a straight needle-like holder or in the shape of a fishhook, with the latter style being more sought after by the collectors of fishing memorabilia.

This trap is rarely found complete and in good or better condition.

From patent text: "The trap is called 'Tarantula,' because it resembles a species of spider by that name. It will catch fish, rats, coons, mink, wild cats, bear, or anything that will bite or take bait. It is easily thrown, and never misses its victim; it hangs when set, and decoys rather than frightens the animal. It advances upon the animal two inches when thrown, and draws or tends to draw the head of the animal within its jaws when it is thrown. On account of its construction, the harder the animal pulls against it the tighter it grasps it."

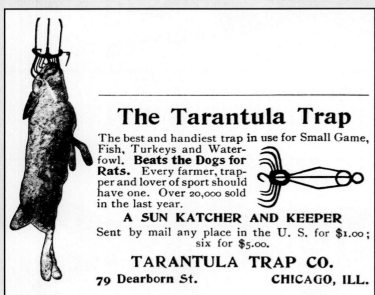

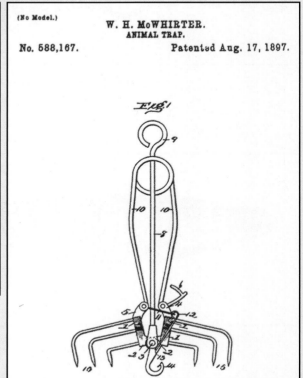

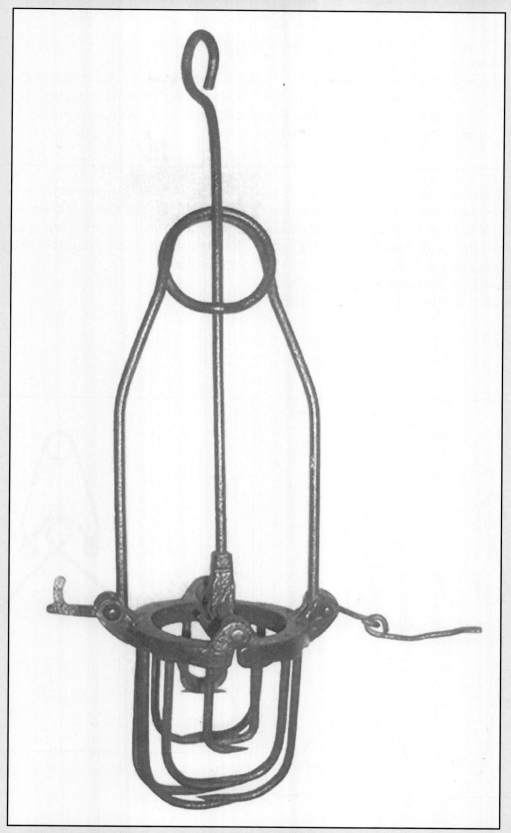

McWhirter's "Tarantula Trap" in the sprung position. The actual size of this trap is 16".

Name:	Great Bristol Automatic Fish Hook
Patented:	November 15, 1898, patent #614,424 by William F. Evans
Origin:	Baltimore, Maryland
Size:	Four sizes advertised as Nos. 1, 2, 3 and 4. The No. 1 is 4" wide when set in the position with the hooks pointed outward and 2½" wide when set with the hooks pointed inward. No other size has as yet been identified.
Material:	Japanned spring-steel wire with brass rivet
Value:	$500.00+

The Great Bristol Automatic Fish Hook is truly an ingenious device. In its one construction, it can be set with the two hooks facing each other or it can be set with the two hooks opposing each other. Both hooks serve as bait hooks.

From patent text: "A twin fishhook….and a spring independent of the said bait hooks…whereby the two hooks have capacity to be set and both baited in either of two positions — in one position so as to move apart when sprung, and in the other position so as to close toward each other when sprung…."

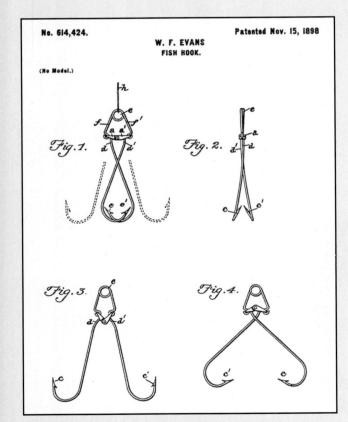

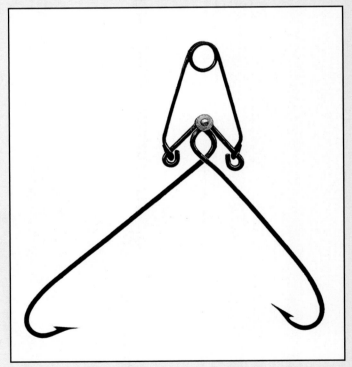

The Great Bristol Automatic Fish Hook, shown in the set, or open, position.

GREAT Bristol Automatic Fish Hook

PAT. NOV. 15TH, 1898.

SUITABLE FOR ALL KINDS OF FISHING.

Parisian Inventors' Academy

Service Special de Representation a l'Exposition de 1900. Bristol Fish Hook award for merit. First-class diploma and great gold medal to WM. F. EVANS, Inventor.

10c. EACH. ANY SIZE.

10c. EACH. ANY SIZE.

ASK YOUR DEALER FOR THE BRISTOL HOOK.

No. 1.

A SURE CATCH

AUTOMATIC IN SETTING.

AUTOMATIC IN HOOKING FISH.

ALWAYS BAIT SHORT HOOK

No. 1, ILLUSTRATED.

The merit in the **Bristol Hook** has been proven by its general adoption throughout the States.

It has a pure mechanical action and does not kill the fish in hooking them.

All fishermen should use the **Bristol Hook** when fishing in rough water or when fish are biting **slow;** it saves bait.

NOTE INSTRUCTIONS.—You can use three different principles in fishing with the **Bristol Hook :** a perfect automatic hook, a trolling hook, an excellent spreader. Bait both hooks. Always reverse the hooks on proper side to give free action, and see that the points of hooks meet as seen in cut.

We do not claim the **Bristol Hook** will catch them all, but we offer you the latest improved and best, practical, patent fish hook, and a fair trial will convince you of its merits.

If you fail to hook the fish with the **Bristol Hook,** the fish are surely small. Use smaller hooks. **You should** always be supplied with No 1, 2, 3 and 4, suitable to catch all medium and small fish.

A fisherman's outfit is not complete without a full set of **Bristol Hooks,** Nos. 1 to 4. They have **been adopted** generally by the sports for rough water fishing.

ANY SIZE HOOKS MADE TO ORDER.

AGENTS WANTED.

SPECIAL RATES IN GROSS LOTS.
ALL ORDERS PROMPTLY ATTENDED TO.

All Hooks have a Medium Temper and are Well Tested as to quality.

FISCHER & EVANS,

PATERSON, N. J.

Name:	The Guillotine or Payton's Automatic Fish Hook
Patented:	Advertised as patented on March 28, 1899; patent # unidentified.
Origin:	Unidentified
Size:	Four sizes: 1/0-3" length in relaxed position; 3/0–3¼" length in relaxed position; 5/0–3¾" length in relaxed position; and, 7/0–4¼" length in relaxed position
Material:	Japanned spring-steel wire with brass rivet
Value:	$400.00 – 600.00 for second, improved model

The Guillotine spring fishhook was relatively mass produced at the beginning of the twentieth century, but not a lot is known about it. The only information on it comes from some magazine advertisements of the time.

Although it was advertised as having been patented on March 28, 1899, the United States Patent Office did not issue patents on that date.

The Guillotine came in two models. The first model had a duplex bait hook and required three rivets for its construction. This model is rare, and its value is twice that of the later model, which has a single bait hook and requires but a single rivet for its construction.

The second model of the Guillotine was also produced with barbless striking hooks (very uncommon) and may be found with a long-shanked bait hook (very uncommon).

To the authors' knowledge, this hook has never been found on a card or in an envelope, but one would think that they exist. Please contact the authors if you have additional information on this sought-after spring-loaded fishhook.

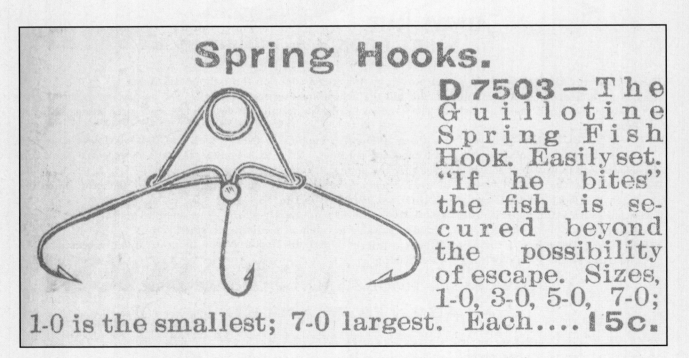

1906 advertisement for the second model Guillotine Spring Hook.

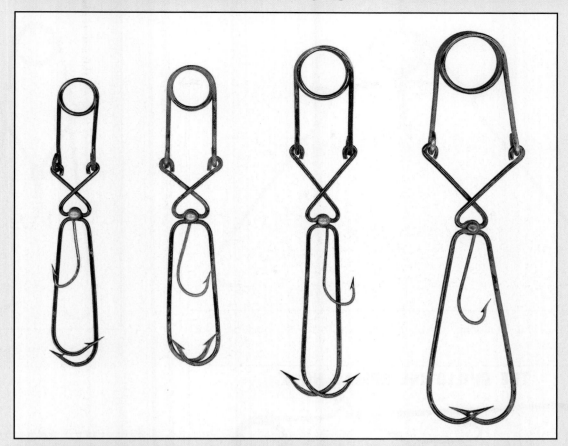

Four sizes of the second model Guillotine Spring Hook, shown actual size and in the sprung position.

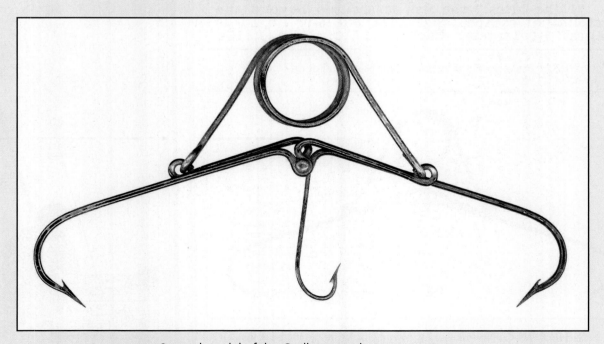

Second model of the Guillotine in the set position.

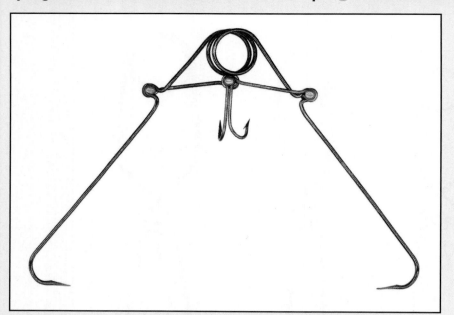

First model of the Guillotine, shown actual size, in the set position. Note the three brass rivets.

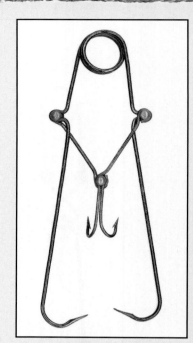

First model, sprung, shown actual size.

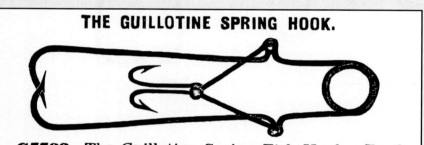

THE GUILLOTINE SPRING HOOK.

G7733 The Guillotine Spring Fish Hook. Easily set. "If he bites," the fish is secured beyond the possibility of escape. Sizes, 1-0, 3-0, 5-0, 7-0, 1-0 is smallest; 7-0 largest. Each............ ... .**15c**

1902 advertisement for the first model Guillotine.

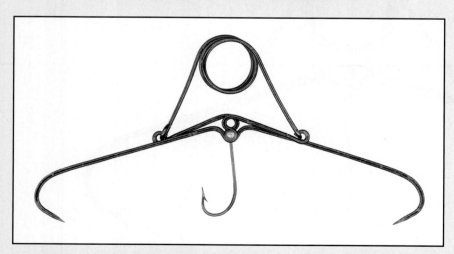

Second model of the Guillotine, set, shown actual size. Rare barbless striking hooks.

Name:	"Old Glory" Sure-Catch Fish Hook and Animal Trap
Patented:	May 30, 1899, patent # 625,742 by Jacob Cartier and Arthur George Pelletier
Origin:	Biddeford, Maine
Size:	3¾" long, 1½" wide
Material:	Brass and steel
Value:	$1,000.00+

The "Old Glory" came in two models. The first (earlier) model was made almost entirely of brass, except for the bait hook and the two "catch hooks" on either side, which were made of japanned steel. In this model, the bait hook is integral to the trap and cannot be removed, with the obvious disadvantage being that should the bait hook break, the entire trap would have to be thrown away.

This first model was originally sold in an envelope, very scarce today, that gave instructions for setting it and pictured the trap in the set and the sprung positions.

The second (later) model of the "Old Glory" was made almost entirely of steel, with the exception being the piece of the trap to which the bait hook was attached and which acted as the dog of this trap, with it being made of brass. In this model, the bait hook is not integral to the trap and can be removed in favor of another size bait hook or to be replaced, a major improvement over the first model.

Stamped on the shank of the "Old Glory" is "PAT. SEPT. 7 97. MAY 30. '99." The first date refers to an earlier patent of Jacob Cartier that was never produced (to the authors' knowledge) and which had a completely different mechanism than did that hook of the 1899 patent. The reason for putting the date of an earlier, different patent on the shank of this trap is debatable, and may have been solely an attempt by the inventor to protect his earlier design.

The mechanism employed to operate the "Old Glory" consists of two wind-up type coil springs, each of which is attached to a catch hook. As the catch hooks are drawn upwards in opposite directions, the attached springs are tightened. When they reach their vertical position, the brass dog to which the bait hook is connected is forced upward by the pressure of a separate contractile helical spring, and the dog then engages cogs on the wind-up type springs, thus setting the trap.

When the bait hook is pulled with enough force to overcome the pressure of the contractile helical spring, the dog becomes disengaged from the cogs, thus allowing the wind-up type coil springs to release their energy, causing the catch hooks to forcibly strike down on the unwitting fish, or — as it more than likely would happen — the fisherman who was trying to use this contraption.

From patent text: "A fish and animal trap comprising a central stem or support, a pair of spring-actuated arms provided with hooks and secured to hubs provided with peripheral notches and arranged to rotate in directions on a pivot pin or support at the lower end of said central stem."

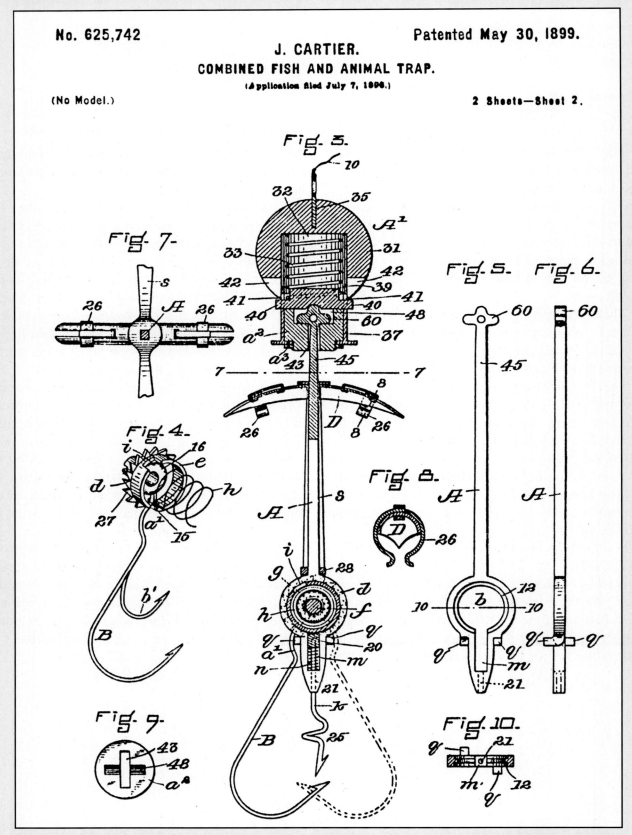

No. 625,742

J. CARTIER.
COMBINED FISH AND ANIMAL TRAP.
(Application filed July 7, 1898.)

Patented May 30, 1899.

(No Model.)

2 Sheets—Sheet 2.

May 30, 1899, Cartier patent for the "Old Glory" fishhook and animal trap. This drawing shows one of the most complicated mechanisms of all the spring hook patents.

First and second model of the "Old Glory" Fish Hook and Animal Trap in the sprung position, and the envelope they were sold in.

Stamped on the shank of the "Old Glory" is "Pat. Sept. 7 97. May 30. '99."

Name:	Unidentified, has six helical springs
Patented:	Unknown, but probably. Circa 1900.
Origin:	Unidentified
Size:	3½" tall, 12" in circumference in the relaxed position, about the size of an orange
Material:	Copper, lead, and steel
Value:	$5,000.00+

This ingenious metal killer fish trap puzzled the authors for a week. It is built around and upon a lead disc, which is ¼" thick and 2" in diameter and has two copper-lined holes near its center, which act as the line-tie. Attached around the periphery of this disc are six pivotally mounted large fishhooks. Overlying the eye of each fishhook, and built into the periphery of the lead disc, is an L-shaped rod of steel, which acts as an "arrestor," and whose function is to not permit the six fishhooks to rotate much above a horizontal plane. Each fishhook has a slidable 1" copper sleeve on it with two "ears" formed into it. These six sleeves are attached to each other by six separate contractile helical springs.

Also attached to alternating fishhooks is a slidable copper T-shaped appendage, positioned between the spring-holding sleeves and barbs of the hook, and which would have served to hold bait.

Thus being so constructed, this fish trap will set automatically when equal upward pressure is applied simultaneously to each of the fishhooks. As this is done, each of the contractile helical springs begins to elongate to the point where they reach a horizontal position. Once above the horizontal plane, the springs begin to automatically contract. They cannot contract completely, which would position the bait hooks in a near vertical position, because they are arrested in their rotation just above a horizontal plane due to the six arrestors that have now come into contact with the spring-holding copper sleeves on each fishhook.

This trap is sprung when any of the fishhooks or bait holders have outward pressure applied to them, and when it does so, it comes together with incredible ferocity.

The use of a lead plate, rather than one of a different metal, would serve to act as a stabilizer under water, preventing excessive swaying of the trap.

The one known example of this fish trap is unmarked.

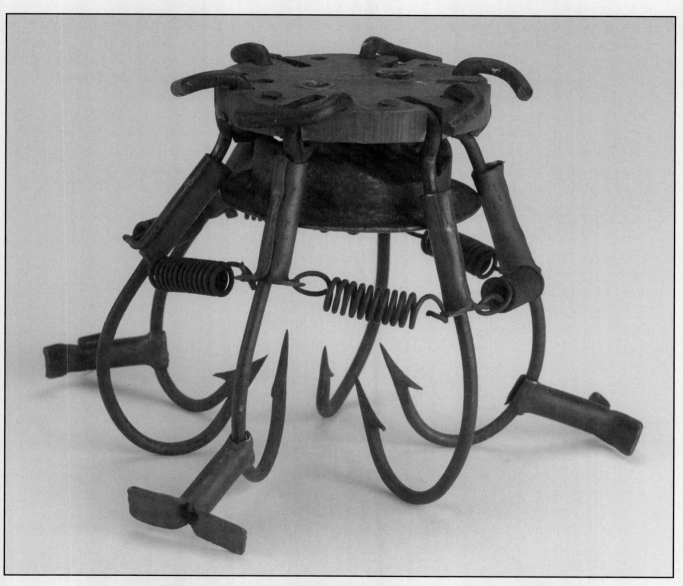

Unidentified trap with six helical springs, shown in the sprung position.

Name:	Unidentified, trap with eight helical springs
Patented:	Unknown, but should have been. Circa 1900.
Origin:	Unidentified
Size:	4" tall not measuring the line-tie, 8½" jaw spread when set
Material:	Steel, spring-steel, and brass
Value:	$2,500.00+

Only a mechanical genius could have envisioned and constructed this metal killer fish trap. It has four striking jaws, which are powered by eight contractile helical springs, all of which must act and perform in harmony for this trap to be effective.

When in the set position, the four striking jaws lay in a horizontal plane with a single bait hook dangling from the center of the contraption. When the fish pulls upon the bait, the entire trap works in unison to strike the fish from four directions.

This fish trap would have to have been used when accompanied by a partner, as it is impossible(?) to set with only one pair of hands. One can only try to imagine the difficulty that would be involved in extricating this trap from a fish's head once it was caught.

This is a finely made, intricate fish trap with a crude line-tie and is the only example known to exist in the hands of collectors.

Unidentified trap with eight helical springs, shown in the set position.

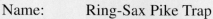

Name:	Ring-Sax Pike Trap
Patented:	Unknown. Circa 1880 – 1920.
Origin:	Sweden
Size:	14" – 20" in length, circular jaws 8" – 12" in diameter
Material:	Steel and spring-steel, hand-forged or (rarely) factory
Value:	$500.00+

As its name implies, the Ring-Sax is big, having been made to capture and kill northern pike and other large fish, including salmon. It is composed of an inner and an outer circular jaw, with each jaw having from eight to eighteen teeth, which are usually attached with rivets. The jaws are rotated 90° to be put in the set position, and at such time look similar to the relaxed position, in that one jaw is concentric to the other.

The Ring-Sax is made of high-quality Swedish steel and is powered by a single long spring, which may be stamped in a variety of ways, including "PATENT" or with any number of blacksmith's names, such as Eriksson, or may have no stampings. A large number of variations occur in this trap, with some having a brass dog, different long spring shapes, and a variety of ways in which the teeth are attached and configured, but all have the same mechanism.

If attempting to set a Ring-Sax Pike Trap, have someone else nearby with a physician's phone number, as you could lose your arm.

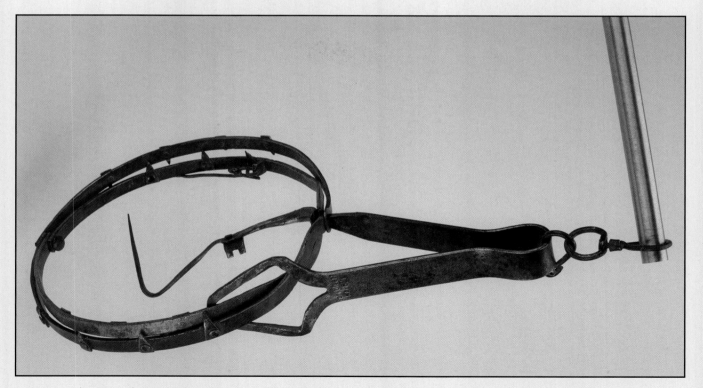

Ring-Sax Pike Trap shown reduced in size. These traps are very large and dangerous. A dead minnow was used on the bait hook. The Ring-Sax was a real killer trap; if a fish took the bait, it was all over for the hapless pike.

Name:	Lundgren's Rex Fish Trap
Patented:	Unknown. Circa 1880 – 1920.
Origin:	Sweden
Size:	12" – 18" long, 5" – 9" across
Material:	Steel and spring-steel, hand-forged
Value:	$300.00 – 600.00

The Lundgren's Rex body is formed by a single rod of spring-steel bent so as to have a coil at its center producing an eye. The terminal ends of the rod have teeth either formed integral to the rod or attached by rivets to the flattened ends. If done by the latter method, any number of teeth could be attached.

A large number of variations occur in this trap, with some having a brass dog or a brass bait hook, different coil-spring shapes, and a variety of ways in which the teeth are attached and configured, but all have the same mechanism.

The Lundgren's Rex was made of high-quality Swedish steel.

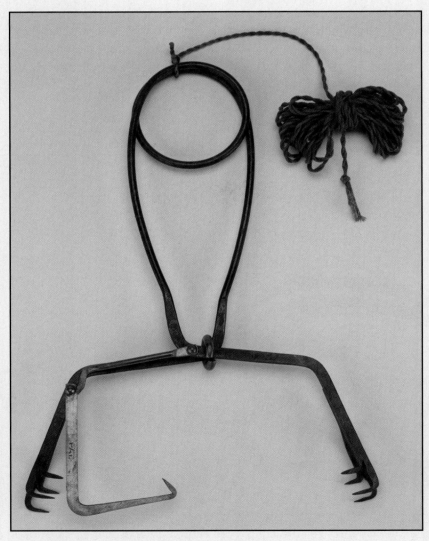

Lundgren's Rex Fish Trap shown reduced in size, in the set position. These traps were used for pike and other large fish and have a hair-trigger setting mechanism. A dead minnow was used on the bait hook. These traps were effective traps to use ice fishing.

Name:	The Greer Patent Lever Fish Hook
Patented:	January 23, 1900, patent #641,857 and December 15, 1908, patent #906,792 by Moses Greer
Origin:	Atlanta, Georgia
Size:	Four sizes; measurements are without the length of the line-tie rod. 1/0, 1¾"; 3/0, 2⅛"; 5/0, 3"; 7/0, 3½"
Material:	Blued steel
Value:	$35.00 – 70.00 each, with the smallest and largest sizes much scarcer and of a different gauge wire.

The Greer Patent Lever Fish Hook was the first fishhook patented in the twentieth century and was sold folded into a white onionskin paper advertisement that listed its size. These advertisements are valued at $125.00 – 175.00 each.

The Greers most commonly found are of the design shown in the 1908 patent. The Greer whose design follows the earlier 1900 patent, called a "slot" Greer, is very rare and is valued at $200.00+.

NEVER LOSE A FISH
BY USING THE GREER PATENT LEVER HOOKS.
SIZE 1/0

SET

SPRING

MANUFACTURED BY
THE GREER MFG. CO., Atlanta, Ga.
——DIRECTIONS:——
Bait the small hook and turn it down, then fasten the clamp in such a manner to the large hook, that when the fish bites, the large hook will release itself easily. By lowering the clamp less force will be needed to throw the Hook forward. The harder the fish pulls, the tighter the Lever Hook holds. Best results are obtained by setting so it will not pull off too easy.

FISHING MADE EASY BY USING THE GREER PATENT LEVER HOOK

SET

SIZE 3/0

The Greer Patent Lever Fish Hook was wrapped in an advertising paper with setting instructions, shown left, and sold in a sliding cardboard box, right.

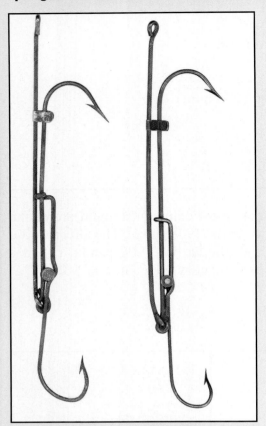

Two "slot" Greers, actual size, shown in set position.

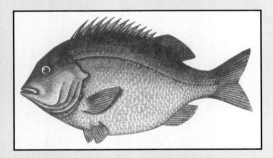

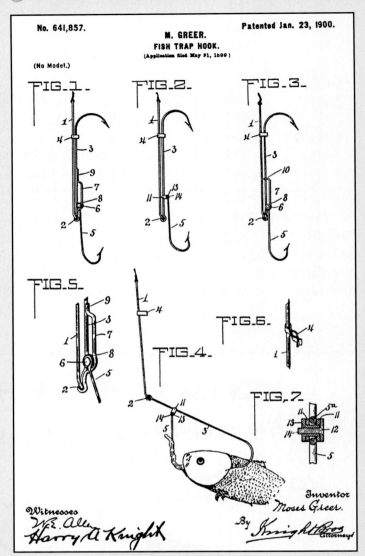

The Greer's 1900 patent drawing shows the slot hook and the earliest standard version.

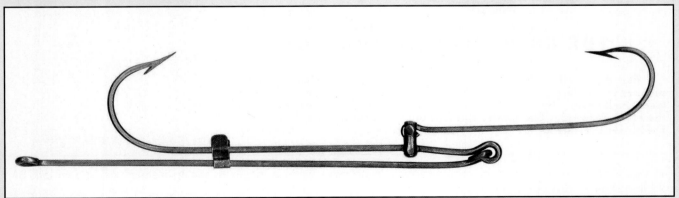

A 1900-style Greer, with a different bait hook assembly than the 1908 patent. These are very rare and valued at $200.00 – 300.00. This one is shown in the set position.

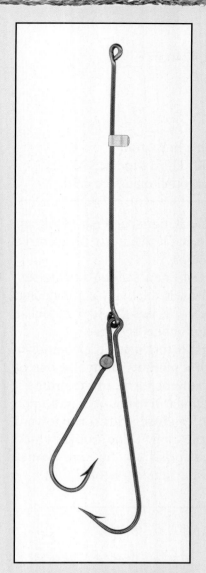

The 1908 model Greer, shown in the sprung position.

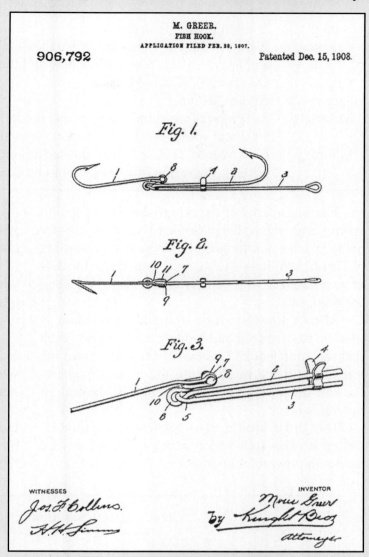

M. GREER.
FISH HOOK.
APPLICATION FILED FEB. 28, 1907.

906,792

Patented Dec. 15, 1908.

Fig. 1.

Fig. 2.

Fig. 3.

WITNESSES
Jos. F. Collins.
H. H. Simms

INVENTOR
Moue Greer
by Knight Bros
Attorneys

The 1908 patent drawing shows the style of the Greer hook most commonly found.

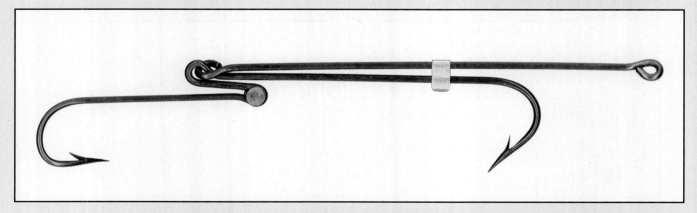

The 1908 model Greer, shown in the set position.

Name:	The Kingfisher Fish Hook
Patented:	February 26, 1901, patent #668,658; October 6, 1903, patent #740,775; and May 9, 1911, patent #991,800 by Frank H. Pardon
Origin:	Owensboro, Kentucky
Size:	About 3" long
Material:	First model, steel and lead; second model, steel and spring-steel; third model, steel and spring-steel with a brass rod
Value:	First Model, $100.00 – 150.00; second model, $50.00 – 60.00; Third Model, $200.00 – 300.00. The value of a hook would be double if the hook was found on a nice card.

The first model of the Kingfisher contained no spring and was a lever hook by design, simply using a lead counterweight to hold it in the set position, whereas the second and third models incorporated a wind-up type coil spring to keep the hook set.

Also of note as to the variations on this hook is that the first and second models are designed such that the "gaff hook" descends from above into the top of the fish's head, while the third model has the gaff hook rising from below into the bottom of the fish's head.

The third model also incorporates into its design a brass rod, which acts as the line-tie and assists in powering the trap.

The springs on the Kingfisher Fish Hook are very delicate and perhaps the most diminutive ever used in a spring hook.

The second model of Frank Pardon's fishhooks, which came in four sizes, is relatively common and may be found on the card, but the first model is uncommon and the third model is scarce.

From Pardon's first patent text: "...a composite fishhook consisting of a plurality of hooks, one of which is adapted to hang pendent, in the ordinary manner, and another under tension of a pull upon the first-named hook to close with force toward the same and gaff the fish." The hook, which hangs in the vertical position, he said would "hereinafter be called the pendent hook."

Kingfisher promotion coupon advertising free premiums.

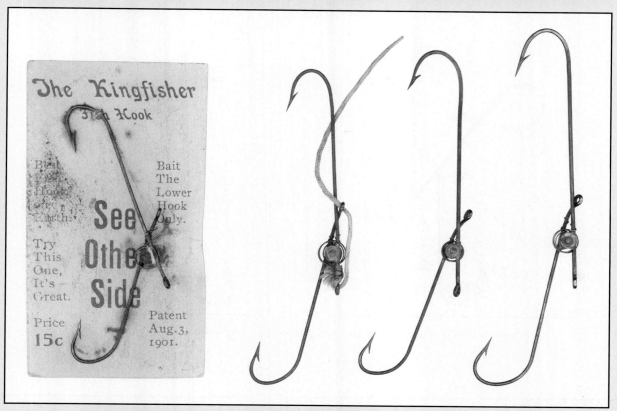

Set of four different size Kingfisher second model hooks and the card that it was sold on. Hooks are in the set position and are shown actual size.

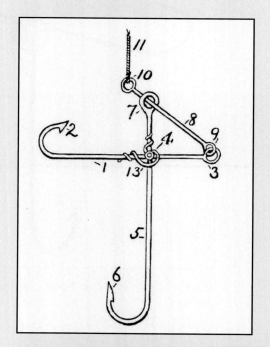

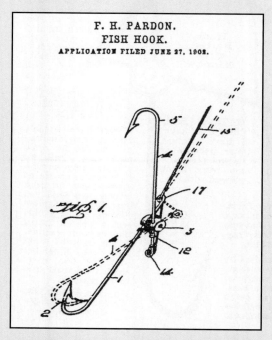

Patent drawings of the third model Kingfisher, on the left, and the second model, on the right. The second model Kingfisher is the most common.

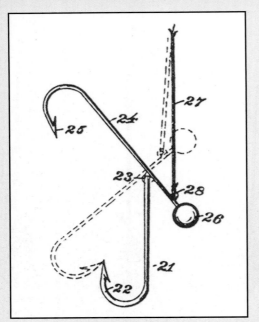

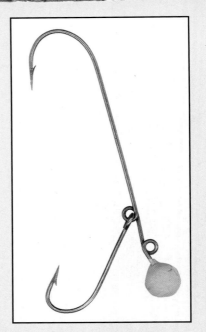

Patent drawing of the first model Kingfisher hook and the hook itself.

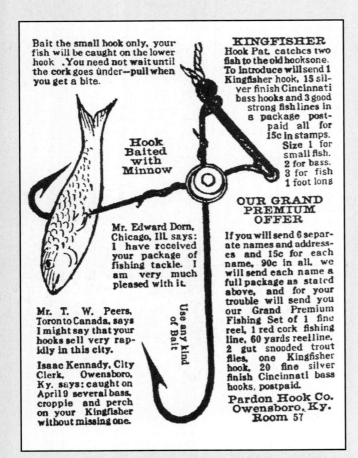

Bait the small hook only, your fish will be caught on the lower hook . You need not wait until the cork goes under--pull when you get a bite.

Hook Baited with Minnow

Mr. Edward Dorn, Chicago, Ill. says: I have received your package of fishing tackle. I am very much pleased with it.

Mr. T. W. Peers, Toronto Canada, says I might say that your hooks sell very rapidly in this city.

Isaac Kennady, City Clerk, Owensboro, Ky. says: caught on April 9 several bass, croppie and perch on your Kingfisher without missing one.

Use any kind of Bait

KINGFISHER
Hook Pat. catches two fish to the old hook one. To introduce will send 1 Kingfisher hook, 15 silver finish Cincinnati bass hooks and 3 good strong fish lines in 8 package post-paid all for 15c in stamps. Size 1 for small fish. 2 for bass. 3 for fish 1 foot long

OUR GRAND PREMIUM OFFER

If you will send 6 separate names and address-es and 15c for each name, 90c in all, we will send each name a full package as stated above, and for your trouble will send you our Grand Premium Fishing Set of 1 fine reel, 1 red cork fishing line, 60 yards reel line, 2 gut snooded trout files, one Kingfisher hook, 20 fine silver finish Cincinnati bass hooks, postpaid.
Pardon Hook Co. Owensboro, Ky. Room 57

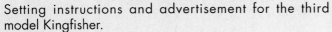

Setting instructions and advertisement for the third model Kingfisher.

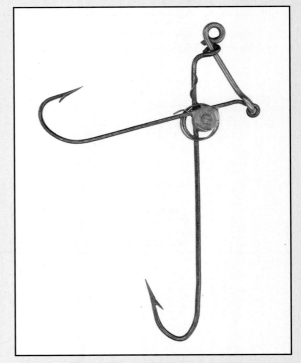

Third model Kingfisher hook, shown in the set position.

Specialty Price List No. 9.

A word to customers. In connection with our Fish Bait we handle a few other specialties for fishermen, and when making up your order, we would be pleased to have you include any of these you may need. We handle nothing but the very best grade of goods, and everything we sell is guaranteed to give perfect satisfaction or money refunded. Send us a trial order and you will be well pleased, and know where to get your money's worth when you want anything in fishing tackle.

How to send money. Postal money orders are the safest way to send remittances. They cost but little and there is no chance for loss. If you cannot purchase a money order at your post office, send money by registered letter, or any way that is safe and convenient. Postage stamps accepted for small amounts, which may be sent safely in an ordinary letter. (One Cent Stamps Prefered.)

We pay the postage. Everything shown in this price list, sent by Parcel Post, Prepaid, and we guarantee safe delivery of goods. Make up your order now while you think of it. Be sure to always write your name and address plainly, so there will be no delay in filling your orders. No foreign stamps will be accepted.

The "Kingfisher" Hook
Makes Every Bite A Catch.

This is an automatic spring hook and is so constructed that when a fish gives the slightest pull on the bait the upper hook reaches down and gets a hold that lands him, every time. It hangs perpendicular in the water, so that the upper hook is entirely out of the way and does not interfere with the fish when taking the bait. The upper hook is larger and longer than the lower one, and gets a deep, sure hold on the fish that saves him. Many fish are safely landed with the Kingfisher where a common hook would have let them get away.

Nothing is more discouraging or disappointing, than to get a shallow hold on a fine large fish and have him splash back into the water just as you are about to land him. That luck never happens when you are using the Kingfisher—he is sure YOUR MEAT whenever he gives it a "yank."

This wonderful hook is automatic in action, and should it fail to catch the fish the first time he touches the bait, it quickly resets itself and is ready for him again; and just as sure as he gives the least pull on the bait he will be your fish, for there is no chance for him to get away after he is once hooked on a Kingfisher. If you want to catch every fish that "monkeys" around your bait use the Kingfisher Hook.

Made in 3 sizes—No.1 for small fish, No.2 for medium, and No.3 for larger fish.

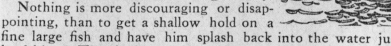
Price Each 15 cts. 2 for 25 cts. 12 for $1.00
A Complete Set of the Three Sizes for 35cts.

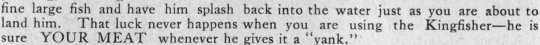

Agents wanted. Send $1.00 for a dozen and you will be surprised how fast they sell. Guaranteed to give perfect satisfaction or your money refunded. Try a dozen.

Early advertisement circular for the Kingfisher hook.

Name:	Monarch Automatic Fish Hook
Patented:	March 25, 1902, patent #696,013 and September 2, 1924, patent #1,507,344 by George H. Doering
Origin:	Brooklyn, New York
Size:	Produced in two sizes, small and large, in various lengths from 3½" to 4½". This hook was manufactured in six different styles.
Material:	Spring-steel, steel, steel and brass rivets
Value:	Style 1, $200.00+; style 2, $65.00 – 100.00; style 3, $65.00 – 100.00; style 4, $20.00 – 40.00; style 5, $20.00 – 40.00; style 6, $20.00 – 40.00.

The Monarch Automatic fishhook, which was made in several varieties, is composed of two jaws, or gripping hooks, which cross each other near their upper ends and are pivotally connected at the point of intersection by a pivot pin (rivet). The bait hook is connected at this pivot point by several means, which are discussed in the text on the six different styles of Monarch hooks. The upper arms of the gripping hooks are connected by a spring-steel wire, which has a coil at its center that also serves as the line-tie eye. When the bait hook is pulled downward, the jaws close upon the fish. The Monarch hook was manufactured in two sizes. The Model B, for small fish, could be purchased with three different bait hook sizes, the striking jaws all being the same size. Model C, for large fish, was offered in two different sizes of bait hooks, the striking jaws being the same size, which was larger than that of the Model B. Therefore, one could collect five different hook varieties in each of the six different styles, or a total of 30 hooks, to have a complete collection of the Monarch Automatic Fish Hook. This is a real challenge. No one has yet put a complete set together. Tim Mierzwa has collected 23 so far, after 15 years of searching. These figures are assuming that style 1 came in five varieties; so far, the only size to surface is the one shown in the text. It is hoped that when these different styles are understood, more of them will turn up.

Style 1 — The whole setting notch is cut out completely on both trap jaws. When the jaws are spread apart, a latch-lug holds them apart. This latch-lug is attached to a trigger plate, which slides up and down between the jaws. The bait hook is riveted to the trigger plate so that when the fish bites, the whole mechanism pulls out of the setting notch, which springs the trap. A small spring keeps the latch-lug engaged.

Style 2 — The setting notch is formed by half the notch being on each jaw; when the jaws are spread apart, the half-notch on each jaw forms a complete setting notch for the latch-lug to set into, thereby setting the trap. A small spring keeps the latch-lug engaged. The mechanism on this hook is the same as that for style 1. The half-notch ends in a point along the edge of the striking jaw, which looks like half a diamond when the trap is in the closed position.

Style 3 — This trap is the same as style 2, except that the half-notch blends into the edge of the striking jaw, giving it a rounded appearance when the hook is in the closed position.

Style 4 — This trap functions the same as styles 1, 2, and 3, except there is no small spring to hold the latch-lug in place and there is no need for a trigger plate. The whole mechanism has been simplified. The striking jaws are ³⁄₃₂" wide, the same width as that of styles 1, 2, and 3.

Style 5 — This trap is the same as style 4, except the striking jaws are ⅛" wide.

Style 6 — This trap doesn't employ a latch-lug to keep jaws apart. The bait hook is riveted to the striking jaws and acts as a pivot point for the jaws. There is no mechanism to set and release the trap. Curiously, this hook sets the easiest of all six styles.

Note: Style 1 is the only Monarch that fully matches the 1902 patent. Styles 2 and 3 employ the mechanism illustrated in the 1902 patent but use a different way of forming the setting notch. Styles 4 and 5 conform to the 1924 patent.

Style 6 exhibits the jaws and spring of the 1924 patent but has no mechanism.

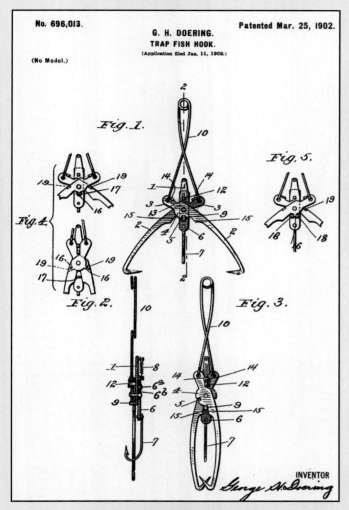

1902 Monarch patent #696,013.

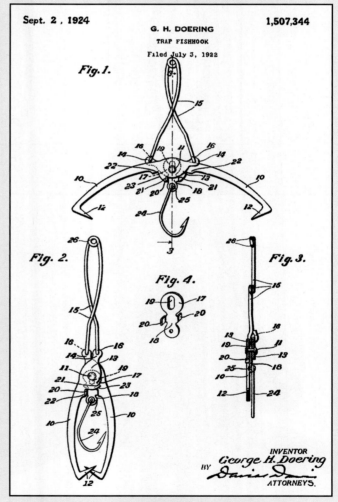

1924 Monarch patent #1,507,344.

Style 1.

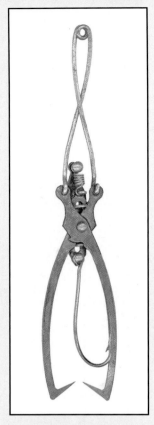

Style 2.

Style 3.

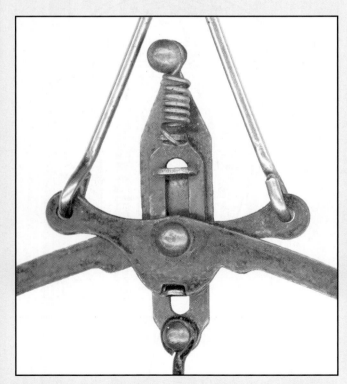

Enlarged mechanism to show setting notch on style 1.

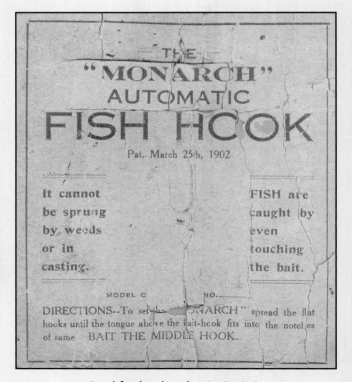

Card for hook styles 1, 2, & 3.

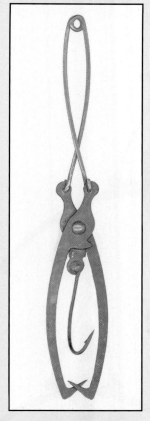

Style 4.

Style 5.

Style 6.

—THE—
"MONARCH"
AUTOMATIC
FISH HOOK

Pat. March 25th, 1902.   September 2nd, 1924.

It cannot
be sprung
by weeds
or in
casting.

FISH are
caught by
even
touching
the bait.

No. 7130

DIRECTIONS—To set the "MONARCH" spread the flat
hooks until the tongue above the bait-hook fits into the notches
of same. BAIT THE MIDDLE HOOK.

"MONARCH"
AUTOMATIC
FISH HOOK

FISH are
caught by
even
touching
the bait.

PAT. MARCH 25, 1902
SEPT. 2, 1924

No. 3612

The more
they pull
the tighter
it holds

DIRECTIONS—To set the "MONARCH" spread the flat
gaff hooks apart until they stay open.
BAIT THE MIDDLE HOOK

Card for hook styles 4 & 5.

Card for hook style 6.

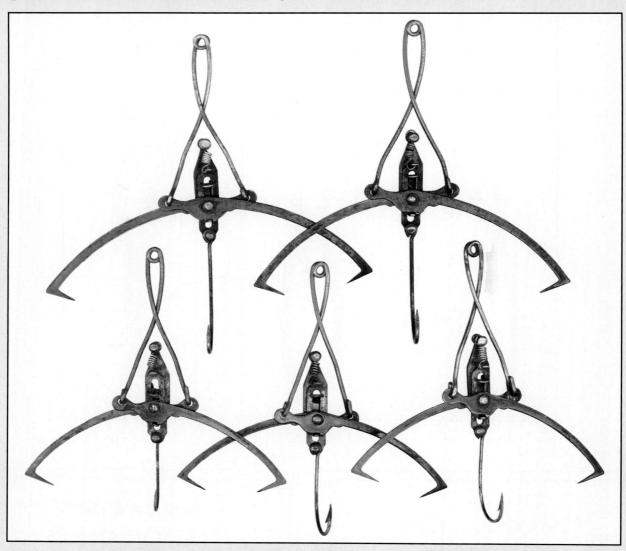

Set of five style 3 Monarch Automatic Fish Hooks, shown actual size.

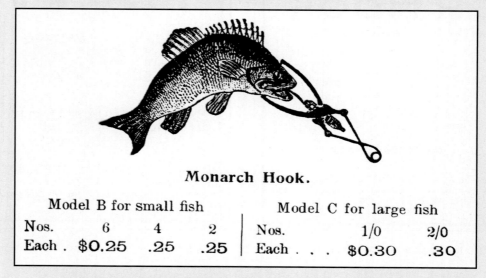

Monarch Hook.

Model B for small fish			Model C for large fish	
Nos.	6	4	2	Nos.	1/0	2/0
Each .	$0.25	.25	.25	Each . . .	$0.30	.30

Monarch advertisement showing the jaw sizes and hook numbers.

1904 advertisement for the Monarch Automatic Fish Hook.

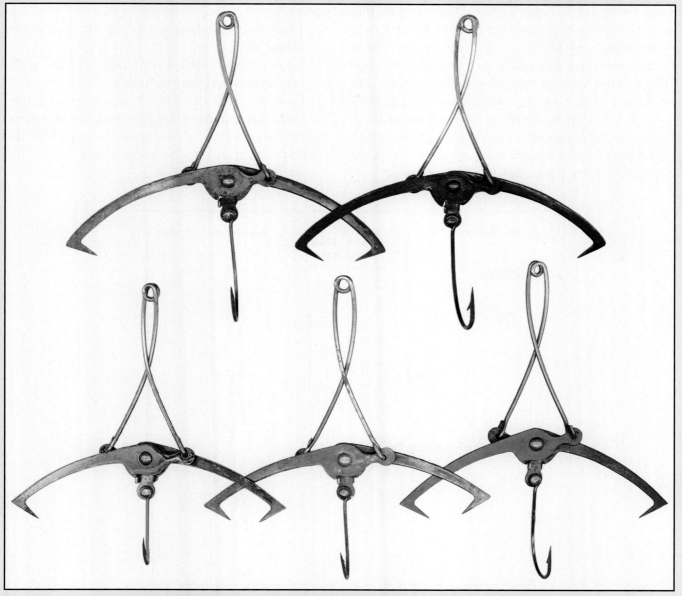

Set of five style 5 Monarch Automatic Fish Hooks, shown actual size.

Name:	The Monopole or Berner's Automatic Fish Hook
Patented:	May 27, 1902, patent #701,132 by Paul B. T. Berner
Origin:	Brooklyn, New York
Size:	3" – 4" in long with four different styles
Material:	Steel and spring-steel
Value:	$500.00 – 750.00

The automatic fishhooks made by Paul Berner, who describes himself in the letters of patent as "a subject of the Emperor of Germany, residing at Brooklyn Borough, New York City," was a puzzlement to collectors for many years. This was due to the fact that these finely made, obviously manufactured spring-hooks came in four different styles that were similar to each other but none of which exactly matched any known patent drawings. These hooks were once referred to as "Timothys," in reference to the name of the spring-hook collector, and co-author of this book, who owned one of each style. It was only in recent years that one of these automatic fishhooks was found on the card, which stated the inventor's name and patent date, with the hook also having the patent date stamped on it.

The two styles of this fishhook that have no real "mechanism" came in blued steel, while the two styles with a mechanism were not blued. Any of the hooks in the four styles may be found unmarked or may be stamped "PAT APPLD FOR," or may rarely have the patent date stamped on them.

These fish traps may be found with bait hooks of various sizes.

Berner's Automatic Fish Hooks, in any style, are very scarce and very desirable.

From patent text: "A fishhook comprising pivoted members, a spring for actuating the members, and a disk-shaped slide made to regulate the action of the spring and to act as a drag."

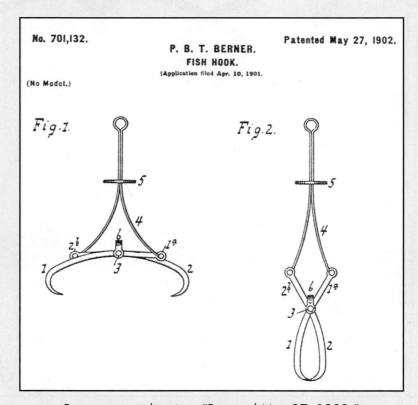

Berner patent drawing, "Patented May 27, 1902."

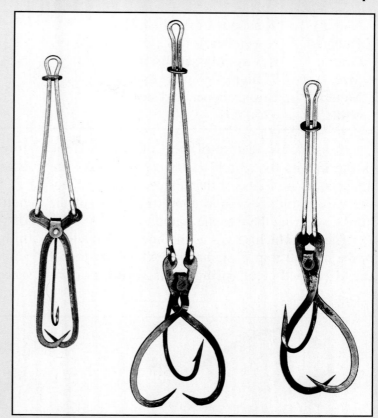

No-mechanism Berner, blued-steel style, actual size.

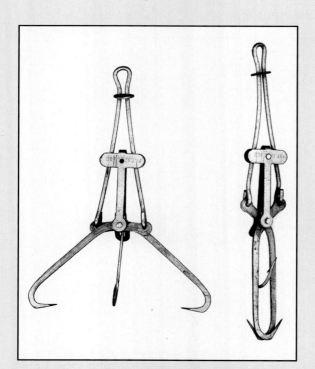

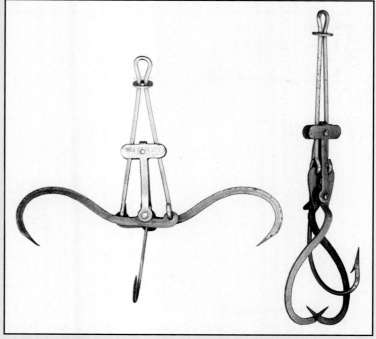

Berner hooks, two different styles, with mechanisms, sprung and set, actual size.

Name:	Thaddeus Coffin Fish Hook
Patented:	November 4, 1902, patent #712,497
Origin:	Revere, Massachusetts
Size:	7" high, 4½" wide expanded
Material:	Brass, copper, and steel
Value:	$750.00+

A distinctive feature of the Coffin Fish Hook is the means by which the two bait hooks are attached to the frame of the device. Very fine copper wire is tightly wound about the shank of the hooks, securing them to the frame.

The rod which serves as the line-tie is made of brass and the trap is stamped "PAT'D" on top of the U-shaped steel spring. This spring is reinforced by another U-shaped steel spring on its inner side, just as described in the patent.

From patent text: "When a fish swallows the bait the line is jerked upward, causing the clip of the slidable shank to leave the pins and permitting the device to expand…The fish can also impale itself when the line is secured to a stationary object."

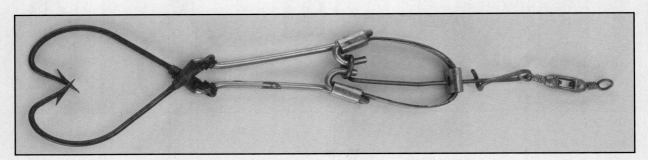

Thaddeus Coffin Fish Hook in the set position.

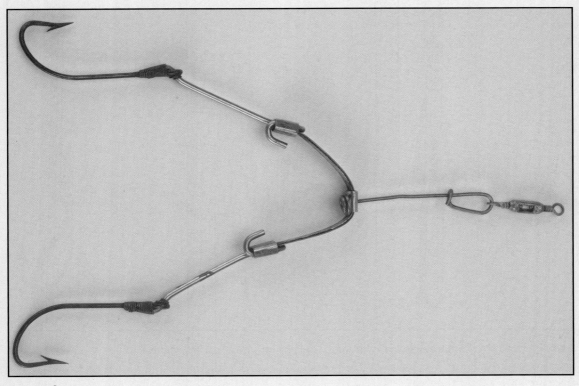

Thaddeus Coffin Fish Hook in the sprung position.

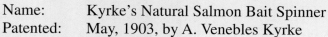

Name:	Kyrke's Natural Salmon Bait Spinner
Patented:	May, 1903, by A. Venebles Kyrke
Origin:	England
Material:	Brass, nickel-plated brass, and spring-steel wire
Size:	4¾" long
Value:	$500.00+

The Kyrke's Natural Salmon Bait Spinner is powered by a spring-steel wire with a coil formed near its center, producing an eye. This eye slides upon the central brass pin, which extends from the painted head. When the spring is compressed, the eye is slid into the head and allows the central pin to engage the loops on the spring hook's arms, thus setting the lure.

Into the head of this nicely made piece are two pivotally mounted L-shaped spikes that serve to help secure the bait by rotating inwardly and piercing the bait's head.

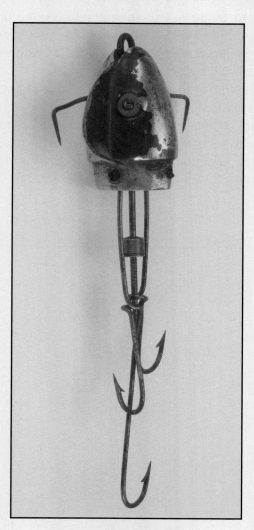

Kyrke's in the set position.

Kyrke's in the sprung position.

Name:	Ward's Fish Trap
Patented:	March 29, 1904, patent #755,726 by Charles H. Ward
Origin:	Jackson, Michigan
Size:	7½" long, 6½" jaw spread when set
Material:	Blued steel and spring-steel with brass pulley
Value:	$4000.00+

The Ward's Fish Trap is perhaps the rarest patented item ever to come out of the State of Michigan with the express purpose of catching a fish. The trap is uniquely designed and depends upon the line attached to the bait hook to be looped over a brass pulley and thence downward to where it is attached to the trap where the two striking jaws pivotally meet. When a fish bites and exerts pressure on the line, the line slides over the pulley and exerts upward pressure on the jaws, thus tripping them and impaling the unsuspecting fish.

This trap also has incorporated into it a "collar," a slotted steel plate, "which is made to encircle the resilient arms and easily traverse upward and downward along the arms, and act by gravity as a follower to hold the grip gained by the closing together of the arms when the jaws are tripped."

The Ward's Fish Trap employs a setscrew near the point where the two jaws are riveted together, which serves as an adjustment to the tension on the trap.

Stamped into one striking jaw of the device is "PAT'D.MAR.29.04."

When found in excellent condition, the bluing on this unique Michigan fish trap has an iridescent shimmer that can best be described as resembling gasoline on water and is quite beautiful.

Less than five of these fish traps are known to exist in the hands of collectors.

From patent text: "...the objects of my invention are to secure the fish when the bait is taken by instantly gripping the fish, the fish tripping the gaff-hooks by slightly pulling on the line."

Ward's in the set position, size reduced.

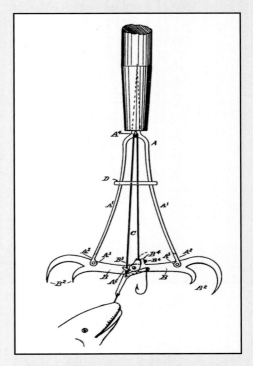

Ward's Fish Trap patent drawing.

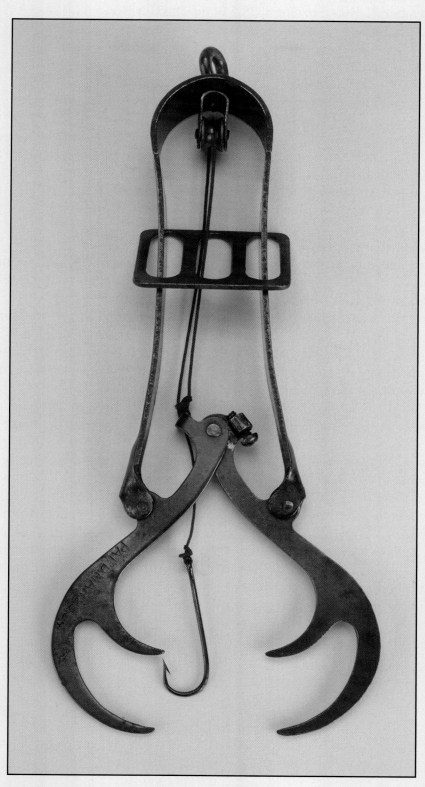

Ward's Fish Trap shown actual size in the sprung position. The patent date is stamped in the jaw.

Name:	The Sure Catch Fish Hook, "Chicago Rake Trap," or Rud Fish Trap
Patented:	December 27, 1904, patent #778,552 by Theodor Rud
Origin:	Chicago, Illinois
Size:	3¼" when folded in half, 5½" extended, not including 3" line-tie
Material:	Nickel-plated brass and spring-brass and steel
Value:	$2,500.00+ without box

This trap is designed in a fashion whereas the distinctive bait pin, which holds the bait, also acts as the dog to this trap. This bait pin is located centrally to two arms that terminate in three teeth each, each arm looking in every way like a garden rake, hence the nickname "Chicago Rake Trap." When the fish pulls on the bait the dog is disengaged, thus springing the trap, which is powered by a brass coiled spring.

An odd design about this trap is that it is articulated, bending in half where the line-tie rod attaches to the trap.

Instructions for the use of this trap are printed on the box in which it was originally sold, the only such box known to exist in collectors' hands. It reads as follows:

The Sure Catch Fish Hook, No. 1 (For Still Fishing Only)

A small bait should be used and placed on the needle inside the arms of the bait hook. No bait should hang down or be outside of the arms; otherwise, the fish can take the bait from the side and skip. Let the hook down slowly, also draw up slowly; so the hook cannot close up. The hook must be very sharp. Always keep a small file in your tackle box. If setting is too tight or too loose, the point of the trigger can easily be fixed to suit.

If hook is used in shallow water use a float on the line so the hook does not reach the bottom.

Manufactured by
T. Rud 629 Artesian Ave.
Chicago, ILL.

Although the "No. 1" on the box would seem to suggest that this fish trap came in other sizes, none are known to exist.

When found in the box, this trap will have an 11" twine leader to which a 3" rod of lead, folded in half, will be attached. This weight acts to stabilize the trap from excessive movement when in the water.

The "Chicago Rake Trap" is stamped "PAT.DEC.27.04" on the frame.

The fish trap invented by Theodor Rud is highly sought after by collectors, but rarely seen.

From patent text: "My invention includes a pair of spring arms or jaws carrying hooks and which may be separated from each other against spring pressure and a trigger arranged to maintain such arms or jaws separated from each other...is designed to be tripped by the fish endeavoring to secure the bait...so as to grasp and hold the fish therebetween."

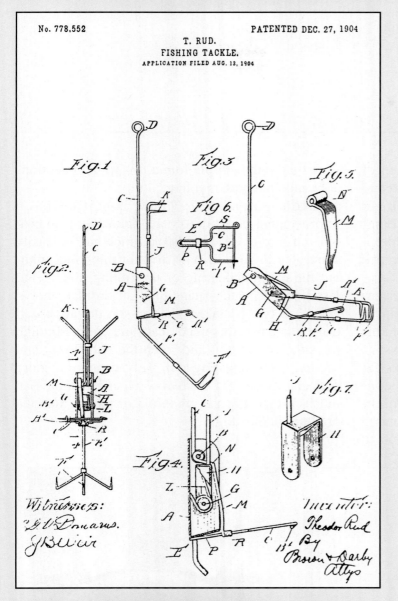

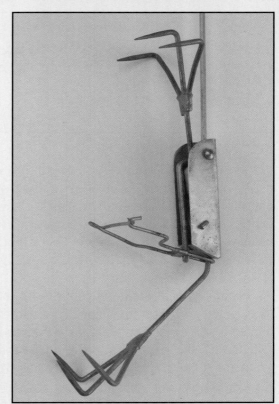

Rud hook in the set position.

Rud enlarged to show date stamp.

Rud box top.

Rud box end.

Name:	Flegel "Throat Trap" Fish Hook
Patented:	February 21,1905, patent #783,253 by Benjamin F. Flegel
Origin:	Racine, Wisconsin
Size:	2½" long
Material:	Nickel-plated steel
Value:	$750.00 – 1,000.00

The Flegel "Throat Trap" is compromised of two exquisitely turned hooks pivotally mounted at the base of a straight shaft that has a "swell," or flattened part, where the barbs come together when in the closed position and keeps them "properly separated." This mechanical hook is stamped "PAT.2.21.05" on the hub.

From personal communication with the inventor's great-grandson and namesake, Benjamin, is related a story that has been passed down from his grandfather, the inventor's son, and is as follows:

A magazine article was written, he thinks for *Field and Stream*, whose subject was the contents of the fishing tackle box of President Theodore Roosevelt. In his tackle box was a Flegel "Throat Trap," and the article goes on to state that many people found this to be objectionable and "unsportsmanlike."

From patent text: "This invention is an improvement in fishhooks: and its object is to provide an improved snare-hook which can be easily concealed in bait, such as frogs or minnows, without the barbs appearing or protruding, thus being less liable to catch snags than an ordinary hook, yet if the bait is 'taken' the jerk on the hook will cause the barbs to spread apart and pierce through the sides of the bait and catch the fish firmly and securely, the resisting pull only causing a more firm engagement of the barbs, which catch the fish much farther down in its throat or mouth than the ordinary hooks do."

 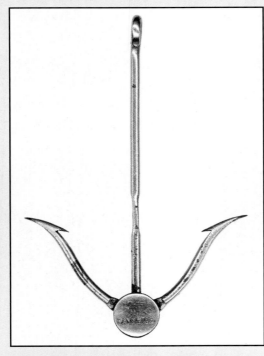 

Left to right: Flegel Hook in the set position, Flegel Hook in the sprung position, Flegel Hook mechanism enlarged to show date stamp.

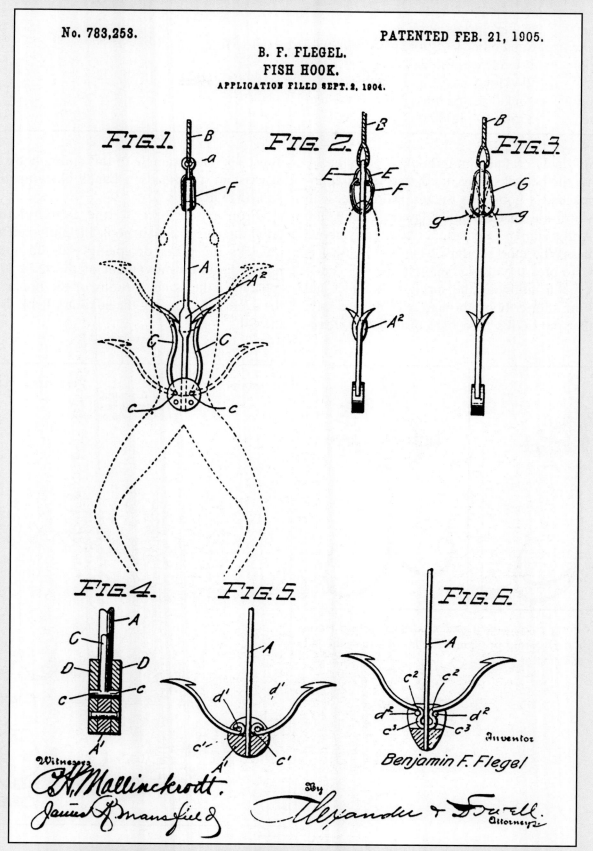

No. 783,253.

PATENTED FEB. 21, 1905.

B. F. FLEGEL.
FISH HOOK.
APPLICATION FILED SEPT. 2, 1904.

Inventor
Benjamin F. Flegel

Flegel Hook 1905 patent showing how the bait is attatched to the hook.

Name:	Miller Spring Hook
Patented:	September 19, 1905, patent #800,001 by Otto Miller
Origin:	Providence, Rhode Island
Size:	2¼" long
Material:	Nickel-plated brass and spring-steel
Value:	$750.00 – 1,000.00

This finely crafted spring hook is powered by a contractile helical spring. It consists of a stationary hook and a hook that rotates 180 degrees. In the set position, the two hooks lay one against the other with a similar orientation, one slightly above the other. When the shorter of the two hooks has downward pressure exerted upon it, the dog is disengaged, thus allowing the spring to contract and "spin" the shorter hook through a 180-degree arc, such that the hooks then face in opposite directions. The one example of this spring hook known to exist in a collector's hands is stamped "PAT APL'D FOR."

From patent text: "…the action of the fish upon striking the bait hook instantly releases or unlocks the other or spring-pressed auxiliary hook, the axial movement of the latter thereby separating the point portions of the hooks and at the same time causing the auxiliary hook to pierce the fish."

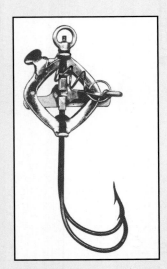
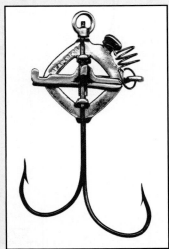
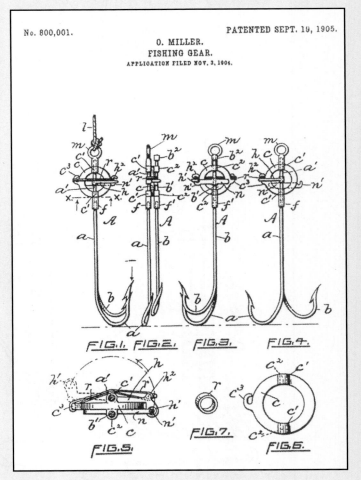

Miller Spring Hook patent and the Miller Spring Hook in the set and sprung positions. The hook is from the Jeff Kieny collection.

Name:	John P. Smith Snag-Hook
Patented:	December 12, 1905, patent #807,135 by John P. Smith
Origin:	New Haven, Connecticut
Size:	7½" tall, 4½" at base with eight steel bait hooks
Value:	$2,500.00+

The construction of the John P. Smith Snag-Hook is that of eight spring-brass rods securely anchored together near the top, with each rod having a replaceable bait hook at its other end. These eight rods are then encircled by a sliding brass ring. When this ring is positioned nearest to the bait hooks, the eight rods of spring brass are compressed together, and the trap is thus in the set position.

To actuate the trap, the fishing line to it is strung in such a way that it wraps around the brass retaining ring in such a fashion that when the line is jerked upward, the ring is forced upward also, thus allowing the eight rods and their attached bait hooks to spring and expand outwardly. Therefore, the mechanism of this fish trap is not integral to the trap itself, but rather, depends on the way in which the fishing line is tied to the trap.

Another novelty of this trap is the way in which it is baited. Bait is not attached to any of the eight bait hooks, but rather is placed in or near the head of the trap. Sometimes this trap is found with a spiral brass wire attached near the line-tie for attaching the bait, as is shown in the patent drawings, while at other times this trap simply employs the brass "cage" near the line-tie for enclosing the bait, as explained in the patent text.

The John P. Smith is sometimes found with the patent date stamped into it near the line-tie, but may also be found with no stampings.

This trap is very desirable, and displays beautifully, as it independently stands upward.

There are less than five examples of the John P. Smith Snag-Hook known to exist in collectors' hands.

From patent text: "This invention relates to an improvement in snag-hooks or combination of fishhooks, and particularly to such as have a series of hooks depending from a head to which bait is attached, and so that if the bait is nibbled a sudden upward movement of the hooks will be apt to catch one or more fish."

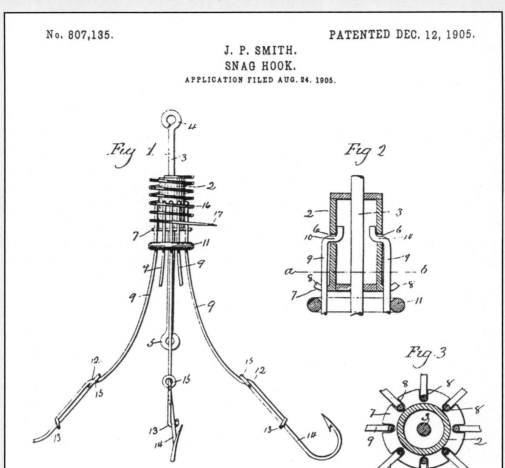

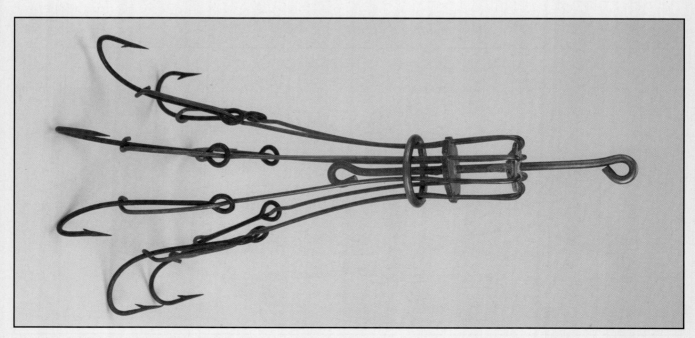

This Smith Snag Hook employs a brass "cage" near the line-tie for enclosing the bait. The hook is shown reduced in size.

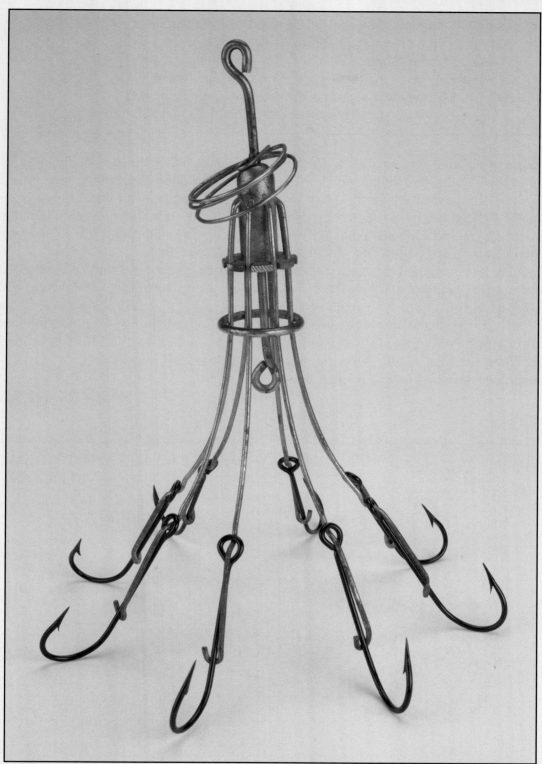

This Smith Snag Hook is shown actual size and has the patent date stamped on the line-tie shank. Note the expandable spring bait holder near the top of the trap.

Name:	Gabriel Automatic-Setting Big Fish and Animal Trap
Patented:	May 15, 1906, patent #820,640 by William Gabrielson
Origin:	Kansas City, Missouri
Size:	8½" long, 5" across
Material:	Steel and spring-steel with delicate brass setting mechanism
Value:	$2,000.00+ when complete, self-setting, and in good or better condition

The Gabriel is a long-spring trap with two rotating round jaws and a bait holder made of a fishhook. It was first advertised by the Missouri Sales Company of Kansas City, Missouri, in 1908 and was called the Gabriel Fish and Animal Trap, with advertisements changed later to call it the Gabriel Big Fish and Animal Trap, and was last advertised for sale in the fall of 1918.

The most distinguishable feature of the Gabriel, aside from its shape, is the exquisitely delicate and complex brass and steel self-setting mechanism. When the long spring is compressed and the two circular jaws rotate 90°, a small brass pin, which acts as the dog on this trap, is automatically sprung into a retaining hole, thus setting the trap. This mechanism was easily broken or worn out and thus, it is rare to find it operational. This is a scarce trap and much more so when complete and self-setting.

From patent text: "my invention...I claim as new...a trap consisting of an outer and an inner jaw, a spring, one end of which forms such pivotal connection...a spring secured to the inner jaw and provided with a lug...and a bait holder supported by the trigger."

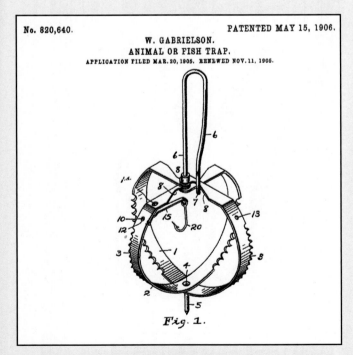

Gabriel Fish Trap patent granted on May 15, 1906.

1907 advertisement for the Gabriel Big Fish Grab Hook. Note that the correct name, Gabriel, is misspelled.

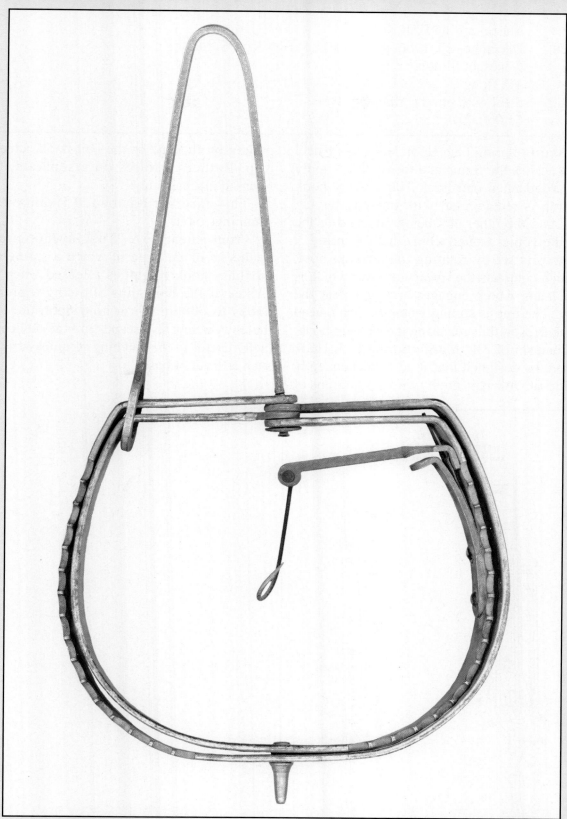

Gabriel Automatic-Setting Big Fish and Animal Trap shown actual size in the sprung position.

Name:	Martin Spring Fish Hook
Patented:	December 25, 1906, patent #839,611 by Azor S. Martin
Origin:	Geneseo, Illinois
Size:	4¾" long
Material:	Steel with brass spring and rivets
Value:	$1,000.00+

The Martin Spring Fish Hook has a solid steel plate that acts as the frame and to which is rigidly attached a japanned bait hook The striking hook on this trap is rectangular, with one end having two jaws and the other end being attached to the frame and pivoting around a brass helical spring.

The trap is set by rotating the striking hook 180°, which contracts the spring and over which is placed a latch, which engages a trigger near the bait hook. The trap is sprung when the fish's head bumps the trigger, thus releasing the striking hook. The mechanism of The Martin Spring Fish Hook is therefore so designed that it acts independently of the line-tie and bait hook, with no amount of pulling on the line or the bait hook actuating the trap. Rather, it relies on a separate, trigger-released mechanism.

This rare spring-loaded fishhook has no stampings on it.

From patent text: "This invention relates to fishhooks of the type in which a spring-actuated auxiliary hook or gaff is released when the fish strikes at the bait, thus allowing a plurality of hooks to obtain a firm hold upon the fish, and thereby prevent its escape, and the device is especially useful in the catching of quick-striking fish, such as trout or bass."

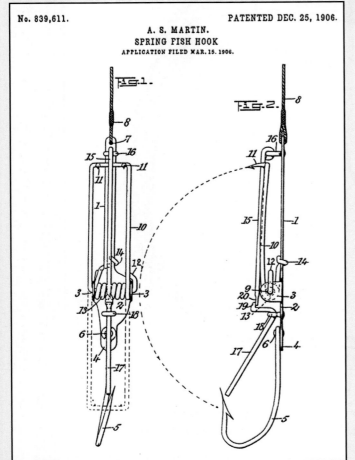

Martin Spring Fish Hook patent issued Dec. 25, 1906.

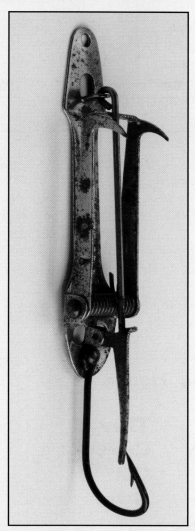

Martin Hook in the set position.

Martin Hook in the sprung position.

Name:	Hartshorn Trap Fish Hook
Patented:	December 10, 1907, patent #873,231 by Joseph Hartshorn
Origin:	Des Moines, Iowa
Size:	Three sizes, 3", 3½", and 4" long when measured without spring
Material:	Blued steel, brass rivets, and spring-steel wire
Value:	$750.00+

The Hartshorn should not be confused with the common Monarch spring-loaded fishhook, as the Hartshorn is larger and has a distinctive bell-shaped line-tie made of spring-steel wire, which has a coil at its center.

Each of the three sizes of the Hartshorn can have any of three sizes of bait hook. Therefore, nine variations occur.

When found in excellent condition, the bluing on this "trap fishhook" has an iridescent shimmer, which can best be described as resembling gasoline on water, and is quite beautiful.

From patent text: "And when a fish has seized the bait and main hook and pulls…the spring will normally expand at its lower end and press into the head of the fish…to securely retain the fish fast to be drawn out by the line."

1908 advertisement for the Hartshorn hook.

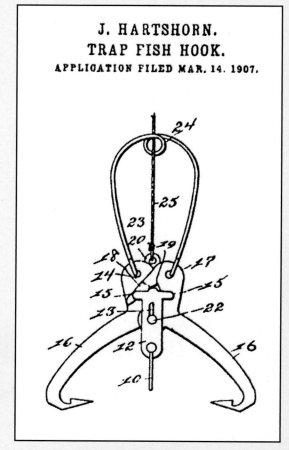

Hartshorn 1907 patent.

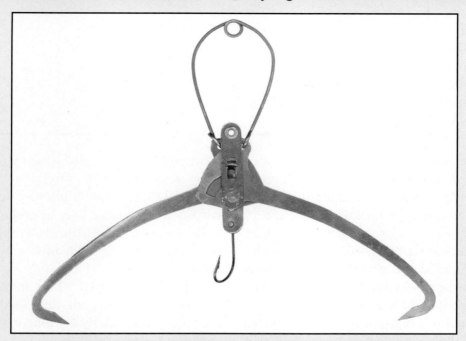

Hartshorn hook shown and in the set position.

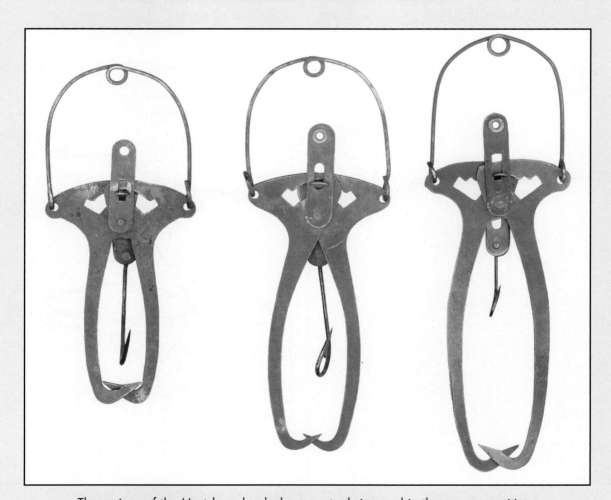

Three sizes of the Hartshorn hook shown actual size and in the sprung position.

Name:	Gilmore Spring-Loaded Fish Hook
Patented:	May 5, 1908, patent #886,794 by Edward L. Gilmore
Origin:	Youngstown, Ohio
Size:	3¼" long when set, 3¼" wide when sprung
Material:	Spring-steel wire, feathers, and yarn
Value:	$800.00 – 1,200.00+

The Gilmore Spring-Loaded Fish Hook is of the design that when struck by a fish, two opposing, outwardly facing hooks are released from a central shaft and spring outward. Onto each of these hooks is attached a "prong or spike," which serves both as the barb to the hook and which also serves to render each hook weedless. This barb is attached using a tightly wound wire that is then soldered to secure it to the shank of the hook.

The one known example of this spring-loaded fish hook has feathers attached to it, secured near the line-tie, which neatly conceal the hook when set. Also attached near the line-tie are a dozen short pieces of red yarn, which would have served as an attractor.

In 1925, Edward Gilmore patented a fishhook whose weed guard was operated by a separate helical spring and usually wrapped with bucktail, patent #1,526,133, now valued at $50.00 – 200.00 each.

From patent text: "This invention relates to fishhooks, and especially that kind of hooks which are adapted especially for long distance casting for catching game fish…a hook of such a nature that it will automatically spring or snap into the walls of the fish's mouth."

Gilmore Spring-Loaded Fish Hook.

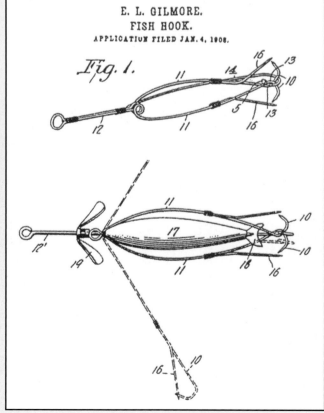

Name:	Unidentified, double clap-bow trap with 17 tacks
Patented:	Unknown, but should have been. Circa 1910?
Origin:	Unidentified
Material:	Steel and spring-steel
Size:	9" long, 4½" wide, 7" jaw spread
Value:	$2,000.00+

This heavy-duty trap consists of two semicircular clap-bows, which have had holes drilled into them to allow for the insertion of 1" long needle-sharp tacks. The heads of these tacks are then soldered onto the clap-bows, with the pointed ends of the tacks being bent inwardly so as to better grasp and hold the poor victim.

The mechanism is powered by two separate coiled springs and is designed so that when a fish pulls on the central bait hook, the two tack-encrusted clap-bows, or jaws, are sprung together. A fish caught in this trap would surely be killed almost instantaneously.

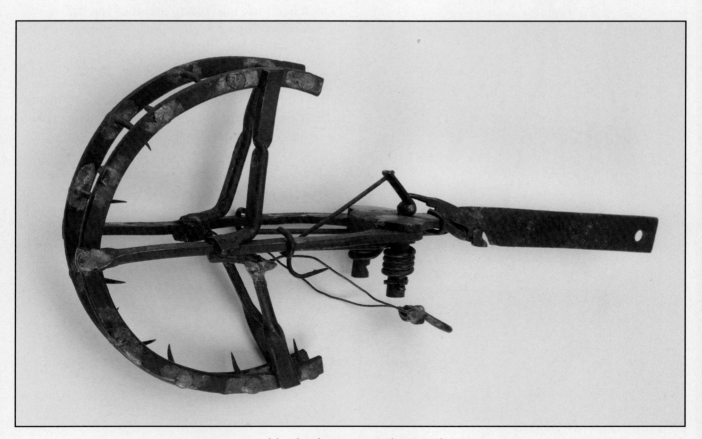

Double clap-bow trap with 17 tacks.

Name:	Unidentified, "Carolina Dogless"
Patented:	Unknown, but probably. Circa 1910?
Origin:	Unidentified
Size:	4½" long, 3" wide, 7" jaw spread when set
Material:	Nickel, brass, steel, and spring-steel
Value:	$3,500.00+

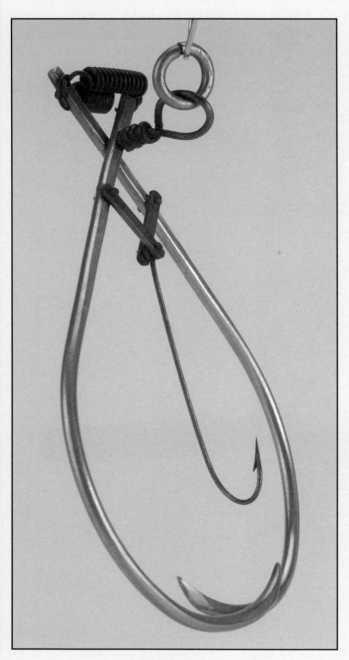

"Carolina Dogless" fish trap.

This fish trap is referred to as a "Carolina Dogless" for the simple fact that it has a dogless mechanism, and the one known example of this trap was found in the Carolinas.

This trap is empowered by two contractile helical springs, although only one would have been required. They are both attached through holes in the upper end of each striking jaw.

When the two striking jaws, which appear to be made from solid nickel, are spread apart, the two-piece brass mechanism to which the bait hook is attached lock into place, and thus the trap is set.

The Carolina Dogless has a unique line-tie, which is a nickel-plated brass ring, attached to a twisted steel wire, which is perpendicular to the trap. This steel wire also acts as the rivet, which holds the two striking jaws together and around which they pivot. When in use, this trap would have hung diagonally in the water.

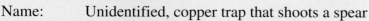

Name:	Unidentified, copper trap that shoots a spear
Patented:	Unknown, but probably. Circa 1910?
Origin:	Unidentified
Size:	4" long
Material:	Copper, brass, and steel
Value:	$2,000.00+

This fish trap is empowered by an expansive helical spring, which is housed in the longer of the two tubes. Attached to this spring is a spear point. The trap is set by compressing the spring with the aid of a rod, which extends from the side of the longer tube and is allowed vertical movement by means of a slot cut into the tube. When the spring is fully compressed, the spear is nearly completely enclosed within the tube, and it is at this point that the L-shaped bend in the bait hook is inserted into

a hole in the longer tube, which prevents the spring from expanding, thus setting the trap.

When sideways pressure is exerted on the bait hook, the L-shaped bend is extricated from the tube, the spring expands, and the spear is thrust into the top of the head of the fish.

The five known examples of this metal killer fish trap are identical, and it therefore would seem to be a manufactured item that was probably patented and sold commercially.

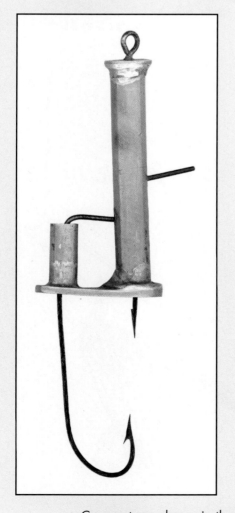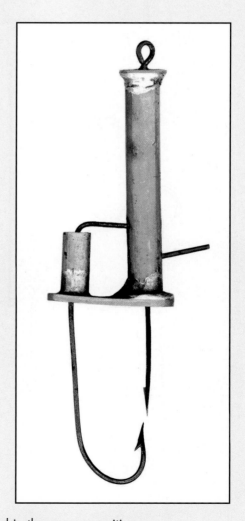

Copper trap, shown in the set and in the sprung positions.

Name:	Marvel Automatic Fish Hook
Patented:	May 31, 1910, patent #959,587 by Andrew Paysen
Origin:	St. Louis, Missouri
Size:	Three sizes: 2½", 2¾", and 3"
Material:	Brass, steel, and cork
Value:	$25.00 – 50.00 each, value doubled when found on nice card

This fishhook does not have a spring and is considered a lever-type hook. It was designed so that the hook with the cork would float on the surface while the smaller, baited hook would be submerged. When the bait was taken by the fish, the floating hook would be pulled into the top of the fish's head.

The Marvel Automatic Fish Hook was manufactured by the Marvel Hook Company of Clinton, Iowa, whose name at one point was the Japanese Novelty Company.

From patent text: "Wherein the gaff hook shall be held up by means of a float."

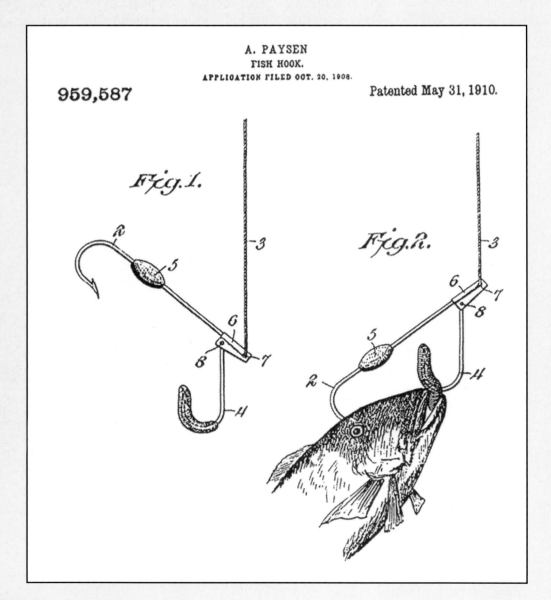

FUNSTEN BROS. & CO.

Cor. Second and Elm Sts.   SAINT LOUIS, U. S. A.

Are You "GOIN' FISHIN'" Soon?

HERE are three things you ought to have. With these three articles in your outfit you will not have to make up any fish stories about the "big ones" that got away. Neither will you have to buy any fish from some one else who has had better luck than you.

THESE THREE ARTICLES BY MAIL, POSTPAID, FOR 45 CENTS

THE "MARVEL" AUTOMATIC FISH HOOK

The "Marvel" sets in a perpendicular position, either suspended or on the bottom, therefore this is the only automatic hook that can be used successfully on pole and trot line. The slightest nibble will make it close, securing the catch. Nothing but a live fish will keep it closed, as it would open instantly if it failed to secure the fish and would get him the next time; but next time never comes for Mr. Fish. He is yours the first time he even nibbles at the "Marvel." Just think of a hook where every bite means a fish to you. Nothing to get out of order; made of the finest steel. Postpaid, each...$0.15

THE WIZARD FISH BAIT

A liquid preparation which will attract fish and make them bite. Can be used on ANY kind of bait for ALL kinds of fish. Per bottle, postpaid. $0.25

R. J. M. GOAT WOOL LINE

Made from the finest fleece of Blue Ridge Mountain Goat. Fifty feet of the best line made for...$0.10

THESE THREE ARTICLES BY MAIL, POSTPAID, FOR 45 CENTS

Fredericksburg, Tex., March 6, 1912

Funsten Bros. & Co.:

Enclosed find 25 cents for which send me another bottle of your Wizard Fish Bait. I am very much pleased with your bait. As soon as I put the hook in the water I get a fish. This makes the fourth bottle I have ordered since the third of February.

Erwin Kusenberger, Route 1, Box 76

Port Hilford, Nova Scotia, Can., Feb. 1, 1912

Funsten Bros. & Co.:

I received the Wizard Fish Bait not long ago. It is great stuff to make them bite. I caught ten Smelt in a hole, while another fellow was catching three.

Earnest Mills.

Funsten Bros. & Co., St. Louis, Mo.: Enclosed please find $ _____ for which please send me the following goods by

To _____

TOWN _____ STATE _____

Sign Here _____

Post Office _____

SEE OTHER SIDE

R. F. D.	Box
State	

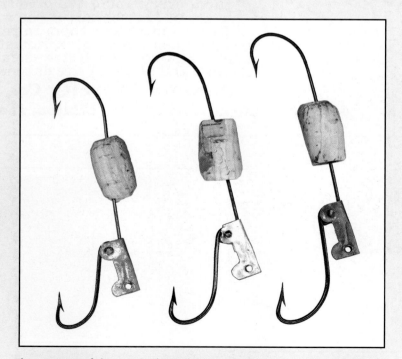

Three sizes of the Marvel Hook, actual sizes, zinc-plated bodies.

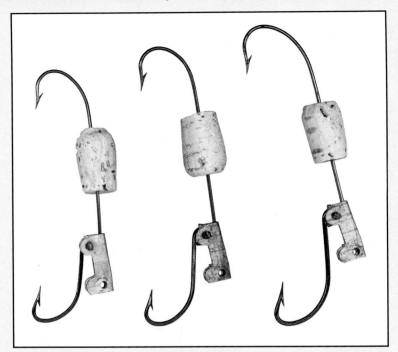

Three sizes of the Marvel Hook, actual sizes, brass bodies.

Two different Marvel Hook cards shown actual size.

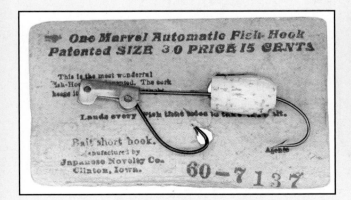

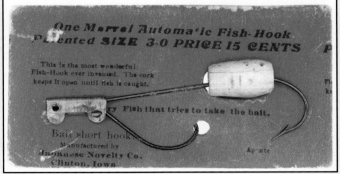

Name:	Calvert's Catch-All Fish Hook
Patented:	July 23, 1912, patent #1,033,755 by Walter Riley Calvert
Origin:	San Antonio Texas
Size:	7" tall when set, 5½" tall when sprung, 2¼" across
Material:	Tin, steel, and spring-steel
Value:	$10,000.00+

This trap is powered by a contractile helical spring on the exterior of the device, with a bait pin attached to it. When in the set position, this bait pin is situated so that it hangs below a circular ring and above a concentric arrangement of fifteen hooks curved upwardly. When a fish pulls on the bait-pin, the trap is sprung, at which instant the helical spring contracts and the arrangement of fifteen hooks is drawn forcibly upward, pinning the head of the fish to the metal ring from underneath.

This trap is stamped "PAT.PEND'G" on the line-tie and was manufactured by Calvert and Franks of San Antonio, Texas, as marked on its box. The box also lists the price of $1.00.

The fish trap invented by Walter Calvert is possibly as odd a device for catching fish as has ever been invented in the history of angling. It is a delicately constructed trap and one that probably would not have lasted long when put to use in the field, or more correctly, under the water. It is not easy to envision how the fisherman using this device, after having caught a fish, was supposed to be able to extricate the fish from the trap without bending or breaking the trap or impaling himself.

Two of these traps are known to exist in the hands of collectors, with one of them having been broken and repaired.

From patent text: "In its broad idea this invention contemplates the employment of two elongated members having a sliding engagement with each other, a trigger connected to one of the members, one…said members having hooks…for snagging the fish…and a spring connected to one member."

Calvert's Catch-All Fish Hook box.

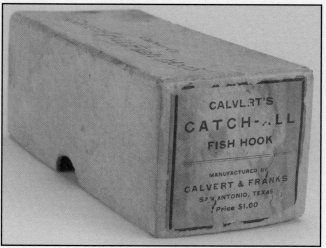

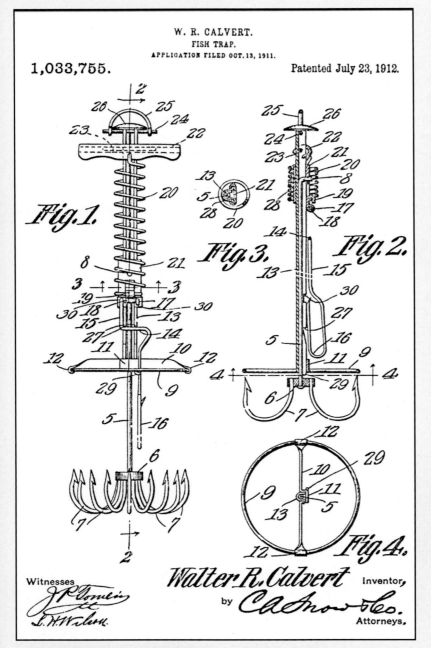

W. R. CALVERT.
FISH TRAP.
APPLICATION FILED OCT. 13, 1911.

1,033,755.

Patented July 23, 1912.

Fig. 1.

Fig. 3.

Fig. 2.

Fig. 4.

Witnesses

Walter R. Calvert Inventor,

by *C. A. Snow & Co.*

Attorneys.

Calvert patent showing the hook in the set and sprung positions.

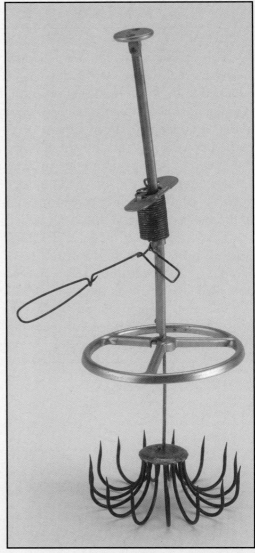

Calvert Hook in a relaxed position.

Name:	Eddleman's Never Fail Fish Hook and Animal Trap
Patented:	September 9, 1913, patent #1,072,672 by Welcome F. Sweet
Origin:	Saint Louis, Missouri, and Mineral Wells, Texas
Size:	7½" long
Material:	Brass, steel, and spring-steel
Value:	$5,000.00+

In the patent title for his "Combined Fish-Hook and Animal Trap," Welcome F. Sweet has already assigned the rights to his invention to "Eddleman's Never Fail Fish Hook and Animal Trap Company, of Mineral Wells, Texas. A Corporation of Texas," which was run by George W. Eddleman.

The fish trap manufactured by George W. Eddleman consists essentially of a hollow brass tube, which encases an expansive helical spring. Attached by a setscrew, at the bottom of the spring, is a spear-shaped "member." When the spring is compressed, the spear is drawn into the tube, where it is maintained by the pivotal dog to which the long-shanked bait hook is attached. When the bait hook is pulled upon, the dog becomes disengaged and the spear is thrust downward into the victim's head.

The commercial manufacturing of Welcome Sweet's patent shows an occurrence that is not uncommon in the production of mechanical fishhooks and fish traps (or any other mechanical device for that matter). Sometimes a modification of the fish trap as it is being produced at the factory allows it to be more efficient and economical than the original design without compromising the integrity of the patent. For example, when the 1914 advertisement for Eddleman's Fish Hook is compared with the patent drawing, an obvious change has been made in the bait hook itself. The inventor had envisioned a somewhat complicated and tedious method for attaching a standard-sized bait hook to the trap, while production showed that simply having a longer shanked hook, which could be attached with a screw to a pivoting bracket on the brass cylinder, would be a simpler, and in fact better, change from the original design.

As with other patented fish traps, the word animal was included in this patent title and text in order to appeal to as large an audience (market) as possible. For example, if this hook would only have been marketed as a fish trap, it would have had no appeal to the housewife with a mouse problem, and in fact, this trap may have been very effective on mice.

This fish trap was also produced with a needle-shaped spearing member, rather than the earlier doubly barbed spear-shaped point as shown in the patent and advertisement.

Less than five of these very desirable fish traps are known to exist in collectors' hands, and all of the traps are the same size and have no stampings.

From patent text: "...the object of my invention being to combine an ordinary fishhook with a device in which is arranged for operation a spring-actuated member carrying a pointed or barbed spear, which is released from its set position and forced outward under spring pressure to enter and impale a fish or animal that bites or nibbles at the bait located on the fishhook."

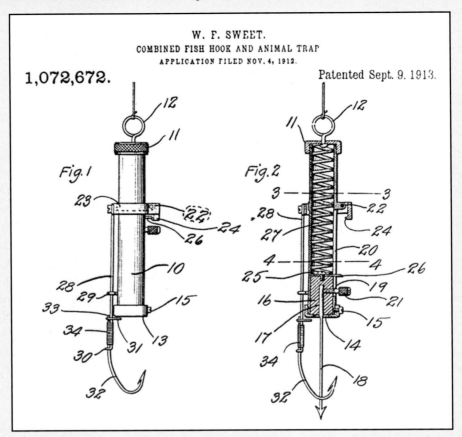

W. F. Sweet patent. All rights to this patent were assigned to George W. Eddleman.

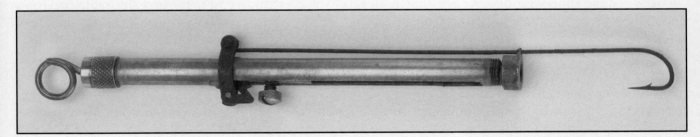

Eddelman Hook in the set position.

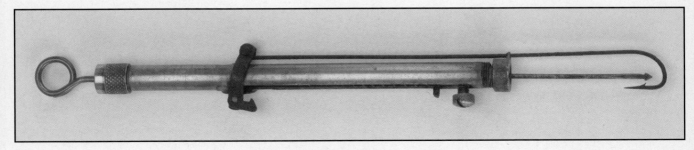

Eddelman Hook in the sprung position.

EDDLEMAN'S
NEVER FAIL Fish Hook & Animal Trap

$1.⁰⁰ $1.⁰⁰

Patent Pending

Fisherman's Delight and Trapper's Profit

"A Bite is a Catch"

No bad feeling over loss of catch when using **Never Fail Fish Hook & Animal Trap**

ESCAPE IMPOSSIBLE

Ready for Action

DIRECTIONS

Bait your hook. Use knob on spear slide to draw spear back to the notch where it will be caught and held ready to discharge. See that spear doesn't catch in side of tube. Next—**Don't hold your hand in front of trigger.** Slide the **hook plate** up against the trigger and if you want an easy release push it gently forward until the trigger is nearly pushed out. Trap is now ready for action.

Address Main Office for all different Sizes, Price List and Particulars

EDDLEMAN'S NEVER FAIL FISH HOOK & ANIMAL TRAP CO.

Factory and St. Louis Office
METAL NOVELTY CO.
1131 S. Broadway, St. Louis, Mo.   Mineral Wells, Texas

Eddleman's Never Fail Fish Hook & Animal Trap advertisement.

Geo. W. Hazlewood, *President*   Geo. W. Eddleman, *Secretary*   Anson Hazlewood, *Treasurer*

Eddleman's Never-Fail Fish Hook & ANIMAL TRAP CO.

HEAD OFFICE, MINERAL WELLS, TEXAS
COKE AND OAK STS.

Presented by *G. W. Eddleman,*

G. W. Eddleman business card.

Name:	No. 1 Alligator Game Trap
Patented:	March 10, 1914, patent #1,089,975 by Bruce A. Shaw
Origin:	Oak Park, Illinois
Size:	8¼" overall length, single bow, or moveable jaw 5½" long and 4½" wide
Material:	Cast iron and steel
Value:	Up – $750.00

There is a larger No. 2 size Alligator Game Trap, but it is not for fish, and only has the cast teeth on one of the iron clap bows, both of which move. The measurements are respectively 11", 7½", and 6½".

The No. 1 Alligator has a one-piece pan and shank combination, with the pan part stamped "TRAPPERS SUPPLY CO." on its upper edge and "OAK PARK, ILL." on its lower edge; "PAT. APD. FOR" is stamped in the center of the pan with the size number stamped beneath it.

The Alligator Game Trap was produced by the Trapper's Supply Company of Oak Park, Illinois, between 1913 and 1916, where either cash or raw furs were accepted as payment.

From patent text: "Another object of the invention is the provision of a chain support on the fixed jaw of the trap and the arrangement of said support, whereby the trap may be suspended in a true perpendicular position from the chain when the trap is used for catching fish or water-living animals."

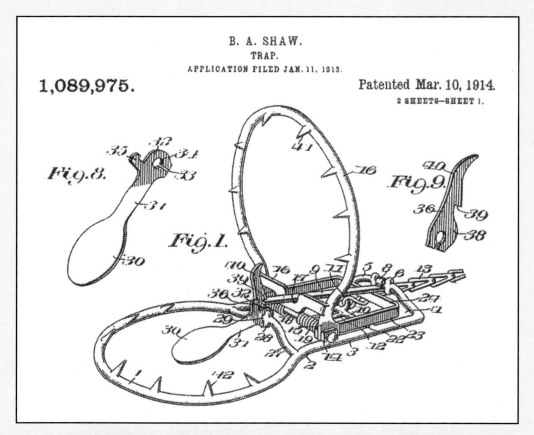

Bruce A. Shaw patent showing the trap pan (left) and the bait trigger (right).

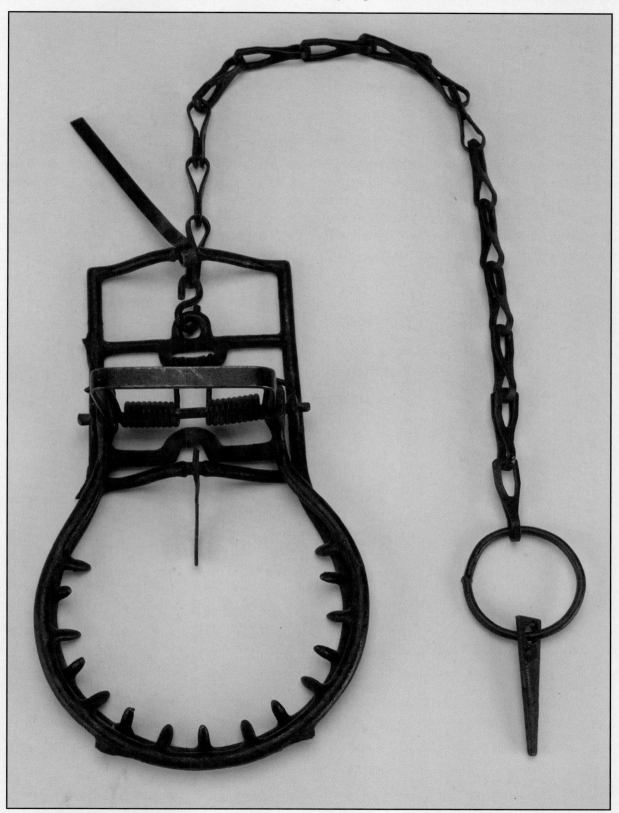

No. 1 Alligator Game Trap set up for fish using the bait trigger after removing the trip pan.

Name:	Unidentified, "Pittsburgh Rake Trap"
Patented:	Unknown, but should have been. Circa 1915?
Origin:	A Pittsburgh, Pennsylvania, tackle box
Size:	2½" tall, 1" wide when relaxed, 3¾" jaw spread when set
Material:	Steel, brass, and solder
Value:	$1,000.00+

This is a finely crafted diminutive trap and one of William Blauser's favorites. It has two striking arms with each arm having three teeth (one arm has a tooth missing on this one known example). These teeth are barbless and attached to each other by a fine, tightly wrapped wire, which is soldered together.

This trap is powered by two brass contractile helical springs and is tripped by a fish pulling on the central bait hook, which has an attachment at its upper end that acts as the dog.

This trap is designed for small fish.

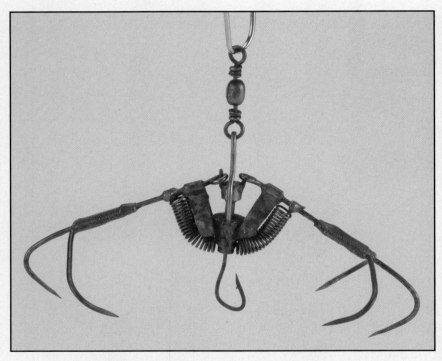 

"Pittsburg Rake Trap" shown in the set and sprung positions.

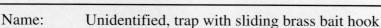

Name:	Unidentified, trap with sliding brass bait hook
Patented:	Unknown, but probably. Circa 1915?
Origin:	Unidentified
Size:	6¼" long, 5" jaw spread when set
Material:	Brass, nickel-plated brass, and spring-steel wire
Value:	$1,000.00+

This spring-loaded fishhook is powered by a single piece of spring-steel wire with a coil at its center, which forms an eye and which also acts as the line-tie.

A unique feature of this fish trap is the bait hook and its attachment to the trap. The bait hook itself is formed from a length of brass wire with a barbless hook formed in one end, while the other end has soldered to it a small brass nut, which allows the hook to slide freely inside of a brass sleeve, which is soldered onto the brass screw and nut, which serves to hold the two striking jaws together and around which they pivot. With this configuration, the bait hook is nearly perpendicular to the trap when in the relaxed position. When the trap is to be set and the jaw to which the brass sleeve is attached is rotated 90°, the bait hook also rotates 90°. This puts the bait hook in a vertical position.

This trap may also be found where the bait hook is not rigidly attached to one jaw. At this point, the bait hook, which acts as the dog on this trap, can be slid upwards through the sleeve to engage the notches cut into the striking hooks, thus setting the trap.

When a fish pulls on the bait hook, it becomes disengaged from the notches in the striking hooks, which are then thrust down into the fish's head from the power of the coil spring.

Less than five of these spring-loaded fishhooks are known to exist in collectors' hands.

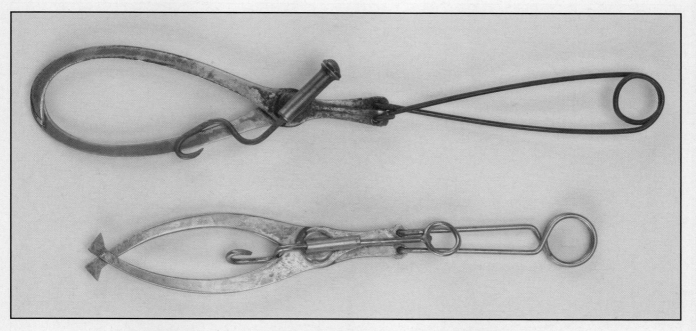

Two varieties of the trap with sliding brass bait hook in the sprung position.

Name:	Unidentified, "the big green trap with 61 teeth"
Patented:	Probably — sister trap has "PAT PEND" painted on it. Circa 1915?
Origin:	Unidentified
Size:	16" long, 7" wide, 13" jaw spread when set
Material:	Steel and spring-steel
Value:	$10,000.00+

This trap was last bought from an advanced collector based on his one-word description — "Awesome" — and it is.

The most powerful metal killer fish trap ever made using a helical spring, it is also one of the most massive. This trap has not only two semi-circular jaws, but also two sets of vertical jaws, each set having been made from a single piece of steel. When combined, this trap has 61 teeth cut into it, along with a large bait hook, which is centrally located.

Being an ex–fishing guide for salmon in Alaska, this author can attest to the fact that this trap could catch and kill a 100 lb. King Salmon.

What is slick about this trap is that it is perhaps the easiest of all to set, since it is self-setting.

There is nothing delicate about this trap. To set it, you merely brace the line-tie against your waist, grab both wire handles on the outside of the jaws with each hand, pull back 90°, and "click," the trap sets itself. (Next comes the tricky part.) Be sure another set of hands and a hospital are nearby when attempting to unset this trap, which is done by pulling on the bait hook, as a fish would do.

A sister trap to this one exists, but it is unset by pushing upon a central bar, rather than pulling on a bait hook. Both of these traps retain coloration from their original green paint, with the sister trap having "PAT PEND" painted on it in white paint.

No other examples of this trap are known to exist in collectors' hands.

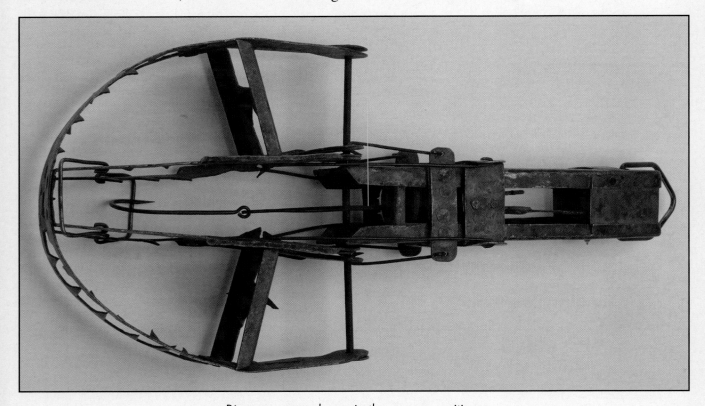

Big green trap shown in the sprung position.

Big green trap with 61 teeth, shown in the set position. This is an extremely dangerous trap to bait and set. If you caught your hand in this trap, you would have a very serious problem.

Name:	Automatic Fish Hook
Patented:	Stamped "PAT. PEND.," purportedly 1915, but letters of patent have not been found as of yet
Origin:	Unidentified
Material:	Mirrored glass, aluminum, and spring-steel wire
Size:	4½" x 2½"
Value:	$5,000.00+

The Automatic Fish Hook is the only fish trap ever manufactured that relied on the use of mirrors. It is, in fact, two separate, independent, identical traps built on one frame, with the two traps positioned back-to-back, being mirror images of each other (no pun intended). Each mirror is in the shape of a trapezoid and positioned so as to face outward and away from the other.

Extending outward from each side of the trap, and centrally positioned below each mirror, are the fish traps themselves. Each trap consists of a spring-steel wire with a coil at its center forming an eye, by which it is attached to the frame of the trap. When the two arms of each spring are compressed together, they can be forced to stay in this set position by a doubly pointed sleeve through which one of the arms extends. This sleeve acts also as the bait-holder. When a fish pulls on this bait-holding sleeve, it slides out away from the mirror, thus releasing the other arm, with both arms now springing outward into the sides of the fish's mouth.

This fish trap came in a plain brown box with "AUTOMATIC FISH HOOK" printed on the top. The trap itself is stamped "AUTOMATIC FISH HOOK" and "PAT. PEND." on the bottom.

The advantages of combining a mirror with a baited hook are perhaps best explained in the 1916 letters of patent for an artificial fish-bait invented by William Zeigler in which he states:

A male fish seeing his image upon looking therein will appear to see another fish approach it from the opposite side with the intent to seize the bait, and this will not only arouse his warlike spirit, but also appeal to his greed, and he will seize the bait quickly in order to defeat the approaching rival.

In the case of a female fish, the attractiveness of a mirror is too well known to need discussion.

Thus the bait appeals to the ruling passion of both sexes, and renders it very certain and efficient in operation.

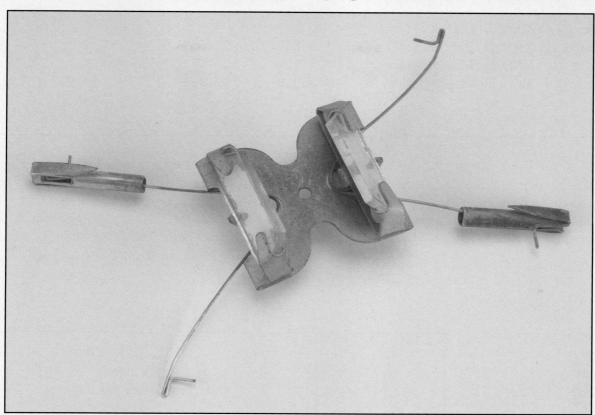

Automatic Fish Hook is stamped "PAT. PEND." and incorporates two mirrors.

Box that the Automatic Fish Hook was sold in.

Name:	Koch Fish Hook
Patented:	April 6, 1915, patent #1,134,622 by William L. C. Koch
Origin:	Dedham, Massachusetts
Material:	Steel, aluminum, brass, and spring-brass
Size:	3¼" long
Value:	$500.00+

The Koch Fish Hook is empowered by a coiled brass spring, which is concealed in a slidable cone-shaped housing. This housing is painted to resemble the head of a frog, and is stamped on the underside "PAT. SEPT. 16, 1914."

When struck by a fish the two hooks, which face each other, are compressed, and thus their pointed, barbed ends are exposed, hooking said fish.

From Patent Text: "...to provide a device which will prevent bait from being put on alive, the device being therefore humane."

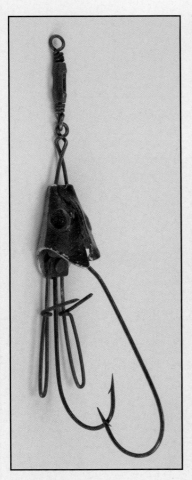

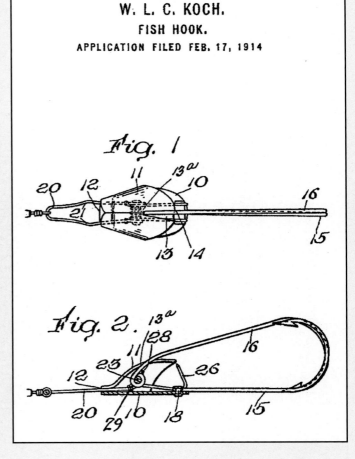

Koch Fish Hook in the open position, used to attach the bait, and in the closed/set position.

Name:	Mau Fish Hook
Patented:	October 12, 1915, patent #1,156,795 by Clayton C. Mau
Origin:	Fredonia, New York
Size:	3" long, 2" wide when sprung
Material:	Spring-steel wire
Value:	$400.00+

The Mau Fish Hook was manufactured to be, as intended by its inventor, "simple, non-encumbering, inexpensive, convenient, practical and efficient." It consists simply of a single piece of spring-steel wire with a coil wound at its center to produce an eye with the terminal ends bent into a barbed hook. Attached to the eye is a short length of wire, which wraps around one arm and produces a catch, or detent, thus completing the spring hook's construction.

The hook is easily set by compressing the two arms so that the one catches under the detent on the other arm. The trap is sprung when these arms are pressed together, which causes them to separate and spring outward.

From patent text: "…a pair of shanks so that the fish in the act of biting or swallowing the bait carried by the hooks will release them, and whereupon the hooks will separate and embed themselves in the flesh of the fish, to facilitate the catching of the fish and to prevent the escape thereof."

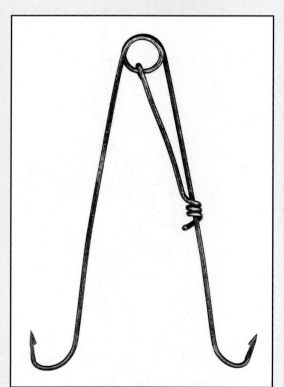

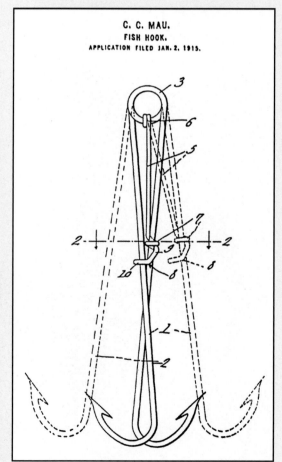

Mau Fish Hook in the sprung and set positions.

Name:	Aspelin Spring-loaded Fish Hook
Patented:	May 30, 1922, patent #1,417,482 by J. O. Aspelin
Origin:	Skandia Township, Murray County, Minnesota
Size:	4½" long
Material:	Steel and spring-steel wire
Value:	$500.00 – 750.00

The spring-loaded fishhook invented by J. O. Aspelin consists of "two metal plates in oppositely disposed parallel relation and partly overlapping each other" that "are loosely mounted on a pivot." Attached to one end of each plate is a bait hook, while at the other end of each plate has attached to it the lower ends of a coil spring. Notches are cut into each metal plate so that when the spring is compressed, the notches latch onto the outside edge of the opposite plate, thus setting the hook and rendering it nearly weedless.

From our personal communication with his then-78-year-old grandson, it was learned that this fishhook, which is normally stamped "MFG. J. O. ASPELIN," was sold with either a straight steel finish, painted gold and red finish, or with electroplating. The electroplating was done using a 32-volt Delco Light Plant. It was not until after WWII, in 1946, that the REA (Rural Electrification Administration) ran electric power lines to J. O.'s farm, providing 110/220 volt service.

J. O. also experimented with incorporating his fishhook into a wooden lure body.

From patent text: "My invention relates to fishhooks including the class of hooks known as trolling hooks, and the object is to provide a light and efficient expanding hook of such construction that the uncertainty of hooking a fish biting at the bait is reduced to a minimum…used with reel and rod…or be used for still fishing."

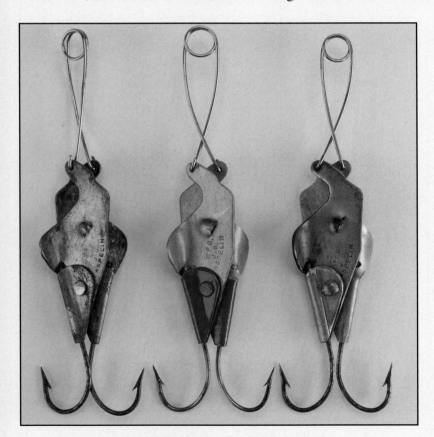

Three Aspelin Spring-loaded Fish Hooks.

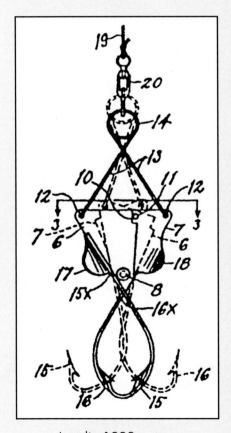

Aspelin 1922 patent.

Julius Oliver Aspelin, circa 1910 – 1920.

J. O. Aspelin at the throttle of a Nicholas and Sheppard threshing separator and engine.

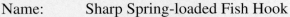

Name:	Sharp Spring-loaded Fish Hook
Patented:	December 9, 1924, patent #1,518,166 by Warren Jackson Sharp
Origin:	Meridian, Mississippi
Size:	4½" long, 2½" wide when sprung
Material:	Copper and japanned spring-steel wire
Value:	$500.00+

The Sharp Spring-loaded Fish Hook is not a complicated device. Its construction consists of merely a single piece of spring-steel wire bent so as to have two "shoulders" near the copper sheet-metal guard and bait hooks on its terminal ends. When the spring is compressed, the shoulders are pushed into the guard and are retained there by the resilient nature of the spring.

A screw that connects the two sides of the copper guard also serves to keep the spring hook from being separated from the guard. When this fish-hook is set, it is nearly weedless. When a fish pulls on the bait hook, it is drawn out of the guard and expands, capturing its prey.

This spring-loaded fishhook is not common.

From patent text: "When a fish…pulls on the prongs…due to the resiliency of the metal…the prongs will deeply embed themselves in the mouth of the fish to insure against the fish releasing itself."

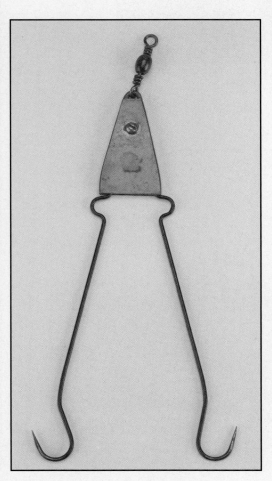

Sharp spring hook in the sprung position.

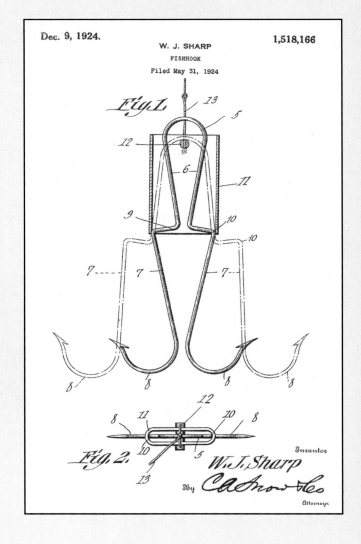

Name:	Sure-Catch Fish Hook
Patented:	Unknown. Circa 1920s.
Origin:	Windfall, Indiana
Size:	Three sizes, 1⅞", 2", and 2⅜"
Material:	Blued spring-steel wire
Value:	$75.00 – 100.00 each

This spring hook was made by the Sure-Catch Fish Hook Company and is a simple device. It is made from a single piece of spring-steel wire, which is coiled at the center to form a line-tie. Onto one arm is soldered a short piece of wire that serves as a catch for the other arm when the two are compressed together.

The box states, "It doesn't require any jerking or pulling. The mere act of the fish closing its mouth, even gently, on it makes a capture."

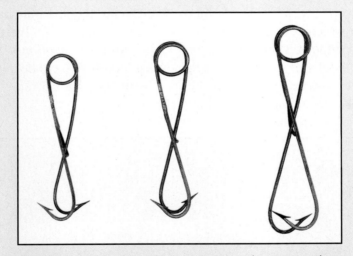

Three Sure-Catch hooks in the set position, shown actual sizes.

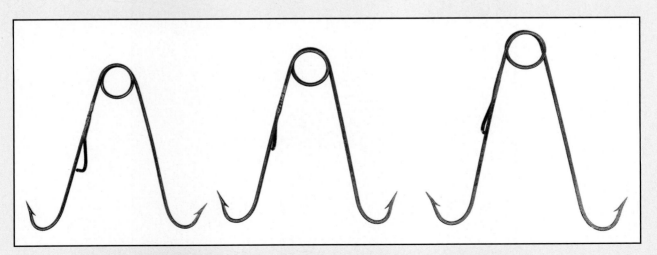

Three Sure-Catch hooks in the sprung position, shown actual sizes.

Name:	The Higgins Grab Hook
Patented:	Unknown, but probably. Circa 1920s.
Origin:	Bellevue, Huron County, Ohio
Size:	3 sizes advertised; the one size known to exist measures 6" long with a 4½" jaw spread.
Material:	Cast aluminum, brass, and steel
Value:	$1,000.00+ without the box

The Higgins Grab Hook has a cast aluminum body with a centrally located stationary bait hook attached. Extending diagonally from the body are two long-shanked grab hooks whose points face toward the bait hook and can move toward it via slots formed into the body. The grab hooks are controlled by a central brass rod, which extends into the body from the top and which acts as the line-tie. When pressure is exerted either on this line-tie or on the bait hook, the grab hooks move toward each other. When pressure is no longer exerted on the line-tie, the two grab hooks spring outward to their extended, relaxed positions. This would be considered a "clutch" trap, as the harder the fish pulls, the harder the grab hooks dig in.

The Higgins Grab Hook was also produced without a central bait hook. In this model, it would be assumed that the two grab hooks were baited, in which case the trap may have been just as effective.

This hook was advertised for sale in the May 1922 edition of *National Sportsman Magazine* and must therefore have been produced prior to this.

This is a scarce trap.

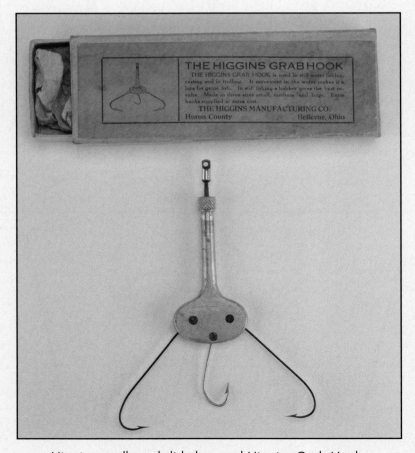

Higgins cardboard slide box and Higgins Grab Hook.

The Higgins Grab Hook

THE HIGGINS GRAB HOOK, as shown, represents a hook that is very positive. It opens and closes automatically and is always ready for action.

Nibbling at the bait causes the hooks to strike from a different angle, which is generally a surprise to the intruder and is most certain to be caught.

In raising and lowering the hooks in the water they open and close according to the tension on the springs, setting the points of the hooks into the desired object when coming into contact with it.

The hooks are very sensitive and are never at rest, as a change in the current or a slight change in the tension of the line keeps the hooks moving.

For casting or trolling, THE HIGGINS GRAB HOOK has no equal, owing to its constant move-ment, and its brilliancy.

The construction of THE HIGGINS GRAB HOOK makes it the most desirable hook to use where there are weeds or other obstructions.

The casing is made of cast aluminum, other parts of brass and steel, whichever serves the place best.

Bait the Center Hook Only

It is not a tin toy, as the best material and workmanship have been employed in its construction. The medium hook will catch a fish from a few ounces to twenty pounds in weight.

Made in three sizes. Packed one in a box, Price $1.00, charges prepaid.
Bait the center hook only for results. Hooks may be taken out and other ones supplied.

The Higgins Manufacturing Company
Lock Box 427, Bellevue, Huron Co., Ohio

Instructions for using the Higgins Grab Hook that were included in the Higgins box.

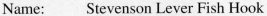

Name:	Stevenson Lever Fish Hook
Patented:	November 30, 1926, patent #1,608,631 by Marcus L. Stevenson
Origin:	Seattle, Washington
Size:	7" long in the set position
Material:	Nickel-plated steel
Value:	$1,000.00+

The Stevenson Lever Fish Hook is a study in vector addition and subtraction. It has no springs, but relies principally on the forces applied to it by fish and man. When set, the striking hook is in a vertical position with the bait hook being completely exposed. The trap is sprung when sufficient forces are applied in diametrically opposite directions in regard to the bait hook and the line-tie, which snaps the striking hook down and imbeds it into the top of the fish's head.

The fishhook was designed for large game fish and is stamped "PAT.NOV.30.1926" on the main shaft of the bait hook.

Less than five of these are known to exist in collectors' hands.

From patent text: "It will now be seen that in addition to being caught in the mouth by the hook, the fish is impaled by the jig hook, thus making his escape a practical impossibility."

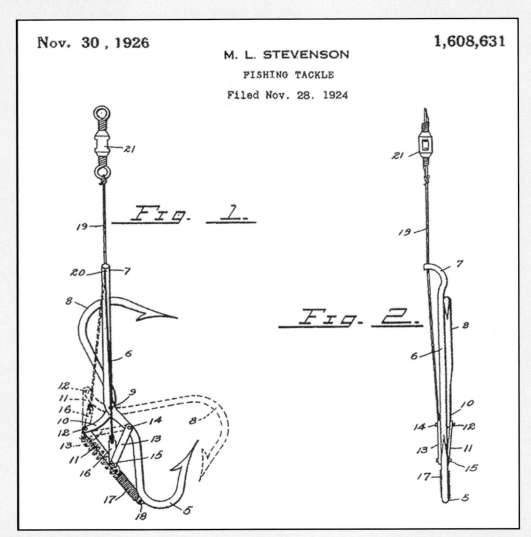

The Stevenson Lever Fish Hook, actual size, shown (above) in the set position and (left) in the sprung position.

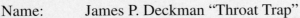

Name:	James P. Deckman "Throat Trap"
Patented:	November 30, 1926, patent #1,609,160 by James P. Deckman
Origin:	Street, Maryland
Size:	4½" long when set, 6" long when relaxed
Material:	Brass, steel, and spring-steel wire
Value:	$5,000.00+

Note: The "Throat Trap" invented by James P. Deckman is similar in appearance to a basic ball-point pen, and in fact, the prototype for this trap was made from a ballpoint pen.

This fish trap was designed so that when a fish pulled on the bait, which was inexplicitly connected to the trap at its lower end and held by means of a flange, a cylindrical bar with two "oppositely shiftable, gravity movable hook elements" was plunged down the fish's throat by means of an internal expansive helical spring. The two hook elements, which are doubly barbed, would then become lodged in the fish's throat "and hold the same until the fish is landed."

In order for this fish trap to be sprung, it was necessary for the fish to rotate the outside sleeve of the trap, which is inseparable from the trap by means of a semicircular arrester. This action would then release an external spring, which had a "tooth" attached and which acted as the dog to this trap, and allow the internal helical spring to expand, thus springing the trap.

At this point, the inventor counted on gravity to pull the two concealed hook elements from the "plunger" and engage the fish. (The plunger on the inventor's prototype was a nail with a slot cut into it and to which he attached two barbed hook elements.)

From our personal communication with the eldest daughter from his second marriage, it was learned that only this one patent model was ever produced.

In quality of construction, this trap pales in comparison to the 1878 John A. Mitchell "Throat Trap."

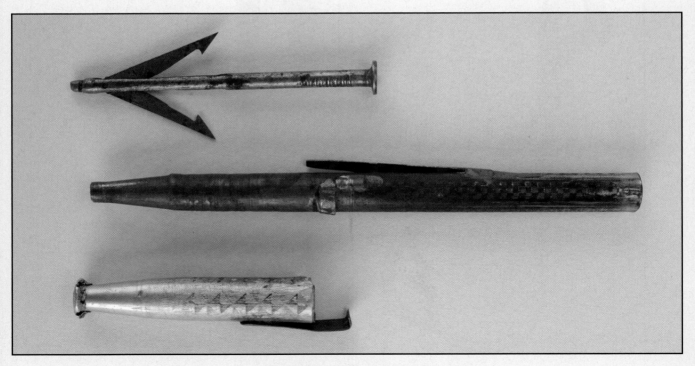

Parts to the Deckman "Throat Trap" prototype.

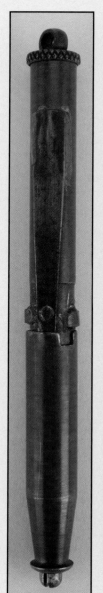

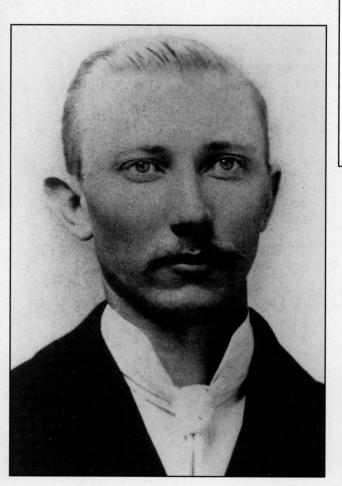

Deckman "Throat Trap" in the set and sprung positions.

J. P. DECKMAN
FISHHOOK
Filed March 17, 1926

Photo of James P. Deckman.

Name:	Howell's Texas Angler
Patented:	August 21, 1928, patent #1,681,407 by John E. Howell
Origin:	Dallas, Texas
Size:	Three sizes, 4⅜", 5", and 6¼"
Material:	Blued steel, rubber band
Value:	$25.00 each. $50.00 – 60.00 when found in the tube or box. Largest size is rarest and has double the value.

The Howell's Texas Angler was designed to be empowered by a rubber band, which if broken could be easily replaced. The small "pilot" hook was to be baited and drawn down to the set position. When the fish pulled on the bait, the rubber band would pull the lower hooks, the "impaling unit," into the fish, thus securing it.

Each size of this fishhook was made of a different gauge steel wire and was sold in a cardboard tube or box.

Sure Catch
For All Ordinary Fishing
PRICE 50c EACH

INSTRUCTIONS:

Put bait on small hook suspended by rubber. Never bait lower hooks. Use sinker only when fishing in swift water. Use of float optional with angler. Never use large float. Jerk while fish is moving with bait as with ordinary tackle. This medium size SURE CATCH operates successfully on fish from 7 to 24 inches in length.

Bait with Minnow, Worm, Cut Bait, Shrimp, etc.

Dry Thoroughly After Every Use.

SLOGAN:
"Be a sport; throw the little ones back."

ORIGINATED AND MANUFACTURED BY
JNO. E. HOWELL

119 No. Marlborough   Dallas, Texas

Advertisement and baiting instructions for the Howell Sure Catch.

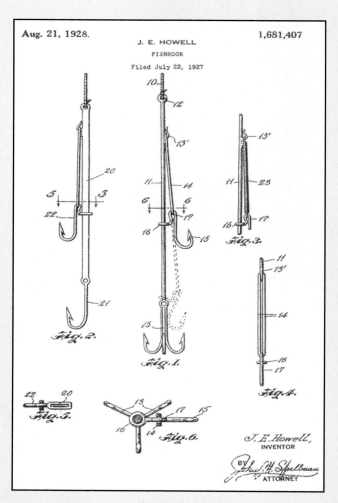

Howell 1928 patent.

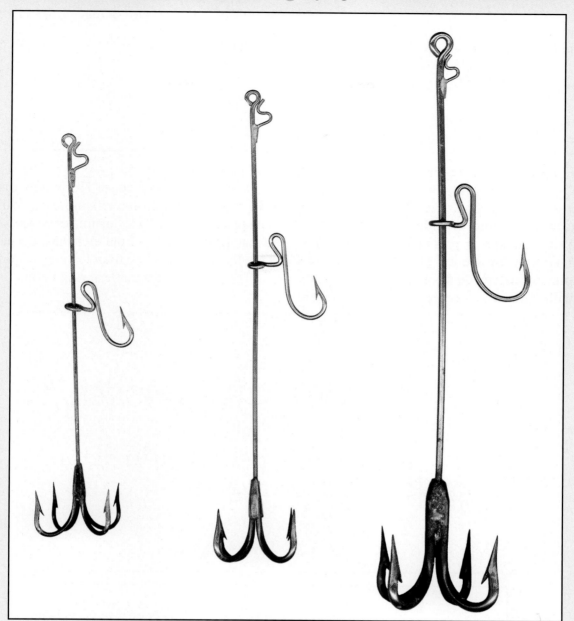

Three Howell Texas Angler Hooks shown actual size. The largest size is very rare.

Manilla envelope that the rubber bands used with the Howell Texas Angler Hook came in.

RUBBER BANDS

This envelope contains several No. 10 rubber bands, one and one fourth inches long, to be used with this size Sure Catch.

INSTRUCTIONS:

Intall rubber band as shown in cut on box. Bait small hook suspended by rubber. Never bait the lower hooks. When using sinker place same on line above Sure Catch. Use of float is optional with angler. Jerk while fish is moving with bait as with ordinary tackle. This small size Sure Catch operates successfully on fish from 5 to about 15 inches in length. Remove rubber and dry thoroughly after every use.

Bait with: Minnow, Shrimp, Worm, Cut Bait, Dough Bait etc.

Name:	Anti-Alibi Trigger Hook
Patented:	Probably, as envelope is marked "PAT. PEND.," but letters of patent have not been found as of yet. Circa 1930s.
Origin:	Detroit, Michigan, made by Al Slack
Size:	4" long
Material:	Brass, spring-brass, and steel
Value:	$400.00+, with premium paid when on nice card

This nicely made spring hook is powered by a piece of spring-brass wire, which has a bait hook attached to each terminal end. These bait hooks were attached by being wound with wire and then soldered onto the spring-brass wire, after which it was painted over by glossy, blood-red paint. The central pin to this spring-hook was also partially wound with wire, which served as an arrestor and was also painted red.

The Anti-Alibi Trigger Hook was originally sold stapled onto an advertising card, which was then placed into a 3" x 5" manila envelope. Because of this protection from the elements, the hook and advertising card may be found in new condition.

This is a very desirable spring hook.

Anti-Alibi Trigger Hook manila envelope and the Trigger Hook on a card.

Name:	Ben-Mer Power Claws
Patented:	Very probably patented by Kenneth D. Johnson of Pasadena, California, on June 4, 1938, as patent #2,120,863. The card, however, advertises this hook as being from West Swanzey, New Hampshire. Because of this discrepancy and no clear link between the two cities, the authors use the word *probably*.
Origin:	United States of America
Size:	2¼" long, 1" wide
Material:	Steel and spring-steel with a brass rivet
Value:	$150.00 – 200.00 when found on nice yellow card

The two "power-claws" of this spring-hook are riveted together and are powered by a separate piece of fine-gauged spring-wire, which is coiled about the rivet.

The Ben-Mer Power Claw originally came with a wire leader and on a yellow advertising card, with store displays each having a dozen of these cards.

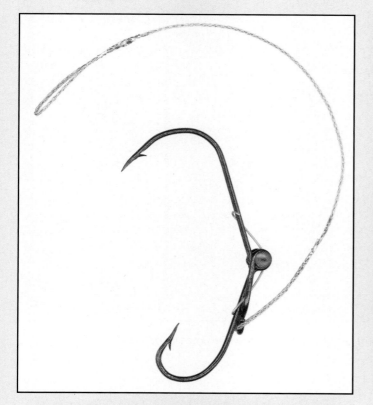

Ben-Mer Power Claw, shown in the relaxed position.

Ben-Mer shown on the original card.

Ben-Mer Power Claw display card that originally held 12 individual hooks on cards.

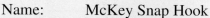

Name:	McKey Snap Hook
Patented:	October 17, 1939, patent #2,176,820 by Charles McConnell
Origin:	Port Norris, New Jersey
Size:	2½" long
Material:	Brass and spring-steel wire
Value:	$200.00 – 250.00

The McKey Snap Hook is made from a single piece of spring-steel wire, doubled back on itself, that is enclosed in a brass housing stamped "McKey PAT PEND." It was designed so that when the fish pulled on the end of the wire, shaped into a bait-hook, the other end of the wire, shaped like a forked tongue, would spring closed and would act as a "securing element or guard portion whereupon its spur-like points penetrate the mouth of the fish and, in conjunction with the point of the bill, securely hold the fish against possible escape."

The McKey is renowned for the exquisitely formed spear-like barbs on the terminal end of the bait hook.

Only 100 of these hooks were ever manufactured.

From patent text: "…a fish and game hook… which will not tear the mouth of the fish and is easily removed there from."

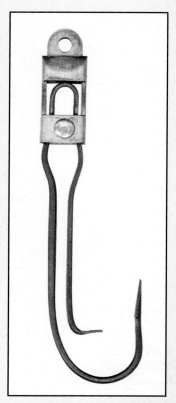 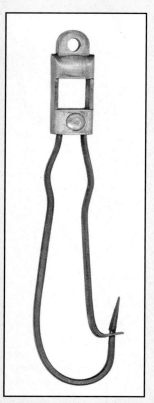  

Left to right: McKey hook in the set position, McKey hook in the sprung position, enlarged view to show McKey stamp, enlarged view of McKey spear-like barbs.

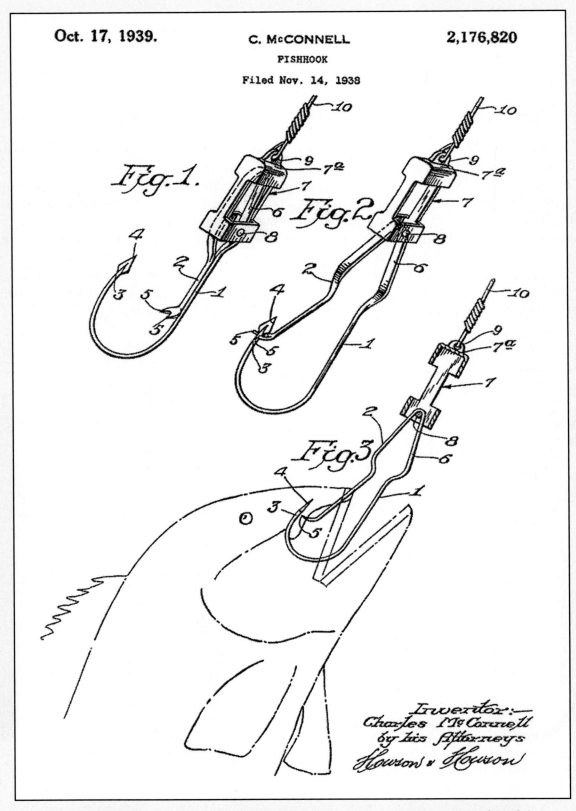

Oct. 17, 1939.   C. McCONNELL   2,176,820

FISHHOOK

Filed Nov. 14, 1938

Fig.1.

Fig.2.

Fig.3

Inventor:-
Charles McConnell
by his Attorneys
Howson & Howson

McConnell patent drawing showing the McKey hook secured in the mouth of the fish.

Name:	Red's Sure-Catch Fish Hook
Patented:	September 3, 1940, patent #2,213,624 by Julius A. Cole
Origin:	Camden, Tennessee
Size:	3¾" long, 2" across
Material:	Brass, lead, and steel
Value:	$15.00 – 20.00, double when on nice red advertising card

Julius A. Cole was retired from the U.S. Postal Service and in his 70s when he invented this fishhook, which was inspired by working on his car's ignition points. He struck a deal to have a local car dealership, Red's Chevrolet, put up the money to have it patented and to supply the money for materials. In his garage, the inventor stamped out and assembled every hook device ever made.

Production was halted on the fishhook with the onset of World War II, and was never resumed.

This fishhook was designed to impale the lower jaw of a fish by using a lever-operated hook with a lead counterbalance. The principle of the device was that when the smaller upper hook was baited and struck by a fish, the lower, larger hook would be drawn upward and impale the fish from below.

These hooks came singly on a red card with instructions on the back, and on a stand-up cardboard advertising display, which held twelve of the hooks. The large advertising display is often found badly watermarked, and should be valued accordingly.

One example of this fishhook, which exactly matches the patent drawing, is known.

From patent text: "…a pair of hooks connected by link and lever, whereby a pull on one of the hooks will actuate the other."

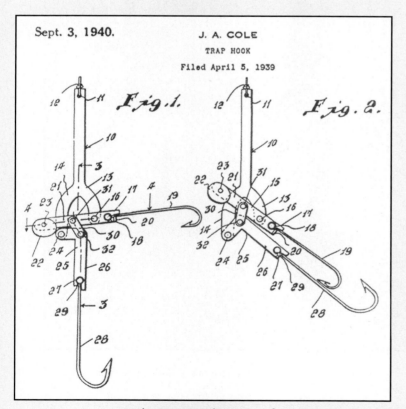 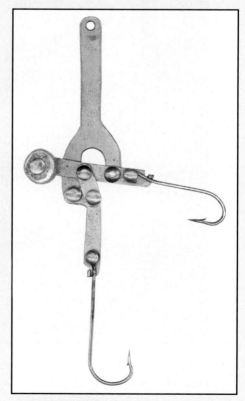

Red's Sure-Catch patent of 1940 and a hook that matches the patent drawing.

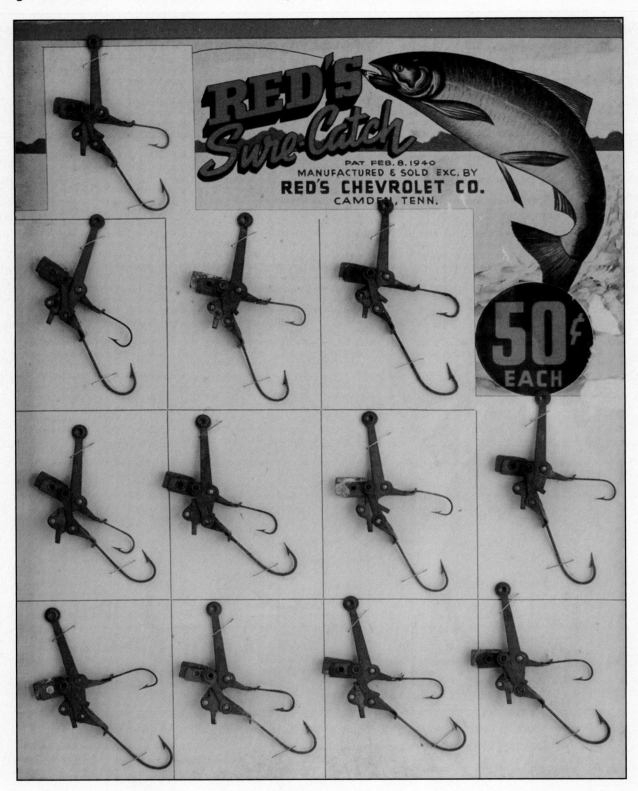

Red's Sure-Catch counter display card with 12 hooks. The hooks on the card are the style that were ultimately manufactured. The card is not actual size.

Name:	Binkowski Expanding Hook
Patented:	December 3, 1940, and May 26, 1942, patents respectively #2,223,946 and #2,284,034 by Andrew Binkowski
Origin:	Lansing, Michigan
Size:	Two sizes; No. 1 is 2⅜" long and No. 3 is 4½" long.
Material:	Spring-steel wire with brass trigger
Value:	$150.00 – 250.00 each

The Binkowski Expanding Hook is a simple device made from a single piece of spring-steel wire with an eye coiled at its center and with the terminal ends bent into the shape of fishhooks, which are barbless.

This hook employs a trigger, a separate piece of metal designed to hold the two shanks of the hook together until a fish strikes, whereupon the trigger is "rocked upon the shanks of the hook," thus allowing the shanks to spring outward.

This hook may be found on a card.

From patent text: "This invention relates to fishhook release triggers, and is intended with elastically connected double fishhooks, which hooks are held in a combined position by a trigger or slide until the fish has taken the bait."

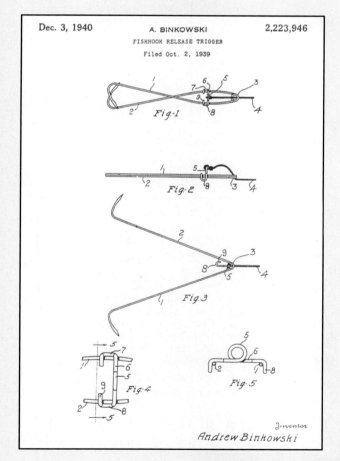

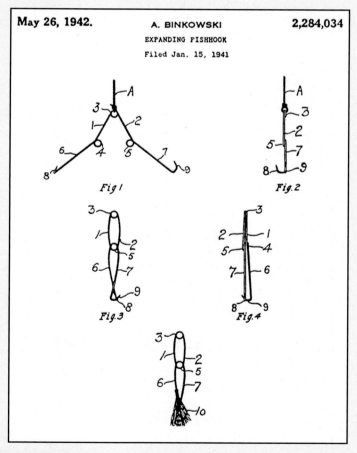

The 1940 and the 1942 Binkowski patents.

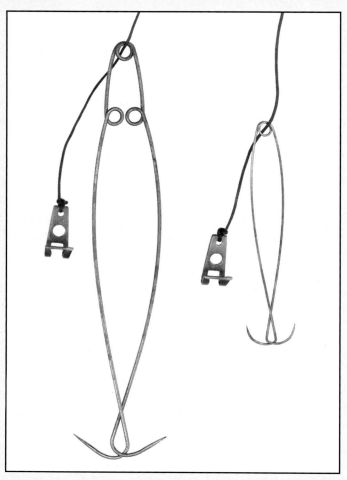

Two different Binkowski Expanding Hooks with setting devices, shown actual sizes.

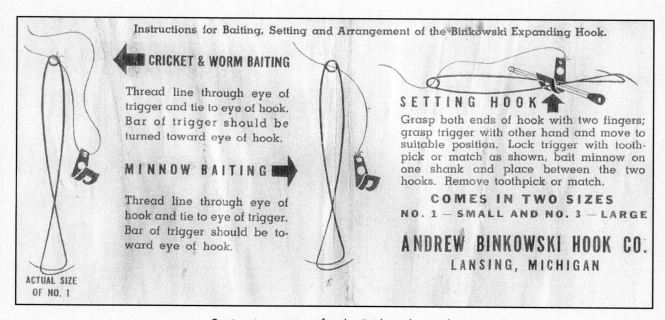

Instructions for Baiting, Setting and Arrangement of the Binkowski Expanding Hook.

CRICKET & WORM BAITING

Thread line through eye of trigger and tie to eye of hook. Bar of trigger should be turned toward eye of hook.

MINNOW BAITING

Thread line through eye of hook and tie to eye of trigger. Bar of trigger should be toward eye of hook.

ACTUAL SIZE OF NO. 1

SETTING HOOK

Grasp both ends of hook with two fingers; grasp trigger with other hand and move to suitable position. Lock trigger with toothpick or match as shown, bait minnow on one shank and place between the two hooks. Remove toothpick or match.

COMES IN TWO SIZES
NO. 1 — SMALL AND NO. 3 — LARGE

ANDREW BINKOWSKI HOOK CO.
LANSING, MICHIGAN

Setting instructions for the Binkowski Hook.

Name:	Jyrkas Fish Landing Device
Patented:	March 18, 1941, patent #2,235,371 by John P. Jyrkas
Origin:	Fergus Falls, Minnesota
Material:	Aluminum, steel, and spring-steel
Size:	12" jaw spread, 8½" tall
Value:	$250.00+

This device consists of a large ring, or bail, to which is attached three large pivotal fishhooks. The bail has a slot to allow it to be slipped over a fishing line, said line being retained within the bail by a "resilient latch member."

A stout line or rope is meant to be attached to the bail, so that when this device is allowed to slide down the fishing line, which has already hooked a fish, the three large hooks will engage the fish, which can then be landed by use of the device.

From patent text: "…may be easily and quickly applied to a fishing line and lowered into engagement with a fish caught on the hook of the line and which will efficiently bite into the fish to assure against the fish getting away or off of the hook and which may be employed along with the fishing line in landing the fish."

Jyrkas Fish Landing Device in the closed position.

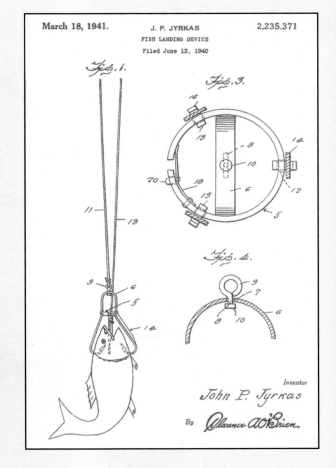

Name:	Voigt Hook Gaff
Patented:	June 3, 1941, patent #2,244,271 by Leon Voigt
Origin:	Galveston, Texas
Size:	2¼" long
Material:	Steel with a brass rivet
Value:	$200.00 – 250.00. Value doubled when found on nice card.

The trap hook patented by Leon Voigt, and pictured in the patent drawings, in no way resembles the manufactured hook as it is found on the card. The patent pertains to a trap hook powered by a helical spring, while the production model is a lever-action hook and has no spring.

The card states that this hook gaff is "essentially a good hook for these times when food is scarce." The card also states that this hook is "a Sheephead's Papa," the meaning of which is not understood by these authors.

This is not a common hook, and is more uncommon when found on the card.

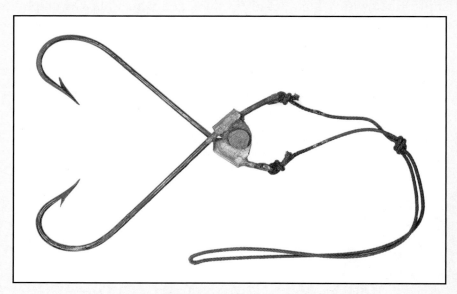

Voigt Hook Gaff, shown in the relaxed position.

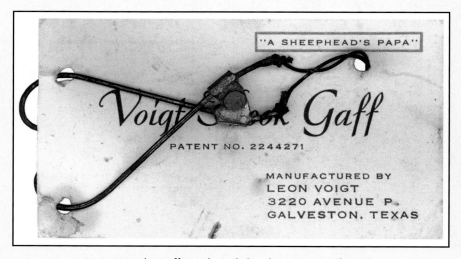

Voigt Hook Gaff card, with hook, as it was found.

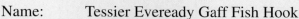

Name:	Tessier Eveready Gaff Fish Hook
Patented:	August 22, 1944, patent #2,356,712 by Joseph D. Tessier
Origin:	Worchester, Massachusetts
Size:	2¾" across when set, 4" long when sprung
Material:	Steel and spring-steel
Value:	$100.00 – 125.00 with clear plastic advertising envelope of equal value

On the envelope in which this hook was sold is printed:

NOVELTY ENGINEERING CO.
Eveready Gaff Fish Hook
"Always dependable sure-catch"
91 Stafford St. Worcester 3, Mass.
Tessier Gaff Fish Hook, Pat. Aug. 22, 1944

From personal communication it was learned that the address given on the envelope was a factory during World War II. (It is now a warehouse.) This factory's main output was survival kits and emergency kits for the armed forces, then fighting in both theaters. It is doubtful these hooks were ever placed in any of these kits, although they might have proved to be very useful.

These hooks have either steel finish or a scarcer galvanized finish.

The line-tie is sometimes riveted.

From patent text: "Objects of the invention include the provision of a frame, a rectilinearly movable fishhook sliding on the frame, a gaff hook pivoted to the frame, and a cam on the rectilinearly movable hook cooperatively with the pivoted gaff hook to swing the latter in it towards the former as the same is moved relative to the frame by the fish as it strikes, so that the fish is gripped by two hooks acting scissor-fashion with the barbs facing each other at the ends of the blades of the scissors."

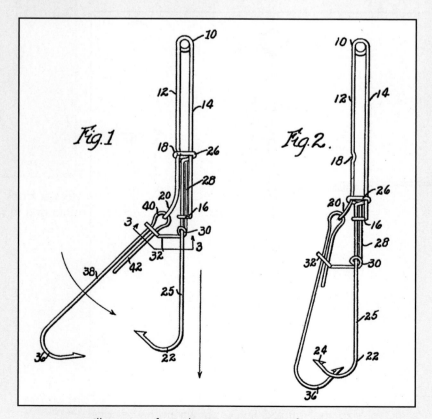

Illustration from the Tessier patent of 1944.

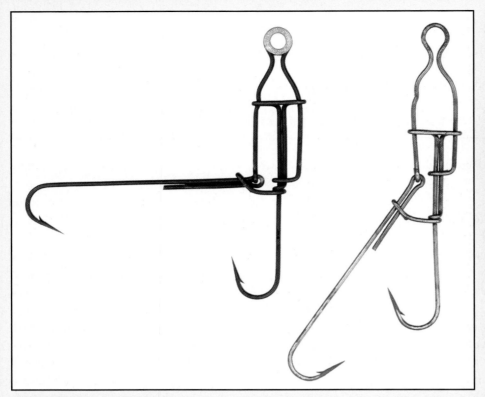

Tessier Eveready Hooks, actual size, steel finish, shown in the set and sprung positions, with and without rivet.

Tessier Hook in original package, enlarged to show details.

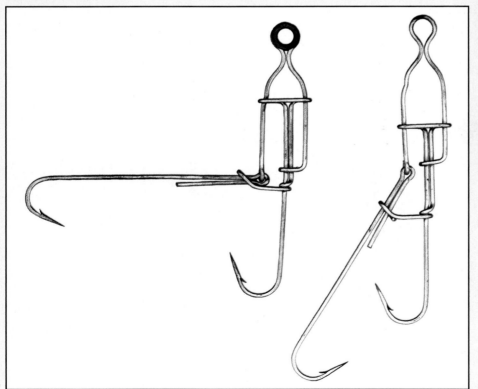

Tessier Eveready Hooks, actual size, galvanized finish, shown in the set and sprung positions with and without rivet.

Name:	Ozark Hooker
Patented:	Probably. Card marked "Patent Pending," but letters of patent have not been found as of yet. Circa 1940s.
Origin:	North Little Rock, Arkansas
Size:	3" long, 3" wide
Material:	Steel and spring-steel wire with a brass rivet
Value:	$200.00+. Value doubled when found on nice original blue card.

The Ozark Hooker, made by the Bracken Manufacturing Company, is a clutch-type fish trap powered by a spring-steel wire with a coil at its center, which forms the line-tie.

The card on which this hook was sold states that, "If you don't ketchum with this hook, it's because they didn't bite."

This scarce hook is even more rare on the card.

Ozark Hooker card and hook enlarged to show details. The hook is in the set position.

Name:	Automatic Safety Fish Hook
Patented:	September 3, 1946, patent #2,406,912 by Fred Schwarzer
Origin:	Pottstown, Pennsylvania
Size:	Two sizes, 2⅜" and 2⅝"
Material:	Stainless steel and brass
Value:	$200.00 – 300.00 when found in red and white box with paperwork

This spring-loaded fishhook was manufactured and sold by the Schwarzer Experimental and Manufacturing Company of Pottstown, Pennsylvania. It is composed of a shank with a barbless fishhook pivotally connected to a double shank with two barbless hooks.

The paperwork for this states that "the Barbless Automatic Triple Hooks will cause all kinds of fish weighing from 1 to 30 lbs. to hook themselves and stay hooked."

This hook came individually boxed and was sold on a cardboard display stand, which held a dozen.

Top of Automatic Safety Fish Hook box.

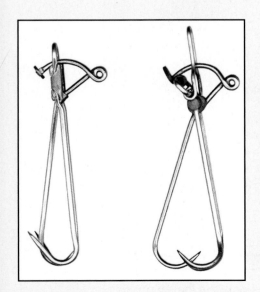 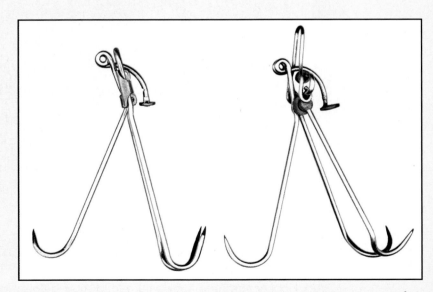

Left to right: Deep Sea Automatic Safety Fish Hook shown in the set position and the Deep Sea Automatic Safety Fish Hook shown in the sprung position. The hook is shown actual size.

Name:	Kayen-Vee Shur Hook
Patented:	December 12, 1950, patent #2,534,152 by Ralph W. VanArkel
Origin:	Oskaloosa, Iowa
Size:	Two sizes, 5¼" long and 4½" long
Material:	Nickel-plated spring and piano wire spring
Value:	Up to $30.00 each, depending on condition. If found on a nice green and white card, the value would double. The small (junior) size is less common.

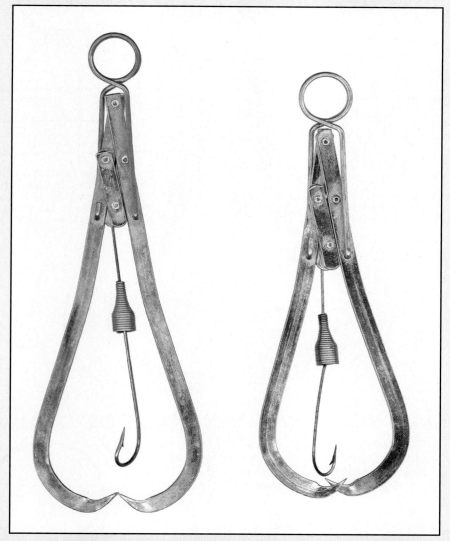

The large and small sizes of the Kayen-Vee Shur Hook. The hooks are each shown actual size and in the sprung position.

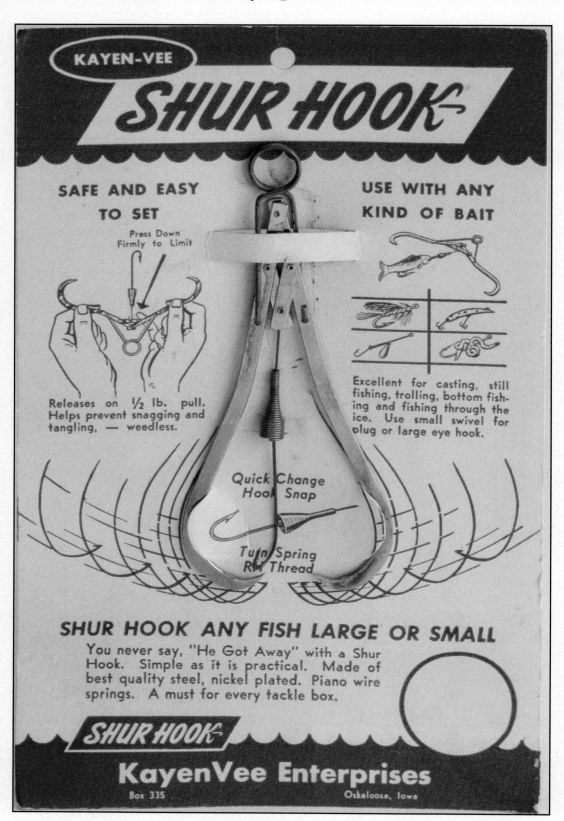

Large size Katen-Vee Shur Hook on the card.

Name:	Penninger Fish Hook
Patented:	December 2, 1952, patent #2,619,759 by Luther S. Penninger
Origin:	Raleigh, North Carolina
Size:	3½" long
Material:	Steel and spring-steel
Value:	$200.00 – 300.00

The fishhook invented by Luther Penninger is of the type that relies upon the configuration of the fishing line and how it is attached to the fishhook to operate the mechanism. The fishhook is so designed that when a fish pulls on the bait hook, a barbed spear point is drawn downward into the fish's head. When the fish is landed, the expansive helical spring automatically extracts the spear point.

From our personal communication with the then-98-year-old inventor, it was learned that he was a steelworker most of his life. He said that he thought these fishhooks were produced over about a five-year period. When asked, he could not remember about how many were made, but thought over 1,000. He and his son had only one of the fishhooks in their possession and knew of no others.

This is a scarce hook now that can sometimes be found on a card but would not be so scarce if a hoard of such hooks appeared, such as a shoe-box full at a flea market near the inventor's town, but this will probably not happen.

The following is what we think is a humorous note that Mr. Penninger sent to us in regard to our request for a picture of him.

"Don't know what you are wanting a picture for. Maybe like a stamp collector. Where did you get my name and Tel #" (he was in the telephone book). "Are anybody making these hooks now in Pennsylvania. I had a royalty contract with a man from Pennsylvania. 'Flim-Flam' man. Never heard from. He come to my house, sign a contract. Never heard from him. He's a Bastard in my book. This is the oldest picture I have."

From patent text: "…said trap hook being in the form of a projectile spear which, when brought into play, harpoons the victim and holds it securely for easy and effective landing."

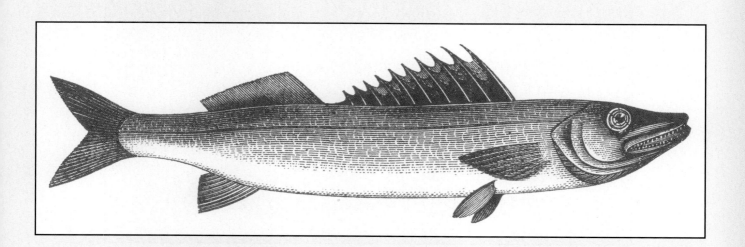

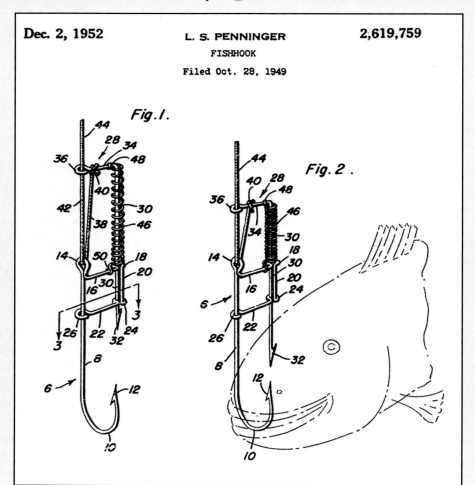

Penninger patent illustration showing the hook imbedded in the fish's head.

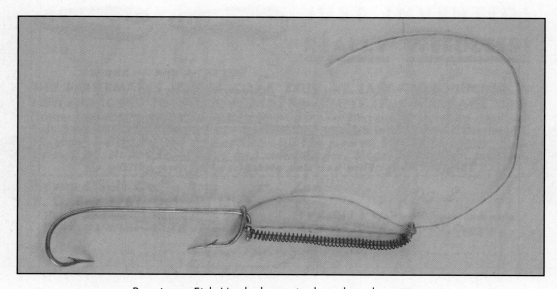

Penninger Fish Hook shown in the relaxed position.

Name:	Thomas Jolley Clutch Fish Hook Advertising Display
Patented:	Hook was patented January 6, 1953.
Origin:	Oskaloosa, Iowa
Size:	Hook is 9" x 14".
Material:	Hook is made with clear plastic tubes attached by copper wire.
Value:	$5,000.00+ with six hooks

This is a painted metal store advertising display with six Jolley Clutch Fish Hooks still on it. The hooks themselves are in their original cellulite tubes with metal caps, along with paper inserts of various colors that read "Adjustable Automatic Clutch Fish Hook, Thomas M. Jolley, Oskaloosa, Iowa, patent #2,624,150, other patents pending, price $1.25."

When the fishhook is removed from its tube, three striking hooks expand to a relaxed position, with a central bait hook extending directly beneath the steel tube of the fishhook, which also encases a helical spring. When a fish pulls on the bait hook, the three striking hooks are forced downward. This and other fish traps of similar design are referred to as "clutch" hooks, because the more fish pull against them, the tighter they contract. This hook is sometimes stamped "PAT PEND" on the steel tube enclosing the spring and also may be found with brass, rather than steel, striking hooks.

A Thomas Jolley Clutch Fish Hook by itself is valued at $400.00+.

Any metal advertising display for a spring-loaded fishhook or metal fish trap is rare.

From patent text: "...a fishhook consisting of a bait hook which, when gripped by a fish, will be pulled downwardly to simultaneously actuate a pair of elongated hooks, which will move inwardly to close about and grip the body portion of the fish. Frequently, a soft-mouthed fish will be able to tear itself loose from a bait hook. Accordingly, the present device is designed to prevent the fish from tearing loose from the bait hook."

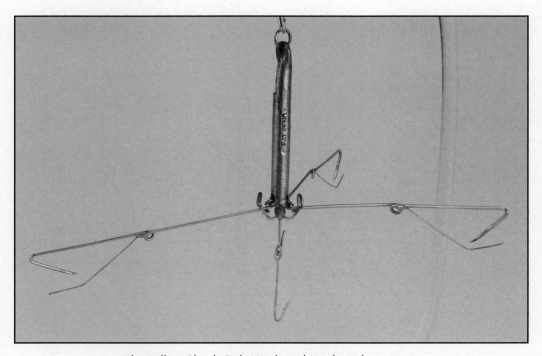

The Jolley Clutch Fish Hook in the relaxed position.

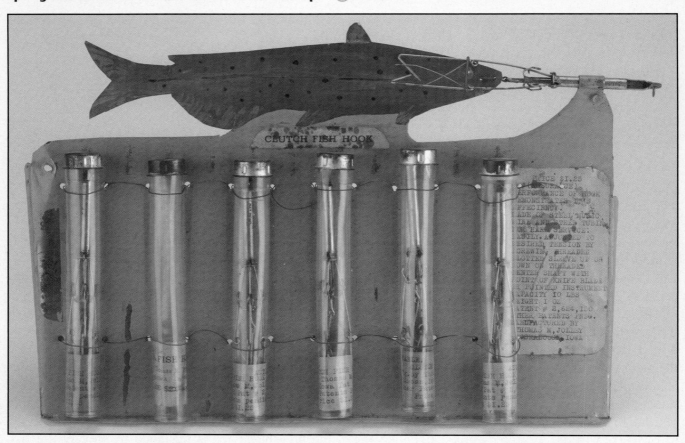

Painted metal store advertising display with six Jolley Clutch Fish Hooks still on it. The hooks themselves are in their original cellulite tubes with metal caps, along with paper inserts of various colors. This is a large display piece measuring 9" x 14".

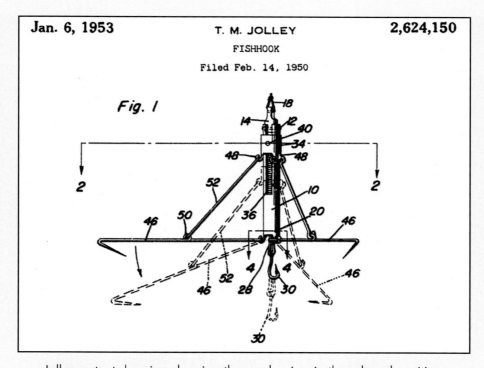

Jolley patent drawing showing the mechanism in the relaxed position.

Name:	Surestrike Fish Hook
Patented:	June 23, 1953, patent #2,642,694 by Bedford Westerfield
Origin:	Detroit, Michigan
Size:	3½" long when set, 1½" x 2" when sprung
Material:	Spring-steel
Value:	$150.00 – 200.00, double when on nice red card

This trap is sprung when the needle-like trigger mechanism is depressed. This "auxiliary pointed member" also has "a piercing action on the fish to firmly lock the fish against removal from the barb."

This is a tricky little device, as evidenced from the disclaimer on the card on which it was sold. It reads, "WARNING — keep away from children, as the force of this spring, if released accidentally, will set the hook barb very deeply in the flesh. NOT RESPONSIBLE FOR ANY INJURY INCURRED."

From patent text: "…to provide snap action means for swinging the barb end of the hook."

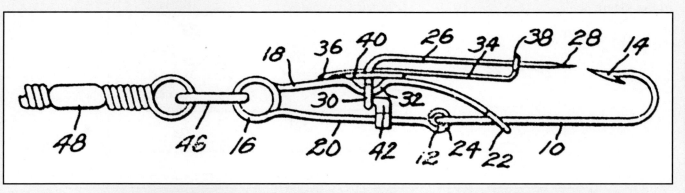

Illustration from the Westerfield patent showing the Surestrike mechanism.

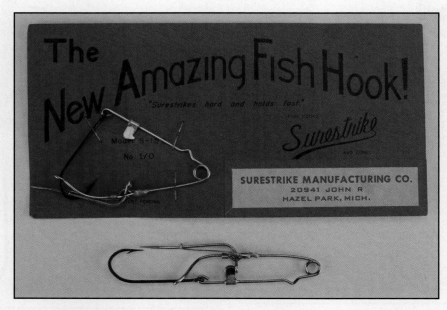

Surestrike Fish Hook in the sprung position, shown on the original card, and the Surestrike Fish Hook, shown in the set position, beneath it.

Name:	Stevenson Trap Hook
Patented:	June 30, 1953, patent #2,643,479 by James E. Stevenson
Origin:	Arcadia, California
Size:	3⅛" and 3½"
Material:	Stainless and spring-steel
Value:	$150.00 – 300.00

The Stevenson Trap Hook came in two sizes. The body of each size is the same, with the difference being the size of the bait hooks attached. These bait hooks could have either a blued finish or a stainless steel finish. This hook is stamped "PAT. PEND."

The two bait hooks on this fish trap are attached in a unique way, which is best described in the patent.

From patent text: "A very simple and satisfactory way to attach the hook is to wrap a portion of the body member…around the shank of the hook and clamp the body member tightly in position. This operation, commonly referred to in the art as 'stoking,' has the advantage that it in no way diminishes the strength of the hook as is apt to occur if the hook is heated as when welded into place."

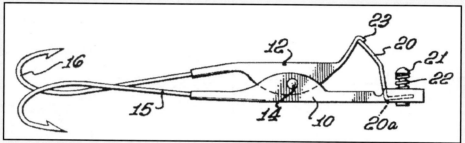

Illustration from the Stevenson patent drawing.

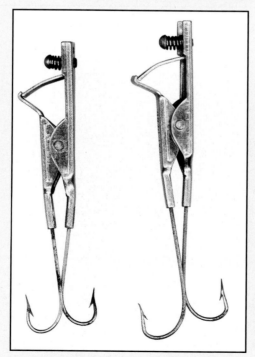

Stevenson Trap Hooks, shown actual sizes of small and large, in the set position.

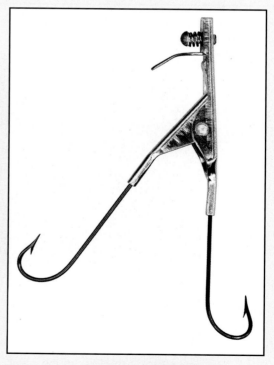

Stevenson Trap Hook, shown actual size, in the sprung position.

Name:	Spread Eagle Fish Hook
Patented:	July 7, 1953, patent #2,644,264 by William H. Heki
Origin:	Pella, Iowa
Size:	Four sizes, 2½", 3", 3½", and 4"
Material:	Spring-steel wire
Value:	$250.00 – 350.00 when in box

The Spread Eagle Fish Hook came in two models. One model number pertained to the two smallest sizes, while the other model number pertained to the two largest sizes. This hook came with either a steel finish or a gold-colored finish.

This hook was made by The Spread Eagle Hook Manufacturing Company of Pella, Iowa, and was advertised as having "won the deep-sea fishing pool at Los Angeles, in July, 1949."

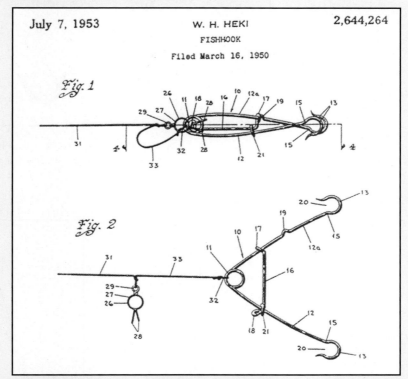

Spread Eagle shipping box that held a dozen hooks in their boxes. The actual size of box is 7¾" x 3".

SPREAD EAGLE

The hook that sets itself when fish strikes and holds fish regardless of slack in line. Available in four sizes.

This hook can be used for all game fish—fresh or salt water—and for all types of fishing—casting, trolling, still and set lines. Any kind of bait may be used. Made of high-grade steel wire. Has been tried and proven.

This hook is a life-saver for small fish, as they are unmolested.

Has won deep-sea fishing pool at Los Angeles in July, 1949.

INSTRUCTIONS

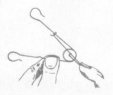

Push trigger up on hook, holding base of hook with thumb and forefinger and compress. Be sure to press upper end of trigger firmly in notch when closed.

WARNING—Do not handle hook without line or leader.

Spread Eagle
Manufacturing Co.
PELLA, IOWA

Setting instructions that were wrapped around the hook in the box.

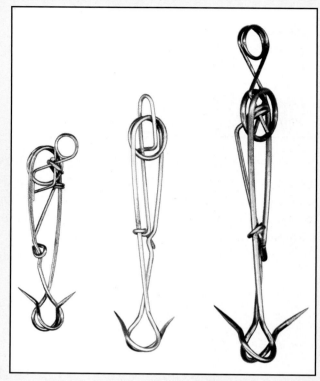

Spead Eagle Hooks No. 1, No. 2, and No. 3, actual size, each shown in the set position.

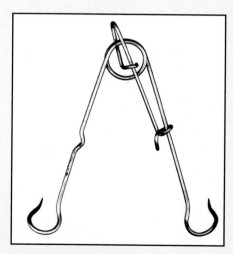

Spread Eagle Hook No. 2, shown in the sprung position.

Spread Eagle hook box.

Name:	Miracle Fish Hook
Patented:	Probably, as card is marked "Pat. Pending," but letters of patent have not as yet been found. Circa 1950s.
Origin:	Chicago, Illinois
Size:	4½" long
Material:	Steel and spring-steel wire with brass rivets
Value:	$250.00+

This spring hook was marketed by the Miracle Fish Hook Company, Inc., and is powered by a single contractile helical spring that can be easily replaced in the event that it breaks.

The line-tie on this spring hook is an elongated piece of flattened steel with an ear on one side, which serves to hold the striking hook in the set position. This line-tie measures 1½" x ⁵⁄₃₂" and serves as the dog to this trap.

This is a scarce spring hook, and may be found on the card.

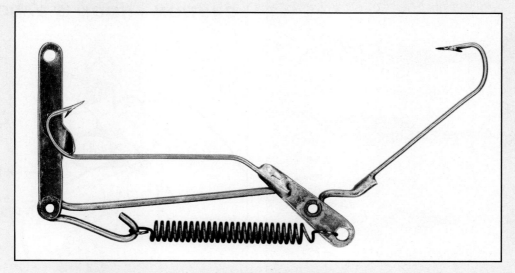

Miracle Fish Hook in the set position.

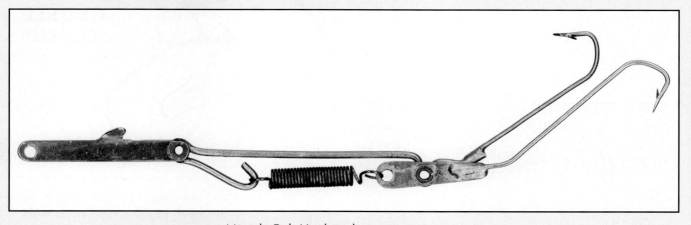

Miracle Fish Hook in the sprung position.

Name:	Trigger Hook
Patented:	Unknown, but probably. Circa 1950s.
Origin:	Denver, Colorado
Size:	2⅜"
Material:	Aluminum, brass, and stainless steel
Value:	$150.00 – 250.00

The Trigger Hook was manufactured by the Keating Advance Corporation and was sold in a clear plastic tube with instructions enclosed. It came in three finishes, red, gold, or aluminum, and it has a 1½" line-tie with a red glass bead and spinner blade.

This is a wicked little trap and one should be most cautious with it. It is humorous that in the instructions it is noted as being "the most humane hook ever devised. They don't get away and die."

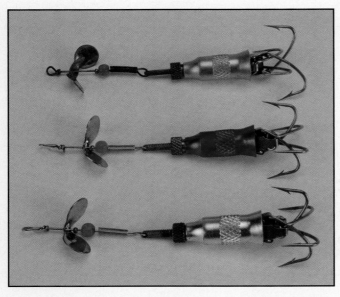

The three color varieties of the Trigger Hook. The hooks are shown in the sprung position.

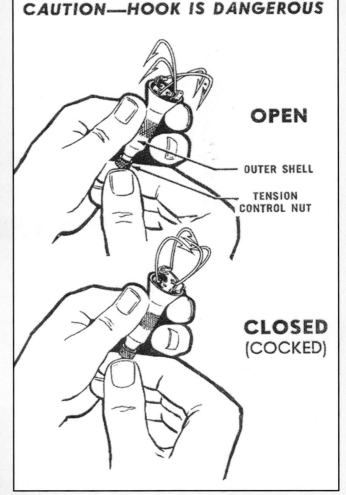

CAUTION—HOOK IS DANGEROUS

OPEN

OUTER SHELL

TENSION CONTROL NUT

CLOSED (COCKED)

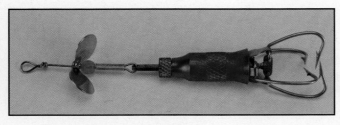

The Trigger Hook, shown in the set position.

Directions for setting the Trigger Hook, which were wrapped around the hook in the clear plastic tube it was packaged in.

Name:	Lite Striking Fish Hook
Patented:	May 22, 1956, patent #2,746,199 by Chester W. Dyckowski
Origin:	St. Paul, Minnesota
Size:	3⅜" long, 1¾" wide when sprung
Material:	Spring-steel wire which may be a gold color
Value:	Steel finish, $20.00; gold finish, $30.00. When found in box with paperwork, add $20.00.

LITE STRIKING FISH HOOK

This hook can be used for all game fish--fresh or salt water--and for all types of fishing-casting, trolling, still and set lines. Any kind of bait may be used. Made of high-grade steel wire. Has been tried and proven.

This hook is a life-saver for small fish, as they are unmolested.

 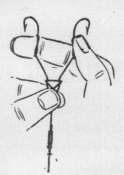

INSTRUCTIONS

Push trigger up on hook holding base of hook with thumb and forefinger and compress. Be sure to press upper end of trigger firmly in notch when closed.

WARNING--Do not handle hook without line or leader.

LITE STRIKE FISH HOOK
Manufacturing Company

Lite Striking Fish Hook setting instructions that came wrapped around the hook in the box.

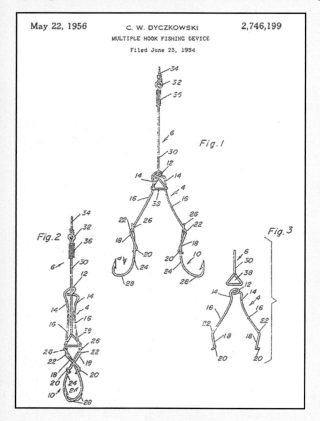

May 22, 1956 C. W. DYCZKOWSKI 2,746,199
MULTIPLE HOOK FISHING DEVICE
Filed June 23, 1954

Fig.1

Fig.2

Fig.3

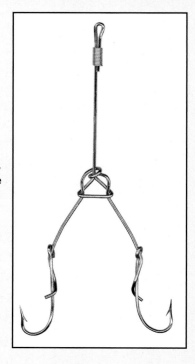

Lite Striking Hook, actual size, in the sprung position.

SELF STRIKING FISH HOOK
THE HOOK THAT HOLDS
PAT. PENDING
146 State St.   Garfield 7926   St. Paul, Minn.

LITE STRIKING FISH HOOK
THE HOOK THAT HOLDS
PAT. PENDING
146 State St.   Garfield 7926   St. Paul, Minn.

LITE STRIKING FISH HOOK
THE HOOK THAT HOLDS
PAT. NO. 2,746,199
146 State St.   CA 4-7926   St. Paul, Minn.

Three different Lite Striking boxes, shown actual size. The Self Striking box was the earliest; then came the Lite Striking with the "Lite" label covering "Self." The last box had a label covering the whole top of the box.

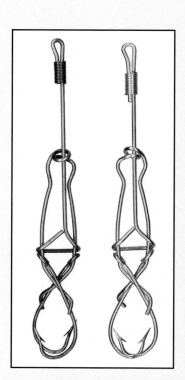

Two varieties of the Lite Striking Hook, actual size, in the set position.

Name:	Parker Self-Setting Fish Hook
Patented:	Unknown, but probably
Origin:	Kansas City, Missouri
Size:	1⅝" long, 1½" jaw spread
Material:	Steel
Value:	$200.00 – 300.00

This is a petite little fishhook made by the Parker Self-Setting Fish Hook Company. It is not a spring-loaded hook, but rather a mechanical one. In the set, or closed, position, the Parker's two hooks lie against each other, facing in opposite directions. When pulled upon by the fish, they slide down a central shaft and spread apart. This hook was advertised for sale in the September 1956 edition of the *Fisherman Magazine*.

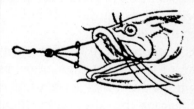

If you use a Parker Self-Setting Fish Hook, those fish that commonly steal your bait will get caught. You set this double hook in a closed position. When a fish bites, the double hook spreads open. It can be used for still fishing and trotline fishing. Hooks are 49¢ apiece or two for $1.00 with instructions.

Advertisement from the 1956 edition of the *Fisherman Magazine*.

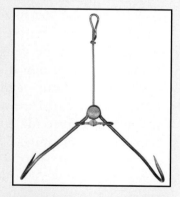

Parker hook in the set position, actual size, and Parker hook in the sprung position, actual size.

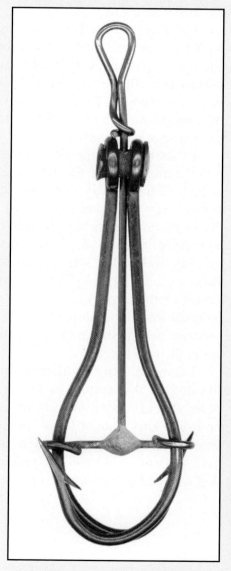

Enlarged view of the Parker Hook, to show detail.

Name:	Reitzel Fish Trap
Patented:	January 29,1957, patent #2,779,125 by George A. Reitzel
Origin:	St. Louis, Missouri
Size:	6" – 8½" across, jaw length 3" – 6"
Material:	Brass, copper, steel, and solder, with brass screen
Value:	$3,500.00+

The Reitzel Fish Trap is possibly the most complex mechanical device that was ever invented to capture and kill a fish, and one can only wonder as to the complexities of the mind of the inventor, George Reitzel. The letters of patent themselves for this fish trap run to five full pages of text and two of illustrations.

The Reitzel Fish Trap was designed so that it would sit on the bottom of any body of water in such a way that the bait and the striking jaws would face upwards, with the brass, circular screen protecting them from any entanglements that might be found on the water bed, such as roots, rocks and weeds, etc.

To set the trap, the brass rod or heavy copper wire, which acts as the line-tie, is grasped and pulled directly away from the screen. Doing so compresses an expansive helical spring while at the same time releasing pressure on the opposing pairs of striking hooks, which then rotate 90° and lay flat against the screen, and at the same time exposes a small vise-like bait-pin clamp at the center of the trap. A small plate of metal is then inserted into the clamp, which is controlled by a separate helical spring. As the clamp is now pried open, the trap is set.

The metal plate, which would be considered the dog of this trap, was preferably tapered in order also to serve as an adjustment of the tension on itself. This plate of metal served best when soldered onto a safety pin, which would then act to hold the bait, as Reitzel showed in his patent. The dog was tied to the trap by a piece of twine. A bare bait hook would also work well, being easily replaced if separated from the trap. The tension on the dog could also be adjusted by a nut on the threaded rod central to the trap.

From our personal communication with his then-93-year-old daughter, it was learned that George Reitzel started work on his fish trap in the early 1900s and patented it as an old man, dying not long afterwards at the age of 94.

He found that his trap proved to be more conducive to the trapping of fish rather than crabs, as crabs would tear his traps and brass screens apart with their claws. He learned this after trying them out in the Chesapeake Bay near Annapolis, Maryland, while visiting his daughter there shortly after WWII. She relates that he would come home from "fishing" all day with his traps and would be up most of the night soldering their repair. She said "he hated those crabs." His profession was that of a stationery engineer with the Rexall Corporation in St. Louis, Missouri. Less than a dozen of these traps were ever produced, and they were never sold commercially.

From patent text: "Aquatic creatures such as fish, crabs, and the like can be caught in nets or seines but can involve many hours of arduous work. They can be caught on baited hooks...but sometimes they can disengage themselves and thus avoid capture...and are thus both objectionable...It is therefore an object of the present invention to provide a trap which can trap and hook aquatic creatures."

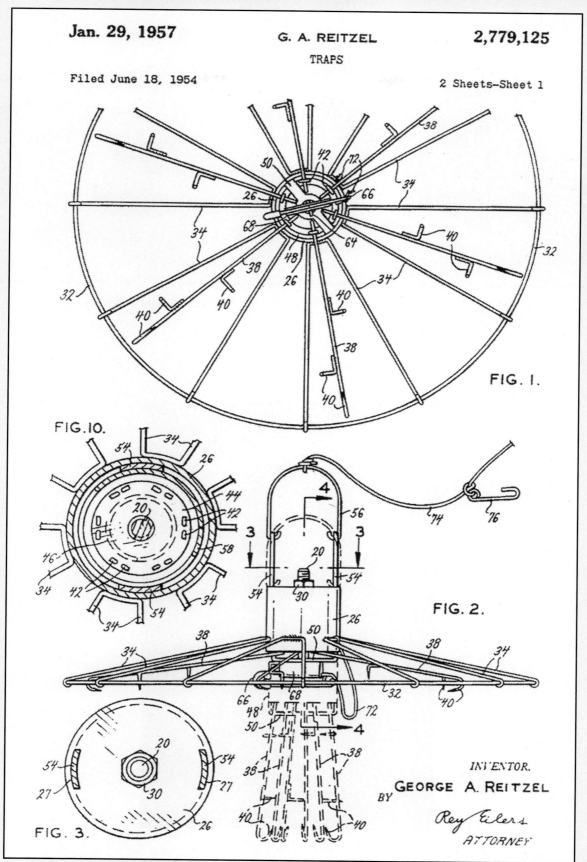

Jan. 29, 1957

G. A. REITZEL

TRAPS

2,779,125

Filed June 18, 1954

2 Sheets—Sheet 1

FIG. I.

FIG. 10.

FIG. 2.

FIG. 3.

INVENTOR.
GEORGE A. REITZEL
BY
Rey Eilers
ATTORNEY

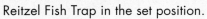

Reitzel Fish Trap in the set position.

Reitzel Fish Trap in the sprung position.

George Reitzel, the Thinker.

Name:	Emmitt Scott's "Sure-Catch Device," which shoots bullets
Patented:	December 24, 1957, patent #2,817,182 by Emmitt Y. Scott
Origin:	Swainsboro, Georgia
Size:	3" – 3½" in length; .22 caliber and .32 S&W caliber
Material:	Brass, steel, and spring-steel
Value:	$5,000.00+ each

The fishing device invented by "Big Emmitt," as he was known, is surely the last word as it pertains to the lying fisherman who speaks of "the big one that got away."

The device consists of a hollow brass tube that is essentially a barrel. To the front of this barrel is attached a fishhook. Inside of the barrel is a slidable spring-loaded hammer, which is designed to strike and fire a cartridge placed in the chamber above the fishhook.

To operate the device, the slidable hammer is pushed toward the rear of the barrel, thus compressing the expansive helical spring. When fully compressed, the rod (which extends out from the slidable hammer) is slid sideways into a slot.

The fishing line is attached to an eye on the front of the device, threaded through an eye on the end of the rod projecting out from the slidable hammer, and thence through a guide eye projecting out from the top of the device. When sufficient force is exerted on the line, the rod projecting out from the slidable hammer is pulled out of its retaining slot and is thereby thrust downward by the force of the spring, thence striking and firing the cartridge.

Another model of Big Emmitt's device was constructed so that instead of a rod being cocked into a slot cut into the barrel, a curlicue-type pin was set into a hole drilled into the barrel. This model had the spring on the outside of the barrel. Ramrods and setting devices were also made in conjunction with Big Emmitt's devices, and are pictured in the letters of patent.

A newspaper article written in 1956 about Emmitt Scott's "Sure-Catch Device," along with a photograph of him holding his invention, quotes Big Emmitt as saying, "Blanks will stun 'em until you get 'em in the boat, live ammo will stun 'em

until fryin' time." The article goes on to state that inventor Scott had not checked on the legality of his device, with his reasoning being "must be legal, because the fish is already caught when it goes off. Just helps you land 'em."

From personal communication, it was learned that these devices were never commercially produced and that less than a dozen were ever constructed. It was also learned that Big Emmitt, who was an automotive mechanic by profession, was not an avid fisherman, but had heard one too many stories about "the big one that got away" from friends who fished the local lakes and rivers. He designed these lures not for any one particular species of fish, but rather for any big fish, and he said himself that he could make his lures in a large enough caliber to "take care of" even the largest catch.

The family tells of how one time, one of Big Emmitt's devices exploded in his hands. It was serious enough to call the town doctor, who in those days made house calls. After examining Big Emmitt, the doctor said that his patient wasn't too bad, but he told the inventor, "Emmitt, you shouldn't be foolin' around with those damn things."

Emmitt Y. Scott was born on May 9, 1893, and died on April 3, 1966, at the age of 73. He was thin as a young man and strong enough to bend a 20-penny nail with his hands. At the time of his death, however, he weighed well over 300 pounds.

In the early 1950s, Big Emmitt Scott was pictured on a postcard promoting Shell Oil Company, one of whose gas stations he owned, in the town of Swainsboro.

Authors' note: The authors would be interested in acquiring one of these original postcards from any reader.

From patent text: "...for firing an explosive charge in the direction of the fish while the latter is held captive by the fishing device. An important object of the invention is to provide a firing mechanism, including a fishhook connected to a cartridge holding firing device functioning to stun and subdue the fish after the same has been caught on the hook."

"Big Emmitt" Scott.

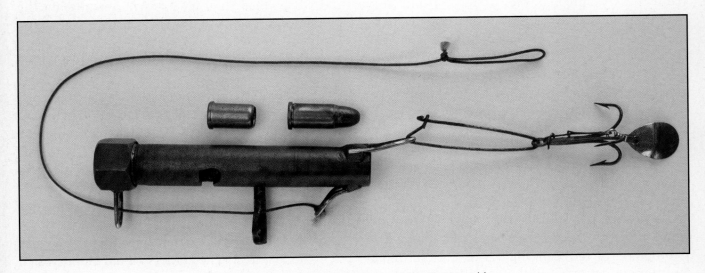

Emmitt Scott's "Sure-Catch Device" 32 S&W caliber.

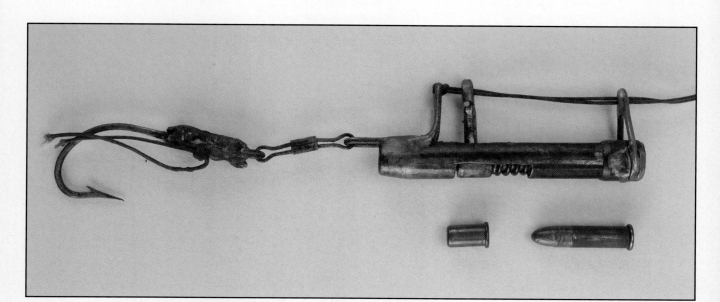

Emmitt Scott's "Sure-Catch Device" 22 caliber.

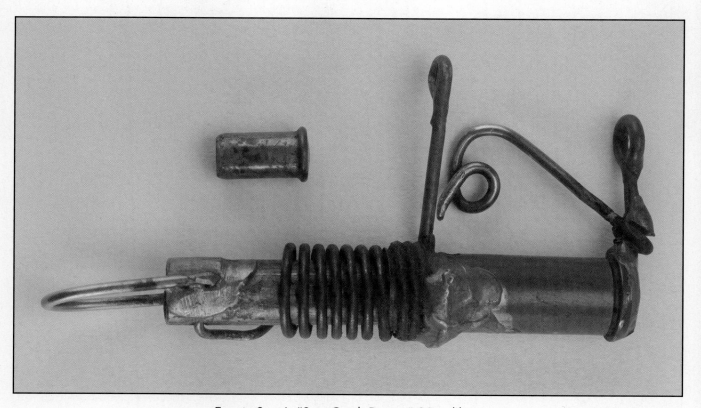

Emmitt Scott's "Sure-Catch Device" 22 caliber.

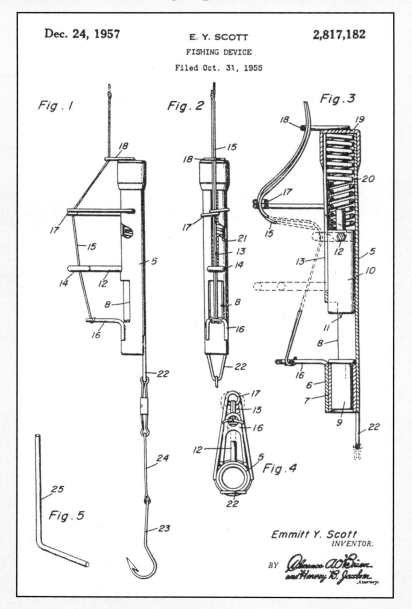

Dec. 24, 1957

E. Y. SCOTT

2,817,182

FISHING DEVICE

Filed Oct. 31, 1955

Fig. 1

Fig. 2

Fig. 3

Fig. 4

Fig. 5

Emmitt Y. Scott
INVENTOR.

BY

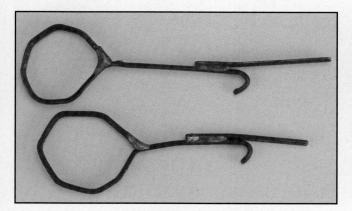

Setting tools for the Emmitt Scott "Sure-Catch Device."

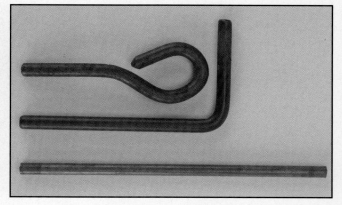

Ram rods shown on the Emmitt Scott patent.

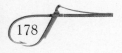

Name:	Reeder Triple Fish Hook
Patented:	February 17, 1959, patent #2,873,548
Origin:	Bayside, New York
Size:	5" long, 6" across when relaxed
Material:	Steel and spring-steel with brass cotter pin rivet
Value:	$200.00+

The Reeder Triple Fish Hook is not a complicated trap. This trap is not so much sprung as it is actuated. This type of trap, when used for fish, is called a clutch trap, because the harder the fish pulls on the bait hook, the more the striking jaws dig in. This trap is expanded in its relaxed position.

This is an uncommon trap and was thought to be much older before patent papers for it were discovered.

From patent text: "Another object of the present invention is to provide a trap hook which will securely grasp both sides of the animal after the main hook has been jerked, thus providing a triple action."

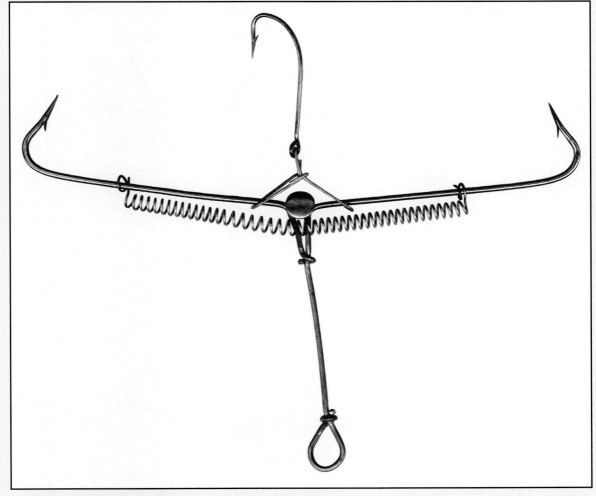

The Reeder Triple Fish Hook shown in the relaxed position, actual size.

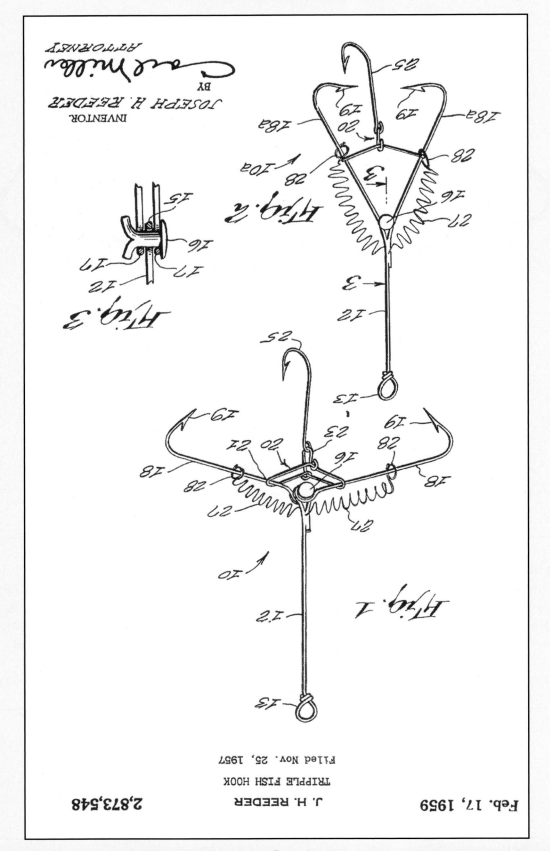

Feb. 17, 1959

J. H. REEDER

2,873,548

TRIPPLE FISH HOOK

Filed Nov. 25, 1957

Fig. 1

Fig. 2

Fig. 3

INVENTOR.
JOSEPH H. REEDER
BY
ATTORNEY

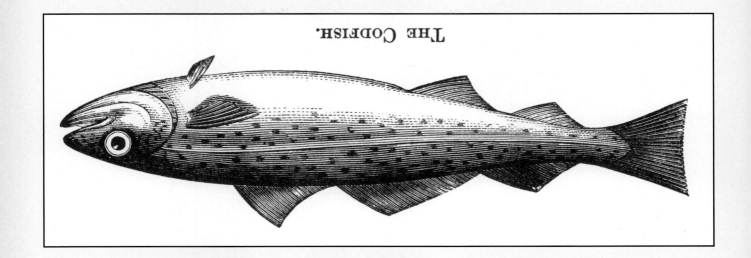

THE CODFISH.

Name:	Thibodeau Commercial Fish Hook
Patented:	August 4, 1959, patent #2,897,628 by Milford E. Thibodeau
Origin:	Scarborough, Maine
Size:	4½" long, 2¼" wide, with a 6½" jaw spread when set
Material:	Galvanized steel and spring-steel
Value:	$500.00+

The metal killer fish trap invented and produced by Milford Thibodeau is powered by "a pair of opposed aligned spring members which are arranged in end-to-end relation with respect to each other."

To each of the two springs is attached a striking hook. These two hooks are symmetrically positioned about the centrally located bait hook, which serves as the trigger for this device.

When in the set position, the two striking hooks are in a horizontal position. When the bait hook has pressure exerted upon it in a direction away from the line-tie, the trap is sprung, sending the two striking hooks down into both sides of the fish's head with "lightning-like speed."

From personal communication with the widow of the inventor, it was learned that fewer than 100 of these hooks were ever produced, with a peck basket of these being discarded as useless trash some fifteen years after the inventor's death on June 11, 1966, at the age of 48.

It was also learned that at the time of his invention, in the late 1950s, Milford was a commercial lobster fisherman in Maine. He had 200 lobster traps, which he ran from a 42' boat that he had built himself. This boat was later sold by him, with the proceeds being used to buy an airplane. He then earned his pilot's license and joined the Aircraft Owners and Pilots Association. His last job was that of a dental technician.

In an advertisement for his fishhook, the inventor states that it "was designed for the commercial fisherman and the men who make their living from the great waters of the world." The origin of this advertisement was South Portland, Maine, and the ad states that this fishhook is "not recommended for minors."

From patent text: "This invention relates to a fishhook assembly...which is especially suitable for use by commercial fisherman."

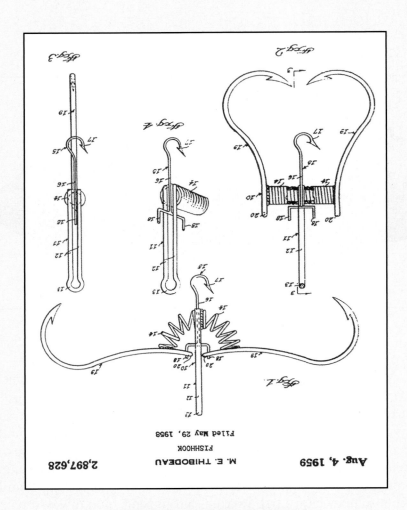

Thibodeau Commercial Fish Hook.

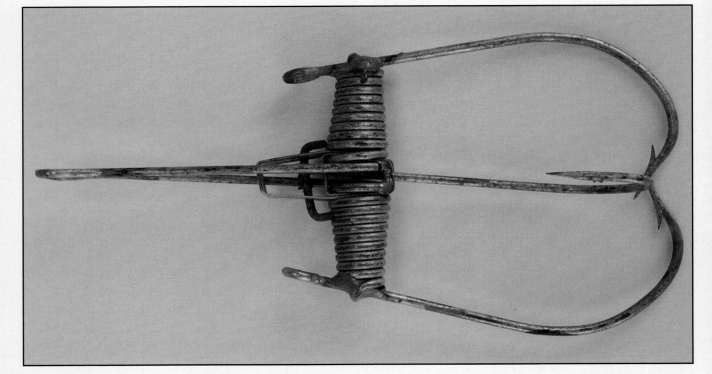

Original picture and enlargement of inventor Milford Thibodeau with his 42' lobster boat, about the time of his invention.

Name:	Wilson Non-Snagging Multiple Hook Fishing Device
Patented:	May 2, 1961, patent #2,982,046 by Roy W. Wilson
Origin:	Bellaire, Texas
Size:	Four sizes, 2", 3", 3½", and 4" long
Material:	Aluminum and steel or brass and steel
Value:	$300.00 – 600.00 each

The spring-loaded fishhook invented by Roy W. Wilson consists of two sets of opposing fishhooks pivotally mounted into a common head. Longitudinal slots are cut into the head, allowing movement of the fishhooks along them. There also is incorporated in the fishhook an outer rotatable collar with slots cut into it. When the slots in this collar are aligned with the slots in the head, the four fishhooks are moved into an expanded condition, each being powered by an expansive helical spring, this easily facilitating the placement of bait upon them.

Once baited, the four fishhooks can then be pivotally rotated back into the head, at which point the outer collar can be rotated so that the slots are not in alignment, thus securing the fishhooks in the set position, essentially weedless.

When struck by a fish, the two sets of opposing hooks are pushed together, thus exposing the barbed points and hooking the fish.

From patent text: "...the provision of a fishing device having multiplicity of hooks which are arranged in a manner to effectively prevent the snagging of the hooks on submerged objects."

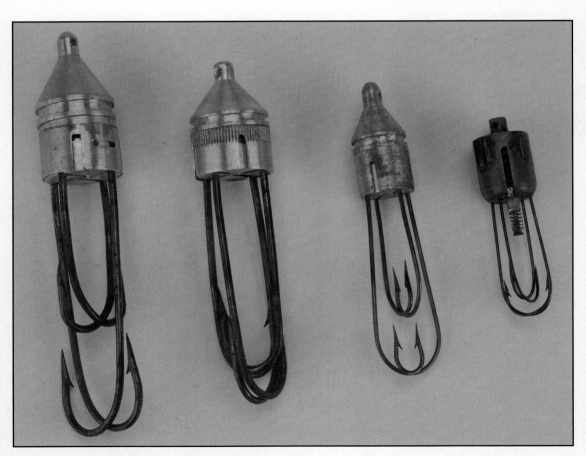

Four different sizes of the Wilson Non-Snagging Multiple Hook Fishing Device, shown in the set position.

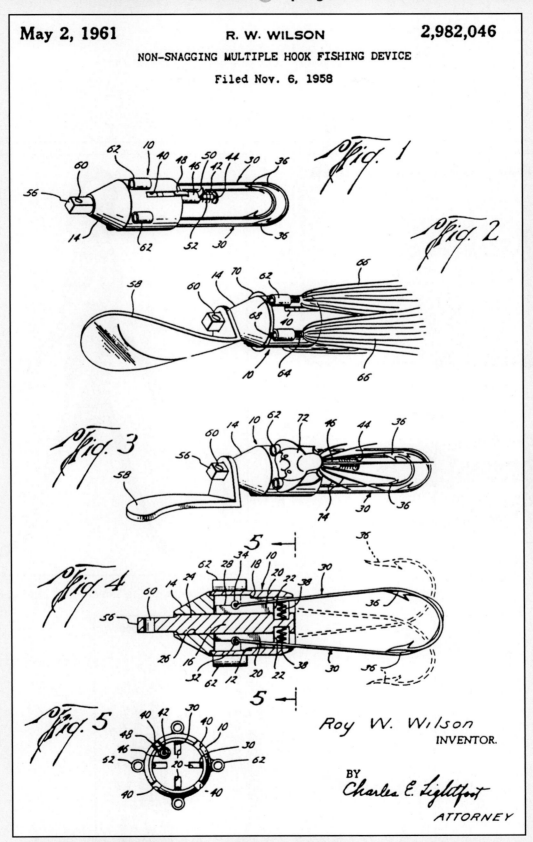

May 2, 1961   R. W. WILSON   2,982,046

NON-SNAGGING MULTIPLE HOOK FISHING DEVICE

Filed Nov. 6, 1958

Fig. 1

Fig. 2

Fig. 3

Fig. 4

Fig. 5

Roy W. Wilson
INVENTOR.

BY
Charles E. Lightfoot
ATTORNEY

1961 patent for the Wilson Non-Snagging Multiple Hook Fishing Device.

Name:	FOLD-A-HOOK
Patented:	May 8, 1962, patent #3,032,909 by William T. Beatty
Origin:	Potsdam, New York
Size:	1½" long, ¾" wide
Material:	Steel and aluminum
Value:	$20.00, usually found in plastic box with blue bottom and clear top

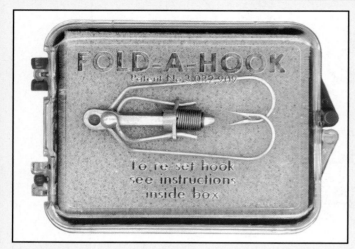

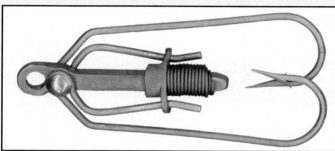

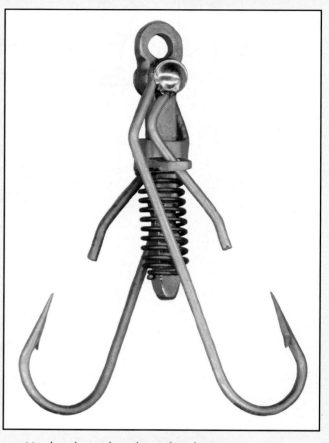

FOLD-A-HOOK box (top) and hook itself (bottom). Box and hook enlarged to show detail.

Hook enlarged to show detail, sprung position.

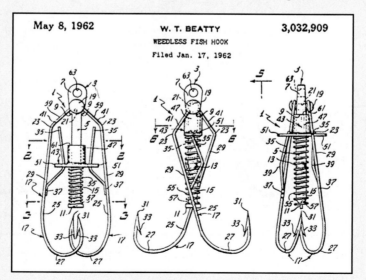

Name:	Katch-A-Matic
Patented:	Yes, according to advertising card, although the letters of patent have not as yet been found.
Origin:	Yuba City, California, post-1963
Size:	1½" long
Material:	Steel and spring-steel wire
Value:	$50.00+. Value doubled when found on nice advertising card.

The Katch-A-Matic consists of two fishhooks connected by a fine-gauged spring-steel wire, which is coiled at its center, forming a loop that serves as the line-tie (painted red). The two hooks are held together in the set position by a clip attached to one of the hooks; the clip could be used to adjust the tension.

This spring hook came originally in a black and clear plastic box that was glued onto an 8½" x 4½" green and white advertising card. This card gives the zip code of Yuba City, thus dating it as post-1963.

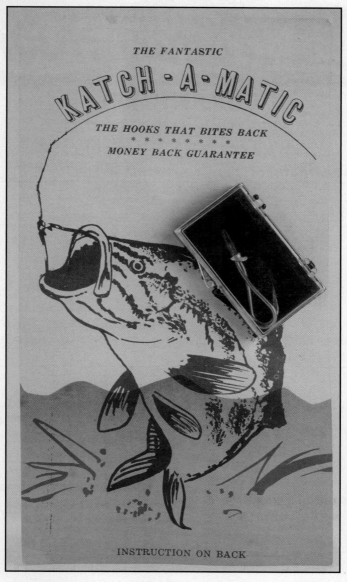

Katch-A-Matic, in the box, on an advertinsing card.

Name:	Ralph's B-Shur Hook
Patented:	Unknown, but probably. Circa 1960s.
Origin:	San Francisco, California
Material:	Nickel
Size:	The 7/0 size is 3" long when contracted.
Value:	$50.00+ on card

This is a simple lever hook whose tension can be adjusted by changing the position of the retaining clip. This hook was manufactured by the Miller Manufacturing Company and was guaranteed rustproof. This hook may have been manufactured in various sizes and can sometimes be found on a black and white card.

Ralph's B-Sure Hook card.

RALPH'S B-SHUR HOOK CO.
SAN FRANCISCO

DIRECTIONS

Push hook on clip. Adjust tension by moving sleeve toward hook for more tension and away from hook for less tension. Keep sleeve oiled to prevent corrosion.

Setting instructions on the back of the card.

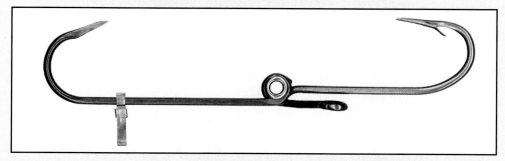

Ralph's B-Sure Hook, actual size, set position. The hook had a line tied at the bottom of the striking hook that the clip on the shank attached to. The hook is folded in half when found on a card.

Name:	Bar-Lou Spring-Loaded Treble Hook
Patented:	December 26, 1967, patent #3,359,625 by Michael Rossnan
Origin:	Silver Spring, Maryland
Size:	Five sizes from 1" to 3½"
Material:	Steel and spring-steel
Value:	$25.00 – 50.00, with the smallest and largest sizes rare.

This spring-loaded treble hook was sold loose on a card as a bait hook, but was also incorporated into jigs and fishing lures. It was manufactured in Korea.

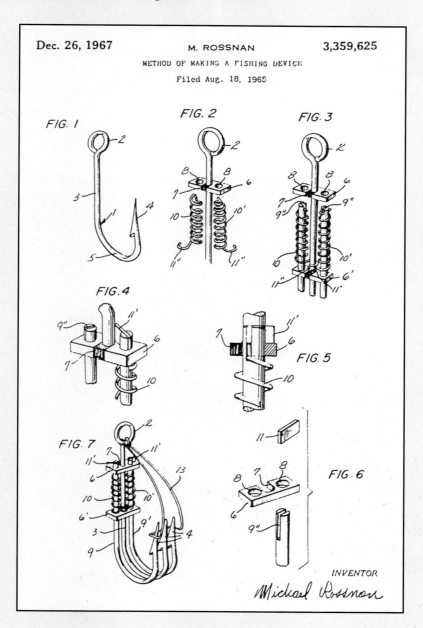

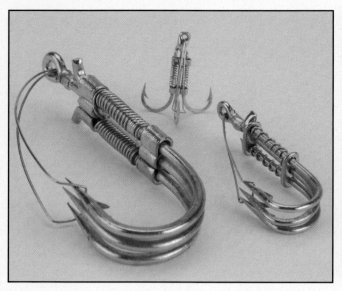

Three sizes of Bar-Lou single hooks. The smallest is in the sprung position.

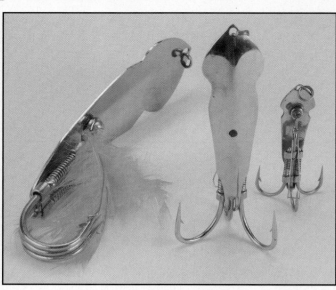

Three sizes of the Bar-Lou Soup Spoon lure.

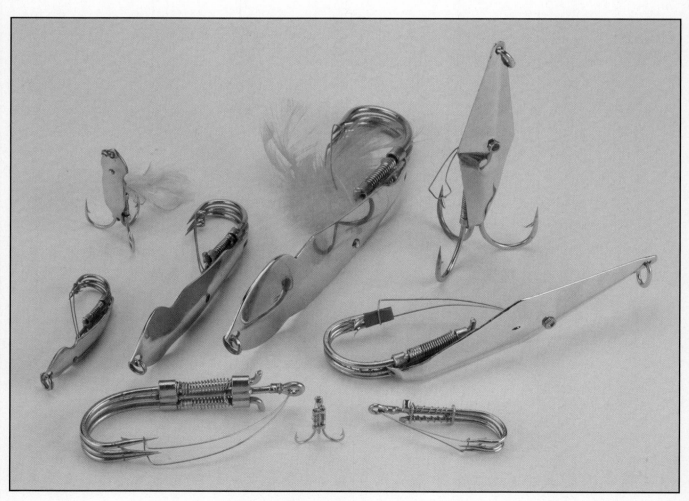

Variety of Bar-Lou hooks and spoons.

Bar-Lou hooks in original packaging.

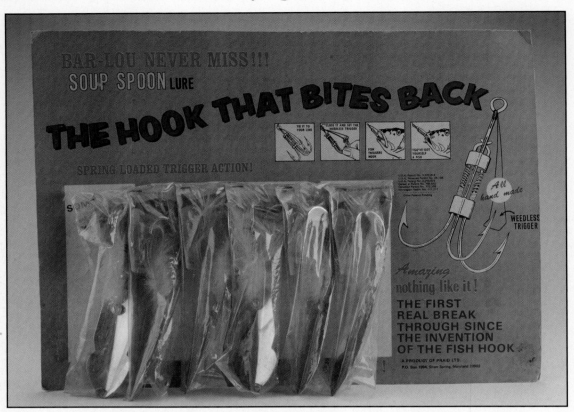

Large display card of six Bar-Lou Soup Spoon lures.

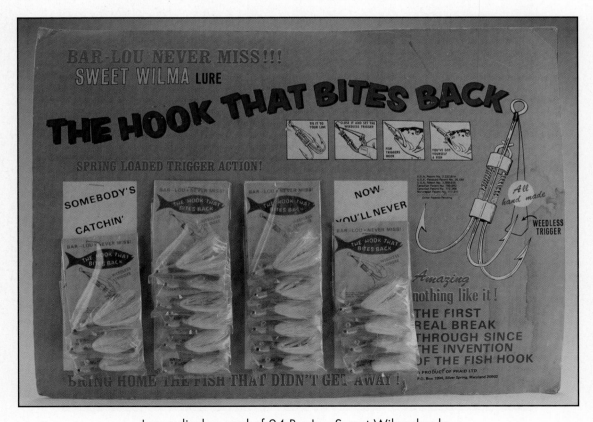

Large display card of 24 Bar-Lou Sweet Wilma hooks.

Name:	Catchmaster Fish Hook
Patented:	April 9, 1968, patent #3,376,662 by Albert J. Harris
Origin:	New Philadelphia, Ohio; manufactured in Hong Kong
Size:	Four sizes, 1¾", 2⅛", 2¾", and 6"
Material:	Cheap spring-steel wire
Value:	$10.00 separately, but $50.00 for all four sizes, or two large ones, on nice advertising card.

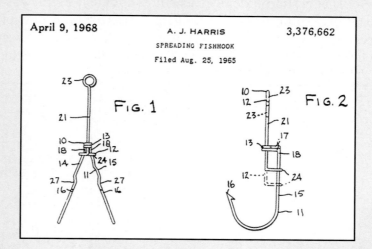

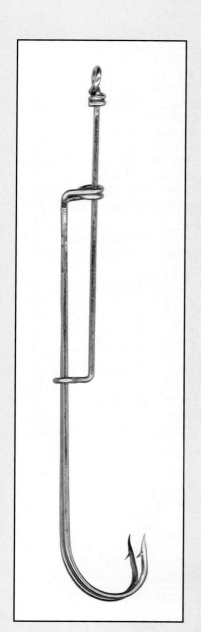

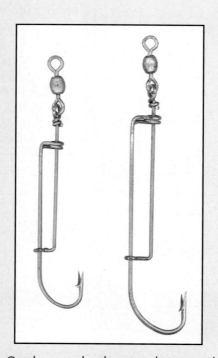

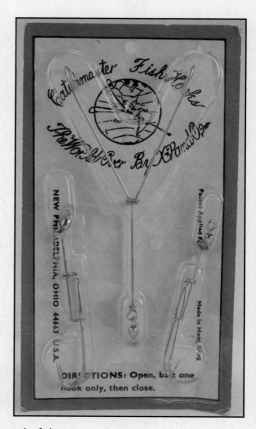

Three Catchmaster hooks, actual size, and a card of three.

Name:	Keeper Hook
Patented:	June 26, 1973, patent #3,740, 890 by Francis J. Aron
Origin:	Mastic Beach, New York
Size:	Two sizes, 2¼" first model, 3¾" second model
Material:	Brass and steel
Value:	$10.00 – 20.00 when found on nice card

The Keeper Hook is a simple device, and it operated by means of a counterweight and its respective balance. The lower, smaller hook was baited, and when a fish exerted pressure on it, the counterweight was overcome, thus sending the striking hook down from above.

These hooks were sold off an orange advertising display that held twelve.

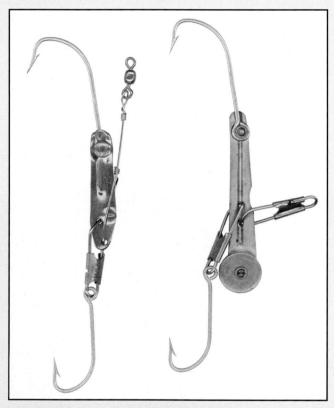 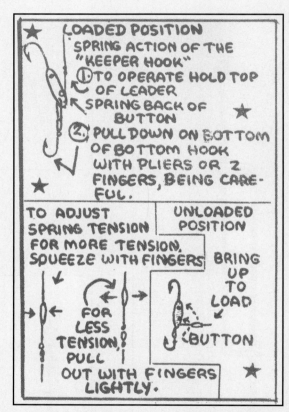

Left to right: Two models of the Keeper Hook, shown actual size and in the set position, and setting instructions.

Two different styles of display cards for the Keeper Hook. Actual size of cards is 12" wide.

Name:	The Gangster Spring-loaded Treble Hook
Patented:	September 13, 1983, patent #4,403,437 by Ervin H. Shuman
Origin:	Ocala, Florida
Size:	1½" long with a companion 2¾" needle-shaped "inserting tool"
Material:	Brass, steel, and spring-steel
Value:	$200.00 – 300.00

The Gangster is a finely crafted spring-loaded treble hook, which is held in the set position by a pivotal weed guard and was manufactured by the Katydid Corporation.

This is a scarce hook with its companion needed-shaped "inserting tool," used for baiting the hook, rarely being found with it.

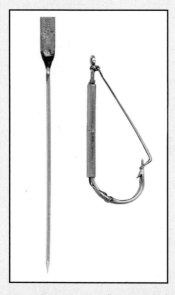

Gangster Hook, actual size, in the set position, and the "inserting tool."

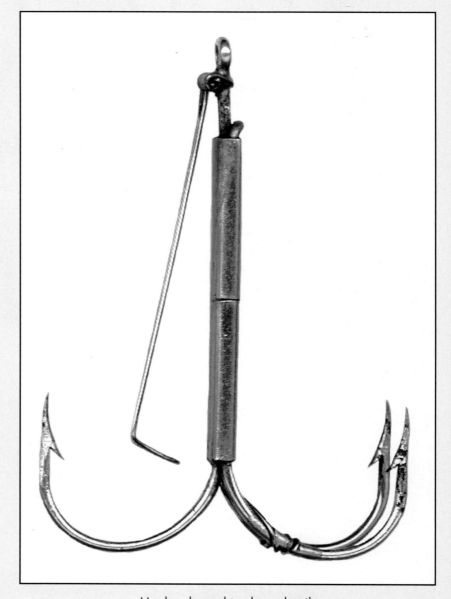

Hook enlarged to show detail.

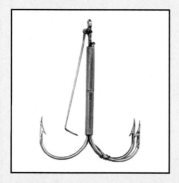

Gangster Hook, actual size, sprung position.

Swedish Spring Hooks

Spring-loaded fishing hooks have been made in Sweden for many years, and are possibly still being produced. There are many variations to them, including number of jaws, number of teeth on each jaw, type of spring used, and the sizes of the hooks themselves. The majority are made of brass, although steel ones are not rare. Even with their many differences, they still resemble each other to such a degree that even someone with a small degree of knowledge and experience may say that a certain spring hook appears to be Swedish.

These spring hooks are generally between 3" and 7" in length and may have no stampings or may be stamped in a variety of ways. Some common stampings are "KISA," "SWEDEN," "A-SAXEN," "ROSTFRI" (which means rust-free), "PATENT," or others.

These spring-loaded metal fish traps from Sweden are very sturdy in construction and would not be considered delicate by any means. Values can be anywhere between $20 and $300, depending upon a hook's scarcity, complexity, size, and condition.

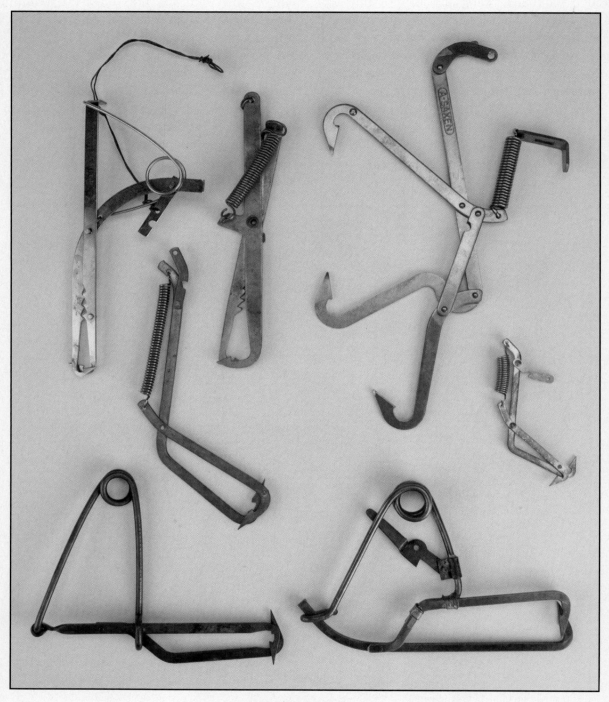

Variety of Swedish hooks.

Unidentified Spring Hooks

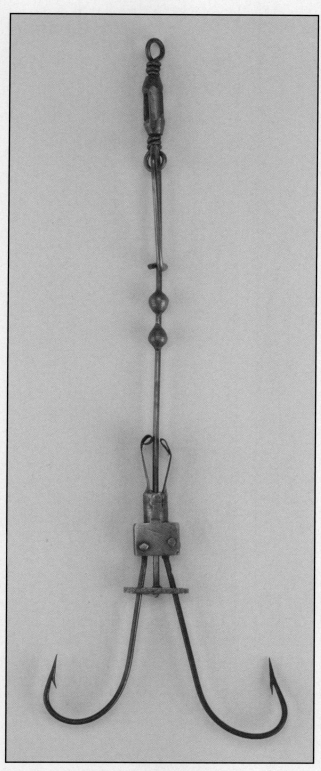

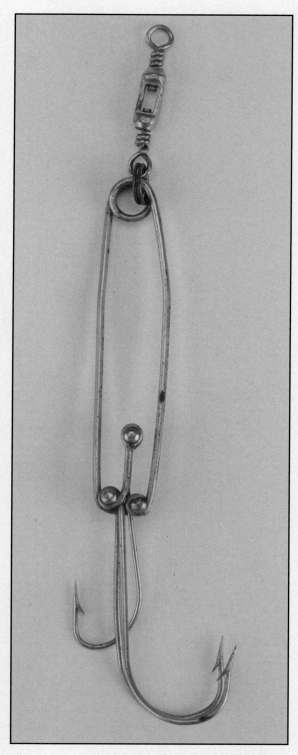

Nicely made brass and steel mechanical hook. When either line pressure or hook pressure is applied, the hooks are drawn downward and forcefully pivoted outward. Only a few of these are known. Value: $500.00+.

The hooks on this nicely made spring hook rotate 90° to be in the horizontal, set position, with two on one side and one on the other. Pulling on any hook springs it. Has early German silver box swivel attached. Only one known. Value: $500.00+.

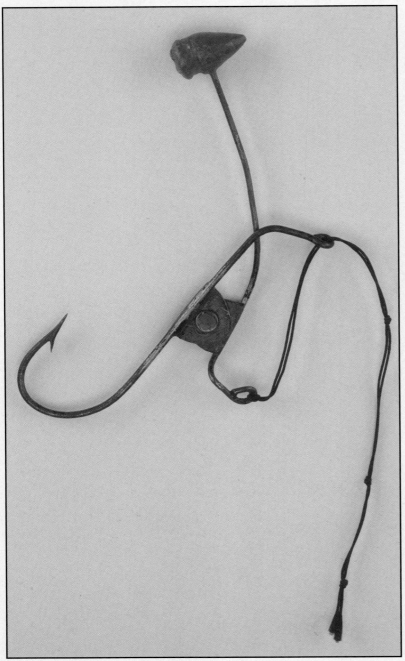

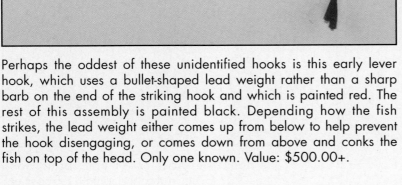

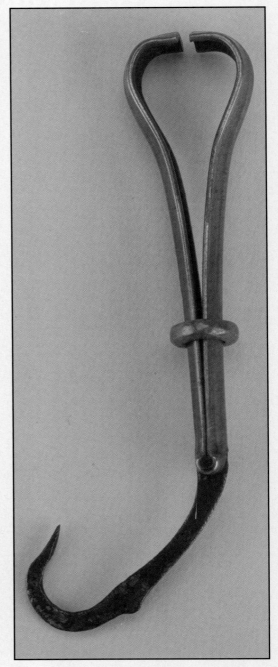

Perhaps the oddest of these unidentified hooks is this early lever hook, which uses a bullet-shaped lead weight rather than a sharp barb on the end of the striking hook and which is painted red. The rest of this assembly is painted black. Depending how the fish strikes, the lead weight either comes up from below to help prevent the hook disengaging, or comes down from above and conks the fish on top of the head. Only one known. Value: $500.00+.

This early fishhook is pivotally attached to a spring-brass assembly that is held open or closed by a sliding brass ring. When not in use, the point of the fishhook is folded into a slot on the assembly, which can then be "locked" shut, allowing for safe transport in one's pocket. Stamping on hook possibly has "N.Y." This may date from the Revolutionary War period. Value: $500.00+.

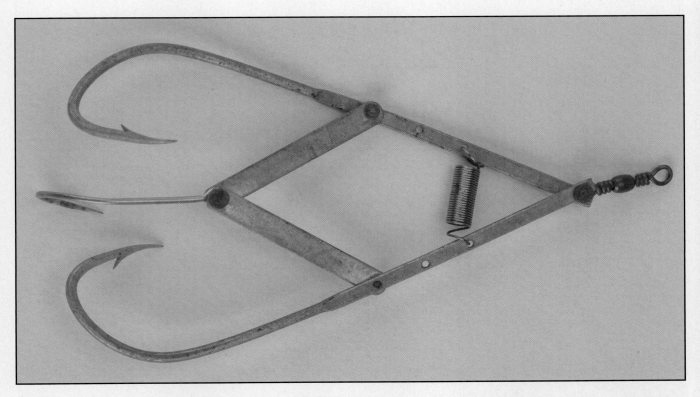

Nicely made dogless spring hook powered by a petite contractile helical spring. An additional set of holes drilled in the striking jaws allows for a different tension setting on the trap. This has brass rivets. Only a few of these are known. Value: $500.00+.

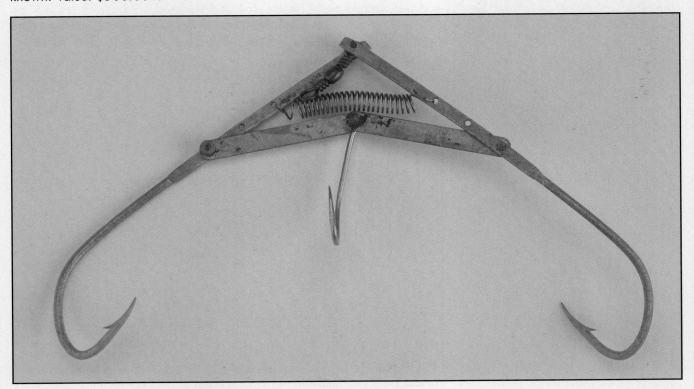

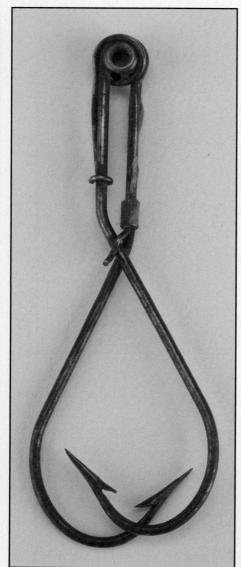

Spring-loaded fishhook made from a single piece of spring-steel wire with a coil at its center forming an eye. Auxiliary fine-gauged spring-steel wire is superimposed at the spring coil and soldered onto it with a catch on one side, which allows the two hooks to be held together. Hollow brass rivet through line-tie. Only a few known. Value: $150.00 – 250.00.

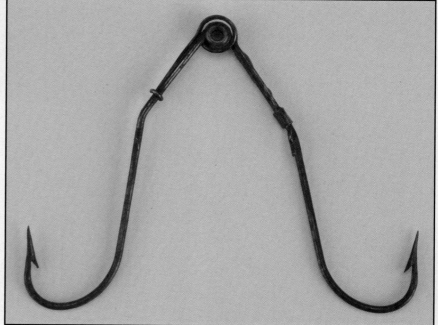

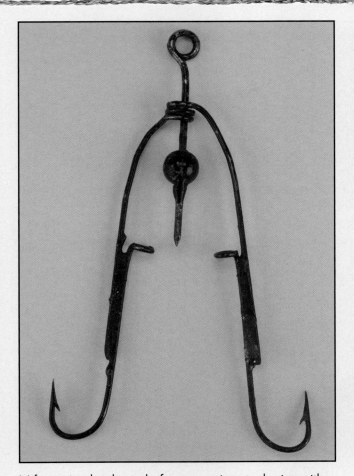

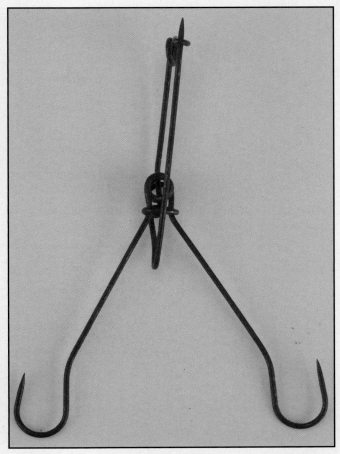

Nifty spring-hook made from a spring-steel wire with a vertical coil formed at its center through which a pin with a spherical brass weight descends. Soldered to each arm is a standard fishhook; their eyes face each other. As the spring is compressed, the eyes come together and overlap, allowing the central pin to be inserted through them, thus setting the hook. This spring hook is painted black and is the one known example. Value: $500.00+.

Very nice barbless spring hook built into a safety pin–type bait holder. Only a few of these are known. Value: $500.00+.

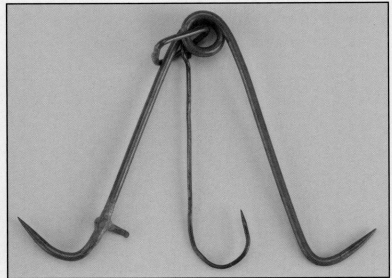

Barbless spring-hook made from single piece of spring-brass coiled at its center to form an eye. Soldered to one arm is a catch into which the opposing arm can latch. Attached through the eye is a separate barbless bait hook that does not affect the mechanism. Value: $200.00 – 400.00.

"DUPLEX HOOK CO., 301 N. Burdick St." The paper label on this Duplex Hook gives the street address, but not the city or state. Made of very fine gauge spring-brass with petite brass slide. Only a few of these known. Value: $500.00+.

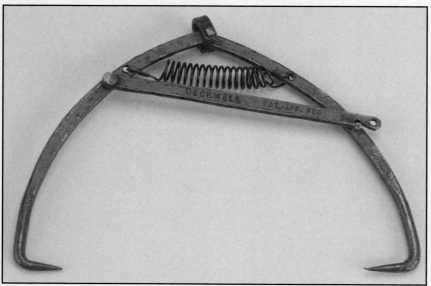

This spring-loaded fishhook is stamped "BECKWELL PAT.APP.FOR" on its crossbar and is powered by a single contractile helical spring. The few known examples of this hook are all printed green. Value: $500.00+.

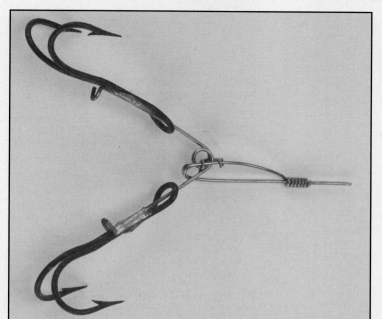

This spring-loaded fish trap is composed of two double hooks, which are each soldered onto the terminal ends of a piece of spring-steel wire, which is coiled at its center. It has a line-tie rod, which inserts into catches on each arm when the spring is compressed. Value: $200.00 – 250.00.

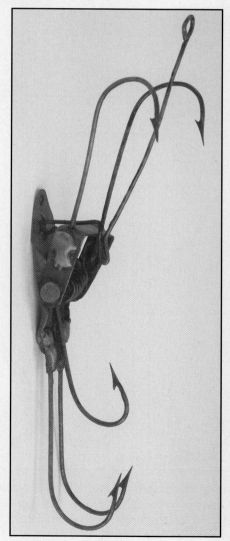

This fish trap has three stationary hooks soldered onto a copper plate. Also soldered onto this plate is a U-shaped copper striking arm with a pair of fishhooks attached, and which is powered by a coiled spring, the type found on a common mousetrap. When set, the striking arm is held in place by a bend in the line-tie rod. This trap, in fact, very much resembles a common mousetrap, and is unmarked. Value: $500.00+.

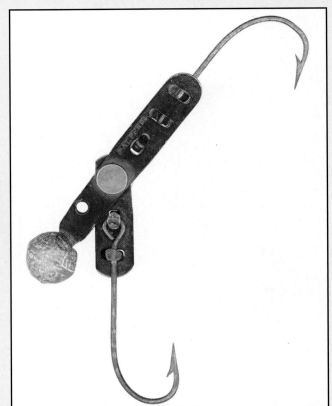

A lever hook of simple construction with a lead ball formed around the end of one of the arms. The arms themselves are elongate metal plates, painted black, and pivotally attached by a brass rivet. This hook is stamped PAT. PEND. Value: $50.00.

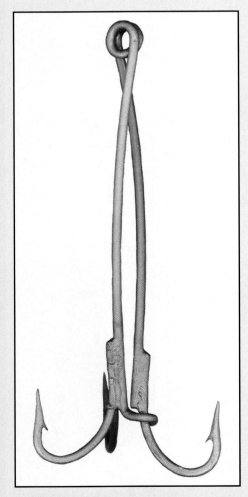

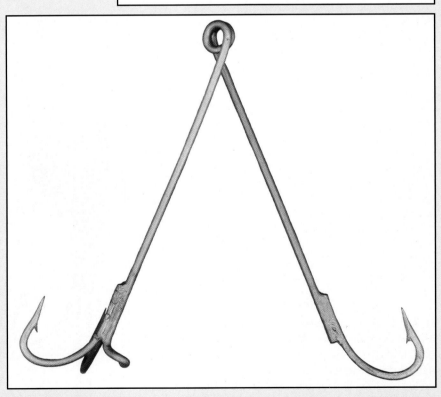

A simply constructed galvanized spring hook made from a piece of spring-steel wire with a coil at its center forming an eye, which acts as the line-tie. Soldered on to one arm are two fishhooks and latch. Soldered on to the other arm is a fishhook, which is retained by the latch when compressed. The few known examples of this spring hook were found together in an Alaskan tackle box. Value: $75.00.

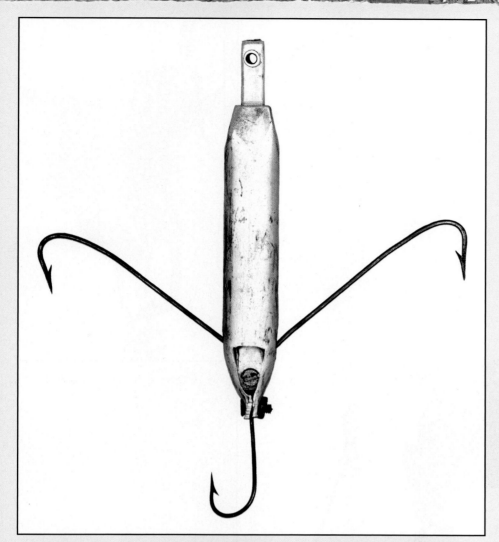

Clutch-type spring hook, designed so that the harder the fish pulls on the bait hook, the harder the two striking jaws are drawn into the fish. This fishhook is empowered by an expansive helical spring encased in a hollow aluminum body. The two known examples of this spring-hook were found together in western Texas. Value: $200.00 – 250.00

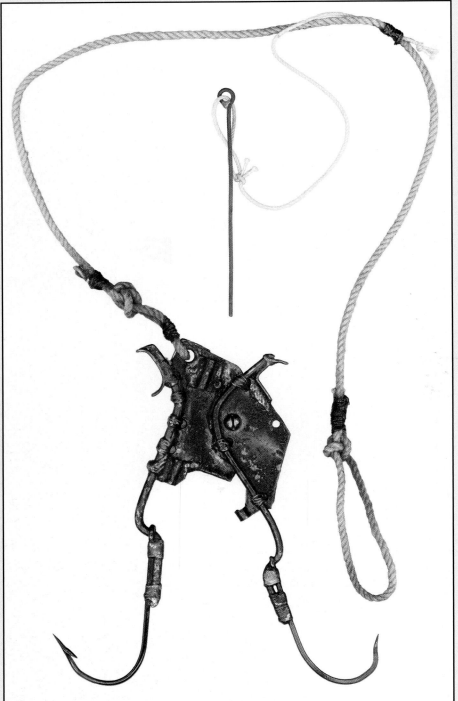

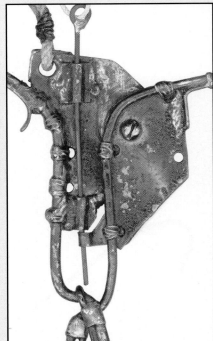

Shows setting pin in place.

This rather crude-looking mechanical hook is designed to be empowered by a rubber band attached at the top, so as to make the two fishhooks move outward, away from each other. The hooks are held in a set position by a separate brass pin, which goes through a sleeve on each arm of the device and which is attached to the main fishing line by a separate line. The two known examples of this were found together by George Ritchy in the northern part of Michigan's Lower Peninsula. Value: $200.00 – 250.00.

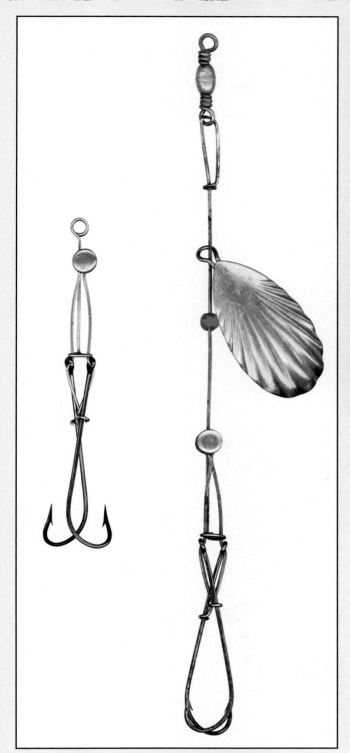

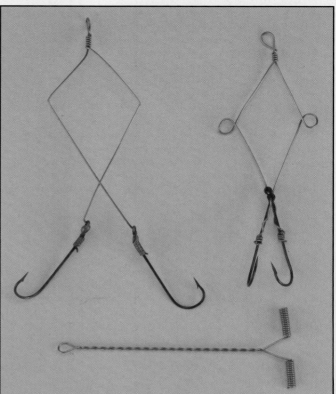

Two nearly identical wisps of a spring hook with intricate bait hook mountings, but no real mechanisms. In use, the bait hooks are pushed together and baited. When either hook is loosened from the bait, it springs outward. These two spring-hooks were found together, along with some type of as-of-yet-not-understood baiting apparatus. Value: $100.00.

Nicely made spring hook of fine-gauged wire whose spring is compressed as it is pushed upward through a ring at the bottom of the line-tie rod. This spring hook may be found with a short unadorned line-tie rod or with a long line-tie rod with red glass beads and a brass spinner blade. This spring hook was probably patented. Value: $300.00+.

This spring hook was referred to by the late George Richey as an Ypsilanti, as all known examples of it came from the Michigan city of that name. It consists of two bait hooks connected by a piece of spring-steel wire, which is then connected to a line-tie rod that has a flat semicircular lead weight soldered to it. Affixed between this distinctive lead weight and the hooks is a Burgess-type spinner. Value: $400.00+.

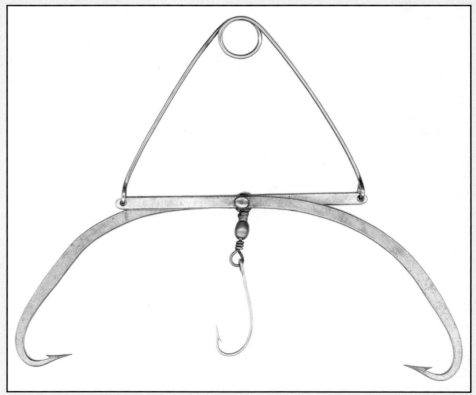

This clutch-type fish trap is powered by a piece of spring-steel wire, which is coiled at its center to form an eye and which acts as the line-tie. The two striking jaws pivot about a brass rivet, to which is also attached a brass swivel with a brass bait hook. Value: $300.00+.

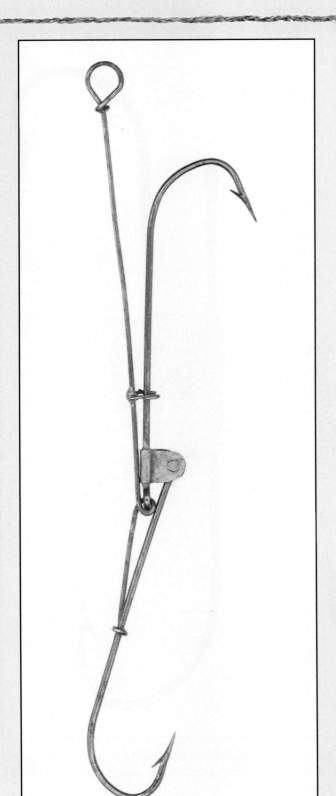
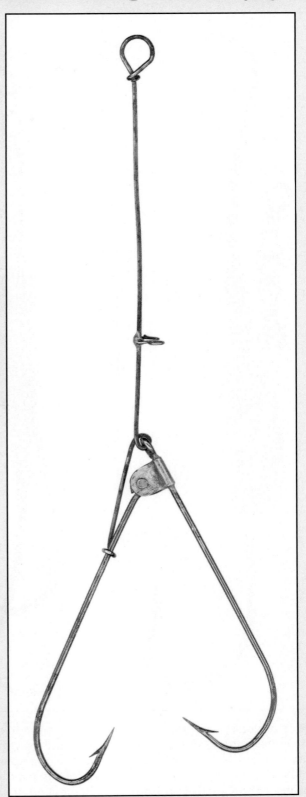

A very delicately made lever hook composed mainly of brass, using fine-gauged wire throughout. When the lower bait hook is pulled upon, the striking hook is forced from its retaining clip by lever action and strikes into the head of the poor victim. This early mechanical hook looks manufactured in every way, shape, and form, and yet no patent can be found for it and only this one example is known to exist. Value: $500.00+.

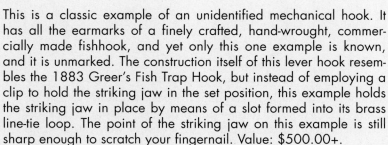

This is a classic example of an unidentified mechanical hook. It has all the earmarks of a finely crafted, hand-wrought, commercially made fishhook, and yet only this one example is known, and it is unmarked. The construction itself of this lever hook resembles the 1883 Greer's Fish Trap Hook, but instead of employing a clip to hold the striking jaw in the set position, this example holds the striking jaw in place by means of a slot formed into its brass line-tie loop. The point of the striking jaw on this example is still sharp enough to scratch your fingernail. Value: $500.00+.

A simple and crudely made lever hook, most probably homemade. Value: $20.00.

Spring-loaded Fishing Lures

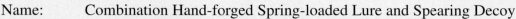

Name:	Combination Hand-forged Spring-loaded Lure and Spearing Decoy
Patented:	Unknown, but could have been due to its unique mechanism
Origin:	Kalamazoo area of Michigan, circa 1880s
Size:	8½" long
Material:	Wood, hand-forged steel and spring-steel
Value:	$15,000.00+

This combination spring-loaded lure and decoy has no equal in either of these two fields of fishing collectibles. It is powered by a flat spring that has a barbed point forged into its one end, and which is set by means of a trigger, or dog, that is located beneath the head of the lure-decoy and into which the hook is latched. When this trigger is compressed, as when bitten by a fish, the hook is released forcibly downward, thus being impaled into the fish's mouth. In this case the fish would have been either a pike or muskie, owing to the shear size of this exquisite piece of American fishing history. An additional aid in securing the fish is a stationary barbed spear point that extends vertically from the top of the lure-decoy's head.

As pertains to its versatility with respect to its use as a spearing decoy, it is the only one known to exist in the hands of collectors that has a spring-loaded hook incorporated into it. This possibly served as an extremely innovative way to ensure that the spear fisherman would not go home empty handed in the event that his expertise with a spear was insufficient or that he had slow reflexes.

This fascinating piece of American ingenuity would be the centerpiece of any collection that pertained to either fish spearing decoys or fishing lures, and so it is no wonder that it has been sought after by so many advanced collectors in both of these fields, as it is no wonder that it has not been separated from its collection or from the hands of its collector, author Timothy Mierzwa.

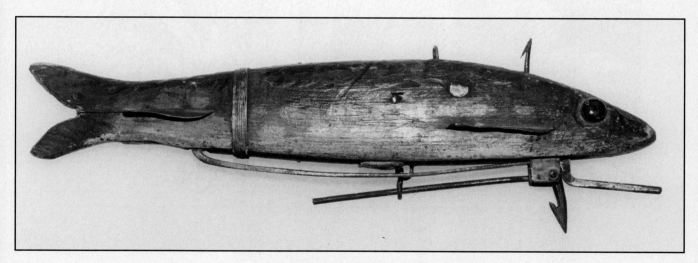

Spearing Decoy in the set position.

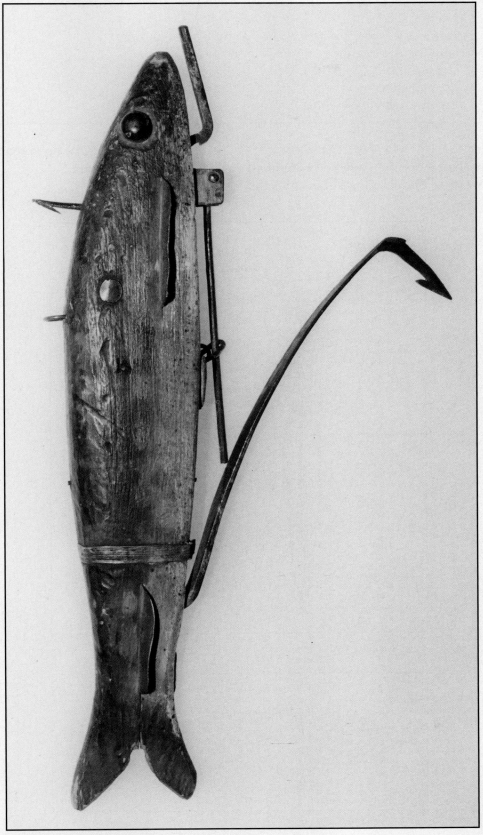

Spearing Decoy in the sprung position.

Name:	Cornelius Lie Bait
Patented:	November 17, 1885, patent #330,793 by Cornelius Lie
Origin:	Trondhjem, Norway
Size:	2½" long
Material:	Brass and steel
Value:	$750.00 – 1,000.00

From patent text: "...when the fish closes his mouth over the bait pressure will be brought to bear upon the tail of the artificial fish, and the points of the hooks will be spread out and catch firm hold upon the game."

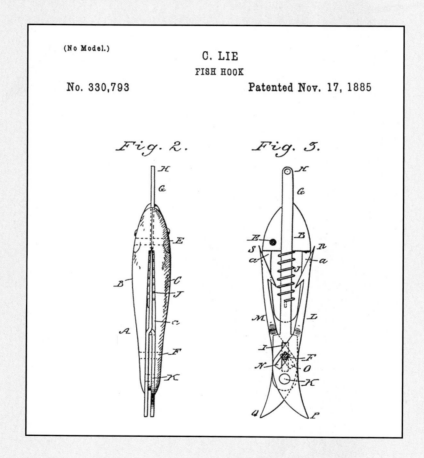

Cornelius Lie lure in the set position.

Name:	Harlow Trolling Spoon Hook
Patented:	February 28, 1888, patent #378,678 by John R. Harlow
Origin:	Auburn, New York
Size:	3" long
Material:	Brass or nickel-plated brass
Value:	$150.00+

From patent text: "A trolling-spoon having a seat for the bill or point of the fishhook and a slot at or near one end through which the hook may protrude when struck by a fish."

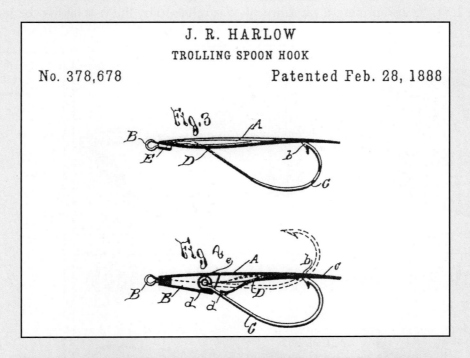

Three different Harlow Trolling Spoons. The one at the top is brass without any nickel plating and is the hardest to find.

Name:	The Chicago Spinner Weedless Hook
Patented:	September 4, 1900, patent #657,387 by Charles Bew
Origin:	Chicago, Illinois
Size:	Two sizes, 3" long and 5" long
Material:	Brass, steel, lead, nickel-plated brass, and spring-steel
Value:	$125.00 – 175.00

This lure is stamped "Chicago Spinner — Patented Sept. 4, 1900."

From patent text: "...comprising a plurality of hooks capable of rotation in opposite directions by spring action and held folded by a mousing which is released by the fish taking the hook."

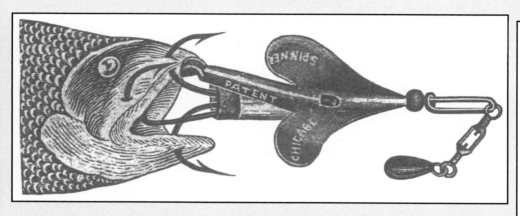

The two images above show the Chicago Spinner in action and the setting instructions.

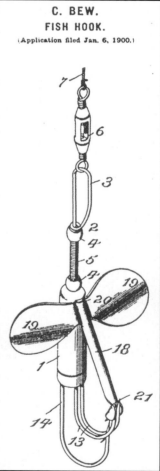

Chicago Spinner patent drawing.

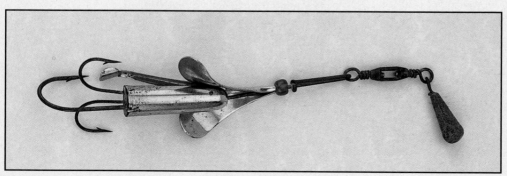

The hook itself.

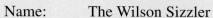

Name:	The Wilson Sizzler
Patented:	August 23, 1904, patent #768,451 by John Hedlund
Origin:	St. Cloud, Minnesota
Size:	Two sizes: 2½" long and 3½" long
Material:	Nickel-plated brass, steel and spring-steel
Value:	$150.00 – 200.00

This lure is painted red on the inside and is usually stamped "Pat. Aug. 24-1904."

From patent text: "In duplex fishhooks the combination of the shank of a hook and a bait-representing plate attached thereto, the shank of another hook and a concave-convex spoon attached thereto, said plate and spoon being hinged together, and a spring secured to one of said hinged members and pressing against the inner side of the other."

Small and large size of the Wilson Sizzler. Note the two different varieties of the large size. The difference is in the tail.

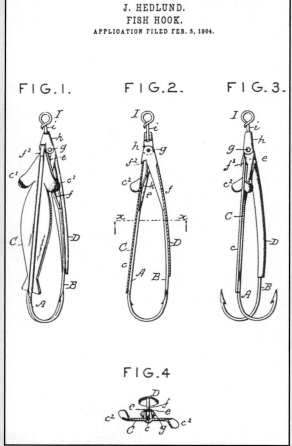

Patent for the Wilson Sizzler.

Name:	Chautauqua Trolling Hook
Patented:	August 31, 1909, patent #932,477 by Alfred J. Krantz and Gustaf E. Smith
Origin:	Jamestown, New York
Size:	3½" long
Material:	Brass, steel, and spring-steel
Value:	$5,000.00+

From patent text: "…a spring trolling hook… which provides means for engaging the points of the hooks so that when so set the device may be drawn through the weeds or past obstructions without catching onto the same, and yet when the fish bites onto the trolling hook, the spring hooks will be immediately released and thrust into the mouth of the fish."

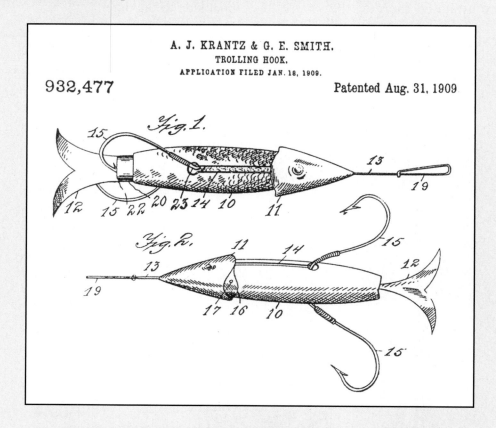

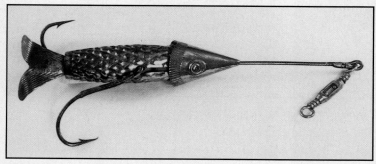

Chautauqua Trolling Hook in the sprung position.

Name:	The Captor
Patented:	Unknown, but probably. Manufactured by The Fischer Schuberth Company in 1914
Origin:	Chicago, Illinois
Size:	4" long and 4½" long
Material:	Wood, brass, and spring-steel
Value:	$400.00+

This lure came in white with either a red head or a blue head.

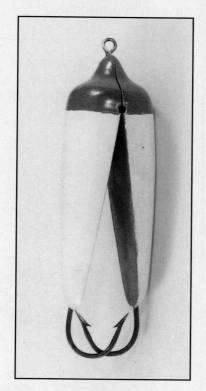
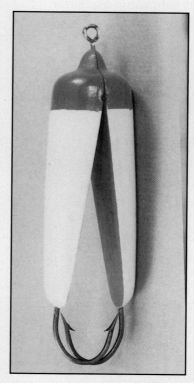

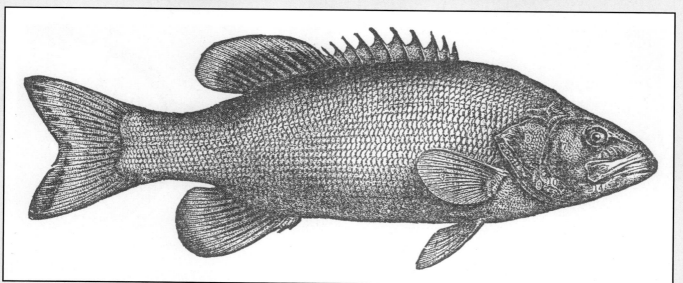

Name:	The Blodgett Bait
Patented:	May 16, 1916, patent #1,183,527 by William G. Blodgett
Origin:	Milwaukee, Wisconsin
Size:	2½" long and 3½" long
Material:	Brass, steel, spring-steel, cork and feathers
Value:	$2,500.00 – 3,000.00

From patent text: "...when a strike occurs, the bite of the fish causes release of the spring-controlled hook member, whereby the same is spread or expanded to thus positively gaff the inner surface of the fish's mouth at two points simultaneously, whereby the catch is insured."

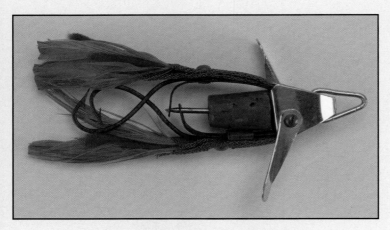

Blodgett Bait in the set position.

Blodgett Bait in the sprung position.

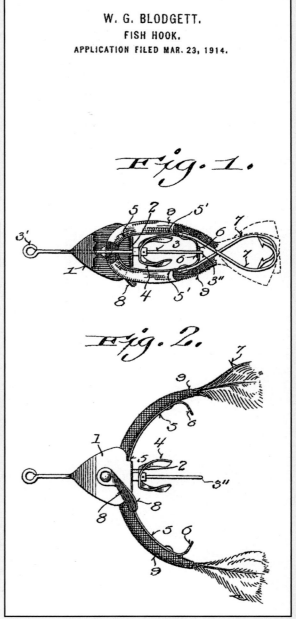

Name:	The Guise Fishing-Bait
Patented:	September 12, 1916, patent #1,197,820 by Clifford Guise
Origin:	Toronto, Ontario, Canada
Size:	3½" long
Material:	Copper and nickel-plated copper
Value:	$500.00+

From patent text: "...my object is to devise a bait which may be used in weedy waters without danger of its becoming caught in the weeds."

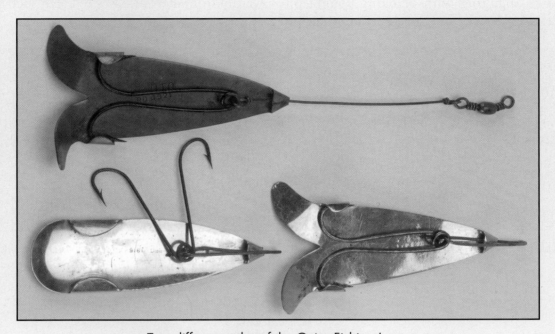

Two different styles of the Guise Fishing Lure.

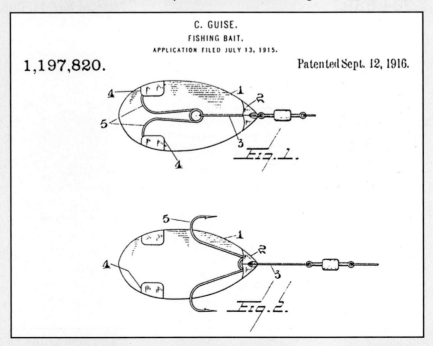

Name:	The Belding Artificial Bait
Patented:	November 14, 1916, patent #1,204,538 by Warren S. Belding
Origin:	Seattle, Washington
Size:	4" long
Material:	Wood, brass, steel and spring-steel
Value:	$1,000.00+

From patent text: "…may be cast in a body of water among weeds and brush without any liability of its hooks engaging with or being caught on such weeds or brush, but if such bait then be seized by a fish…then such mechanism shall be actuated to project its associated fishhooks outwardly from their recesses to catch such fish."

The Belding Artifact Bait in the relaxed position. The hooks come out when you pull on the line-tie.

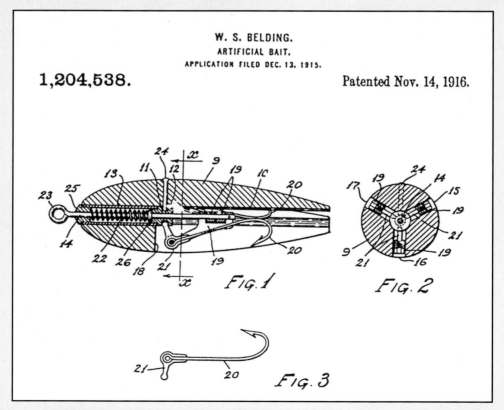

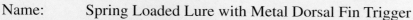

Name:	Spring Loaded Lure with Metal Dorsal Fin Trigger
Patented:	Unknown, but could have been due to its unique mechanism
Origin:	Found in a pre-1920 Michigan tackle box
Size:	4½" long
Material:	Wood, lead, brass, steel, and spring-steel
Value:	$5,000.00+

This early, ingenious spring-loaded lure is designed so that the single barbed fishhook, which is soldered onto a strip of spring-steel, can be pushed upward and concealed in the hollowed-out, one-piece wooden body of the lure. The hook is held in place by the rotatable steel dorsal fin whose curved end on the inside latches over a small wire appendage which is soldered onto the inner side of the strip of spring-steel, opposite the barbed fishhook.

The hook is released and allowed to spring downward when the dorsal fin "trigger" has pressure applied to it in such a way as to cause it to rotate into the body of the lure, as would hopefully occur when struck by a fish.

On a personal note, this spring-loaded lure is considered by me to be American folk art at its finest, and is my favorite.

Lure is shown in the sprung position.

Name:	E-Z Way Fish Lure
Patented:	July 13, 1920, patent #1,346,674 by George E. Pickup
Origin:	Newark, Ohio
Size:	5" long in the relaxed position, 3" long when set
Material:	Wood, lead, steel, and spring-steel
Value:	$750.00+

From patent text: "The bait comprises a body, a pair of hooks having arms, a coiled spring on the end of each arm and anchored in the forward end of the body, and a latch for locking the hooks together...and arranged to release...when the bait body is seized and pulled by the fish."

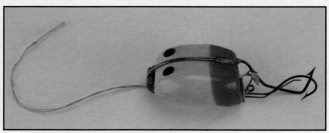

E-Z Way lure in the set position.

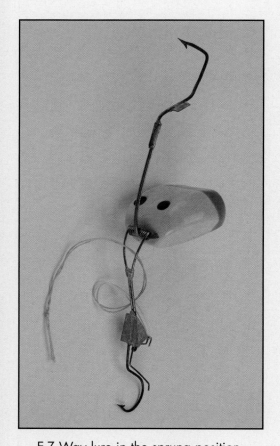

E-Z Way lure in the sprung position.

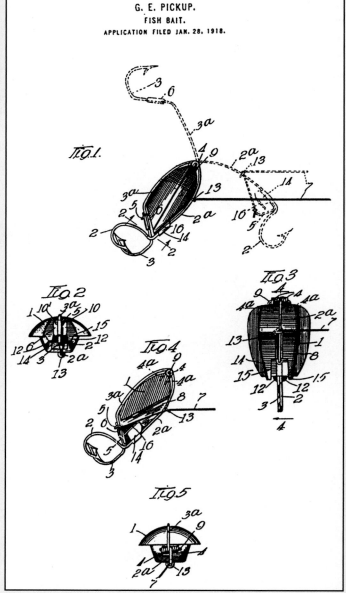

Name:	The "Hookzem" Automatic Weedless Wobbler
Patented:	September 6, 1921, patent #1,389,644 by Henry L. Gottschalk
Origin:	Chicago, Illinois
Size:	3½" long
Material:	Wood, steel, and spring-steel
Value:	$500.00 – 750.00. When found in nice picture box, add $500.00

From patent text: "…fish bait consisting of a buoyant body carrying hooks which normally lie close to the body and which are projected into the mouth of the fish when the latter seizes the bait, whereby the hooks positively take hold and the fish is effectually prevented from getting clear of the hook and escaping."

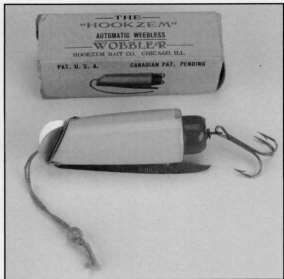

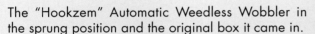

The "Hookzem" Automatic Weedless Wobbler in the sprung position and the original box it came in.

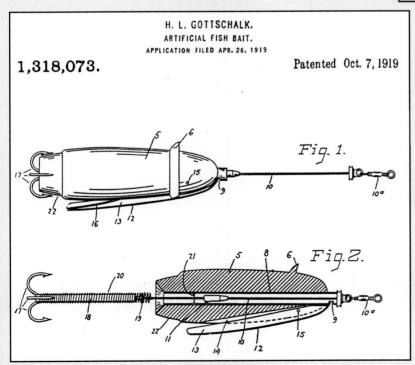

Name:	Toledo Weedless Fish Bait
Patented:	May 12, 1925, patent #1,537,266 by Dennis P. Ryan
Origin:	Toledo, Ohio
Size:	3½" long
Material:	Wood, steel, and spring-steel
Value:	$400.00+

From patent text: "...an exceedingly efficient fish bait that is so constructed that the end of the hook is completely covered, so as to prevent it from engaging weeds over which the bait may be drawn, and yet when a strike is made the hook will be uncovered and catch the fish."

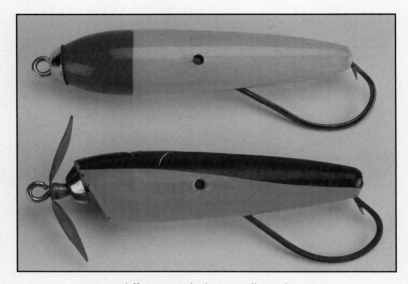

Two different "Toledo Weedless" lures.

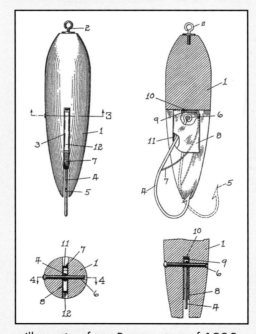

Illustration from Ryan patent of 1925.

Name:	The WAB Artificial Bait (with WAB being the acronym for Weedless Artificial Bait)
Patented:	February 2, 1926, patent #1,571,770, and January 25, 1927, patent #1,615,747 by George E. Fenner
Origin:	Oxford, Wisconsin
Size:	2¼" long
Material:	Celluloid, steel and spring-steel
Value:	$40.00 for the red and white version, $250.00+ for all other colors

The WAB was produced in a variety of colors, with red and white being the most common by far. Other colors and combinations of colors are:
• Tortoise-shell top and bottom
• Tortoise-shell top with gold glitter bottom
• Gold glitter top and bottom
• White top with gold glitter bottom
• White top with silver glitter bottom
• White top with black bottom

Lures with any combinations of the above colors may exist, but have not been seen by these authors.

From patent text: "…a bait in which the hooks are ordinarily guarded and the barbs thereof housed, but in which the hooks become exposed upon the bite being taken by a fish."

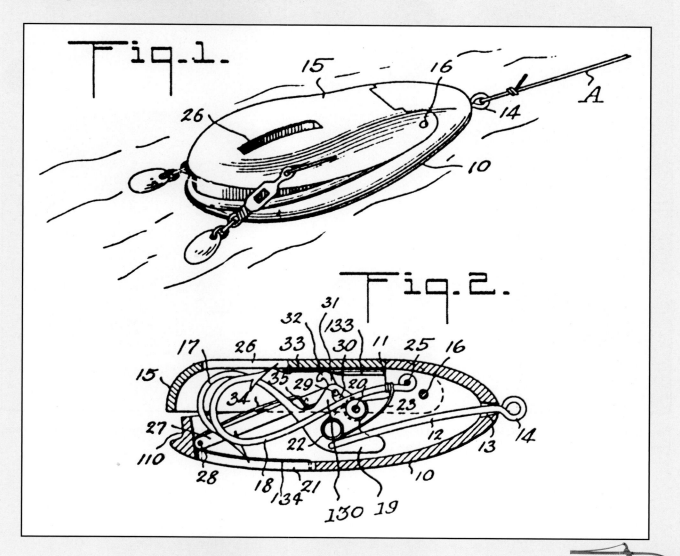

Five different color combinations of the Fenner Weedless Artificial Bait and a box. Note the separate mechanism, bottom right. This mechanism is inside the lure.

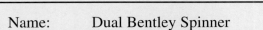

Name:	Dual Bentley Spinner
Patented:	September 21, 1926, patent #1,600,618 by John B. Bentley
Origin:	Jamestown, New York
Size:	9" long
Material:	Brass, steel, and spring-steel with various metal spinner blades and feathers
Value:	$200.00+

A smaller version of this had just a single spinner blade.

From patent text: "…to provide means which will prevent securing the hooks in juxtaposition without a certain amount of relative lateral shifting."

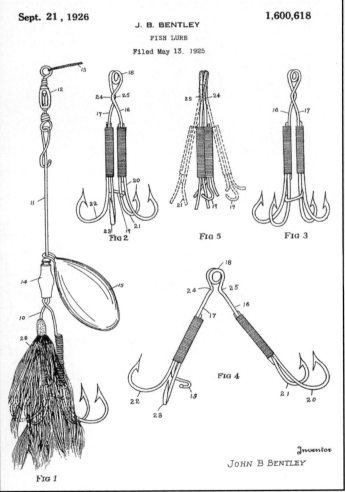

A single Bentley Spinner lure, a dual Bentley Spinner lure, and a hook by itself.

Name:	Danielson Minnow
Patented:	August 16, 1927, patent #1,638,923 by Rubin Danielson
Origin:	Chicago, Illinois
Size:	4¼" long
Material:	Aluminum, brass, steel, and spring-steel
Value:	$500.00 – 750.00

From patent text: "...the novel feature of concealing spring actuated fishhooks within the body of the inanimate bait, and there secured until at such time as they are released by the hungry victim which grabs the supposed fish, or fish-like bait."

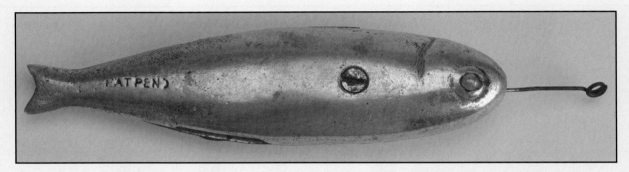

Danielson Minnow in the relaxed position. When you pull on the line-tie, the hook pops out.

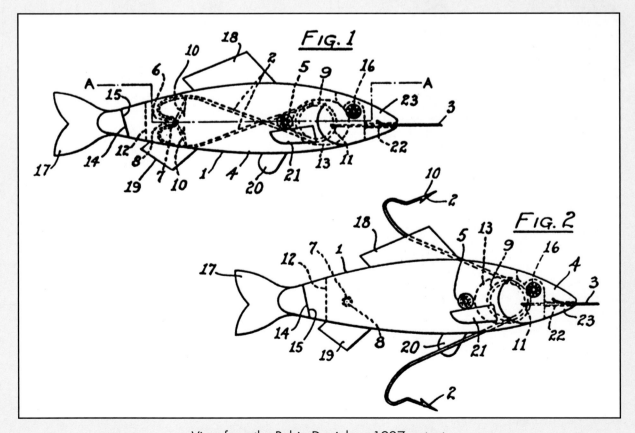

View from the Rubin Danielson 1927 patent.

Name:	Babbitt Automatic Weedless Fish Lure
Patented:	May 13, 1930, patent #1,758,817 and October 26, 1937, patent #2,097,221
	by Elwin J. Babbitt
Origin:	Los Angeles, California
Size:	Four sizes: 4½" long wooden body with three larger saltwater aluminum sizes
Material:	The body of the smaller size may be wood or aluminum, while the large
	two sizes are always aluminum. Bronze counterweight and glass eyes.
Value:	$300.00 – 500.00

From patent text: "…a fish lure which has an over-balanced hook that tends to remain sheathed in the body of the lure, but which is automatically swung out when the lure is grasped by the fish."

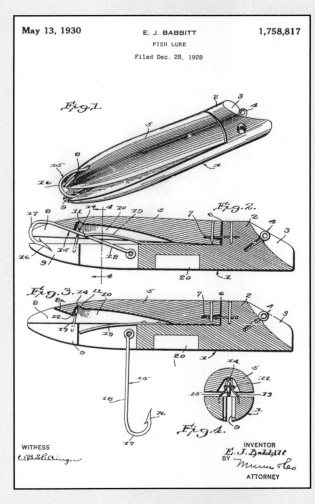

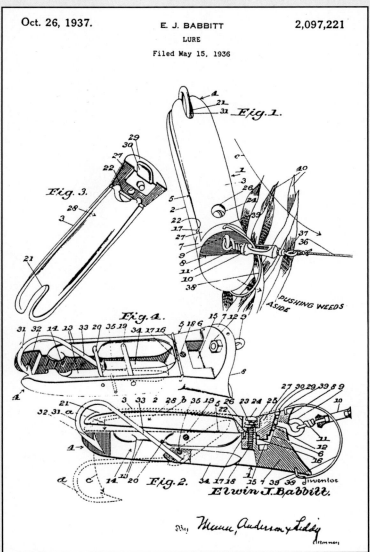

Two different patents issued for the Babbitt Automatic Weedless Fish Lure.

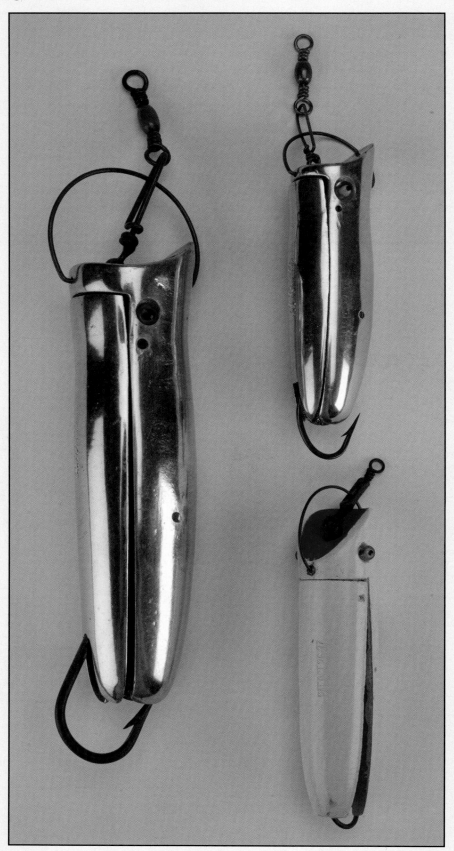

Three Babbitt lures; the two at the top are aluminum and the one bottom right is wooden.

Name:	The Sheik Metal Minnow
Patented:	July 7, 1931, patent #1,812,906 by Herman G. Swearingen
Origin:	California, Missouri
Size:	3" long
Material:	Aluminum
Value:	$1,000.00+ if found in its yellow box.

From patent text: "…said body is bifurcated, the furcation constituting the tail portion thereof and forming a sheath to conceal and accommodate the duplex spring hook arrangement."

The Sheik Metal Minnow and the box it came in.

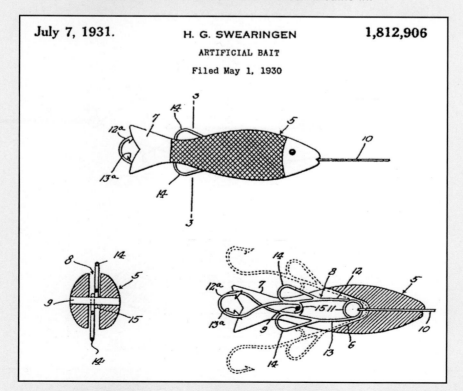

Name:	Fogelson Fish Lure
Patented:	May 22, 1934, patent #1,959,911 by David J. Fogelson
Origin:	West St. Paul, Minnesota
Size:	4" long
Material:	Wood, steel, and spring-steel
Value:	$750.00+

From patent text: "…to impel the fishhook inwardly and outwardly by corresponding outward or inward action."

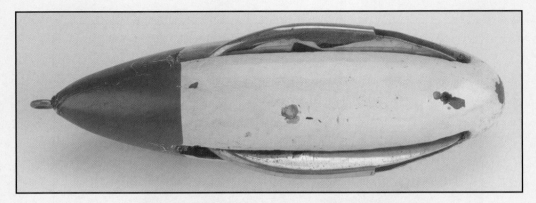

Fogelson Fish Lure in the relaxed position.

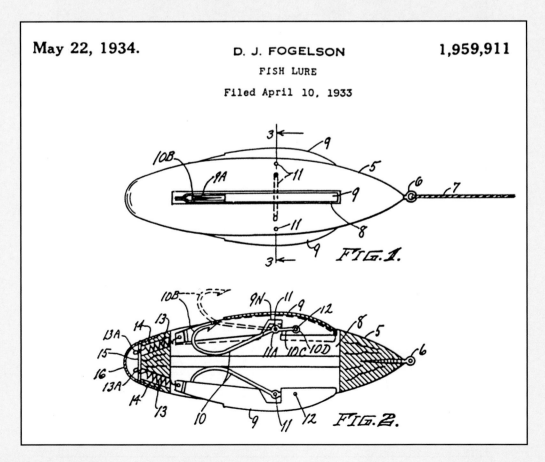

Name:	The Rocket Lure
Patented:	Unknown, but probably
Origin:	Livonia, Michigan? About 1930s?
Size:	4½" long
Material:	Hard rubber(?), brass, steel, and spring-steel
Value:	$150.00 – 200.00

The late George Richey said that this lure came in four color schemes: green and white, yellow and white, all yellow, or red and white. He also said that every one of these lures that he had ever seen came out of Livonia, Michigan.

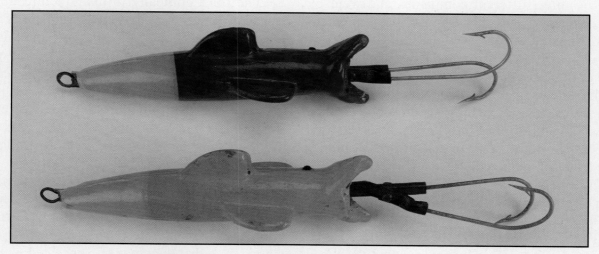

The Rocket Lure in the sprung (top) and set (bottom) positions.

Name:	The Weed Queen
Patented:	March 12, 1935, patent #1,994,168 by John Boyko
Origin:	Hamtramick, Michigan
Size:	2¾" long
Material:	Wood, steel, spring-steel, glass eyes
Value:	$50.00 – 75.00, with scale patterns being much rarer and valued at $200.00+ when in excellent condition.

The spring-loaded lure patented by John Boyko in 1935 was manufactured over the next 25 years by three different companies and went by three different names. The first company to manufacture this lure was the Neptune Bait Company of Detroit, Michigan, with the lure going by the name of the "Sure-Getter."

This lure came in a variety of colors, including red head/white body, white head/red body, green head/white body, orange head/green body, and red head/orange body, none of which had a spinner blade attached to the rear.

This lure may be found on a cardboard advertising display which held six lures.

The second company to manufacture this lure was The Evans Walton Tackle Company also of Detroit, Michigan. This lure was called the Weed Queen, incorporated a rear spinner blade, and came painted with either a red head and white body or in a tight scale pattern. The scale patterns include perch, pike, blue mullet, pearl and frog.

The third company to manufacture this lure was The Kingfisher Products Company of Baseline, Michigan. They called the lure the Weedless King. This lure also incorporated a rear spinner blade and came painted with either a red head and white body or in a scale pattern. This scale pattern is larger than that found on the Weed Queen, and was produced in additional colors than that of the Weed Queen, including the very desirable blue scale pattern.

The Weedless King may be rarely found made of plastic; these versions are valued at $150 and up.

From patent text: "…an automatic trolling hook that will operate by outwardly expanding members so that they may be concealed within the trolling body, but will instantly expand and seize the fish throat or mouth walls when released."

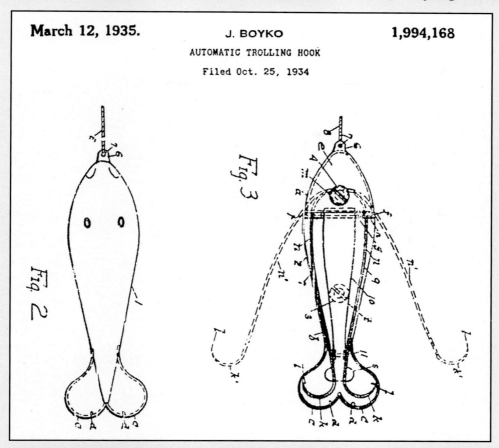

March 12, 1935.

J. BOYKO

1,994,168

AUTOMATIC TROLLING HOOK

Filed Oct. 25, 1934

Fig. 2

Fig. 3

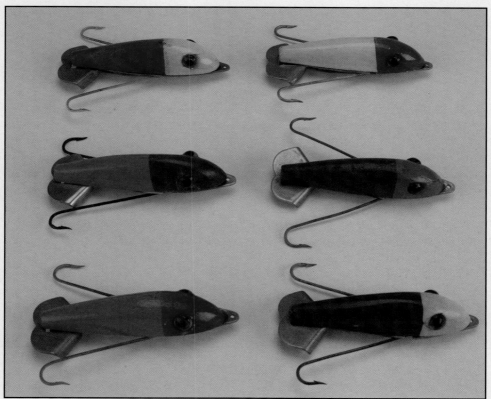

Six color combinations of the Neptune "Sure-Getter."

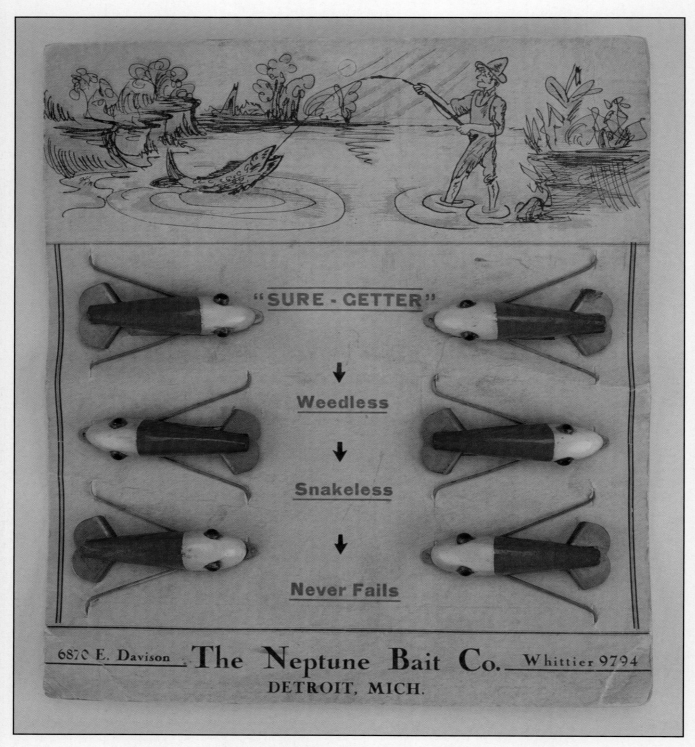

A display card with the six Neptune "Sure-Getter" lures.

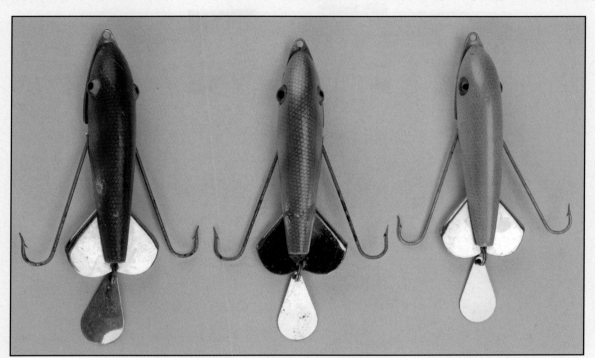

The Weed Queen lure in three different colors.

Note the different sizes of the scale paterns. The larger scale pattern, top, is found on the Weedless King, and the smaller scale pattern, bottom, is found on the Weed Queen.

Six different colors of the Weedless King lure.

Weed Queen lure and the original box that it came in.

Six different colors of the plastic Weedless King lure.

Name:	Smith and Dietz Spring Hook Lure
Patented:	March 19, 1935, patent #1,994,878 by Worden L. Smith and Andrew A. Dietz
Origin:	Jackson, Michigan
Size:	4¼" long
Material:	Wood and spring-steel, with glass eyes
Value:	$1,500.00+

This lure is known to have come with a red head and white body and also in green with a white belly.

From patent text: "…a hook normally concealed in said body, direct linked connections between said hook and said head, said connections upon relative movement of said head and body moving said hook to an operative position, and resilient means, normally retaining said hook concealed."

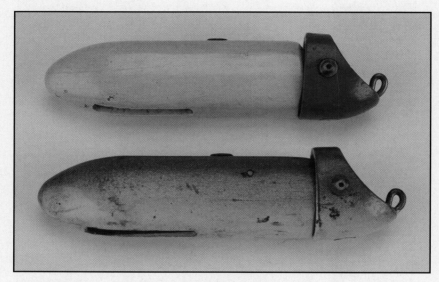

Two different colors of the Smith and Dietz Spring Hook Lure. Two hooks pop out of the bottom when you pull on the lure.

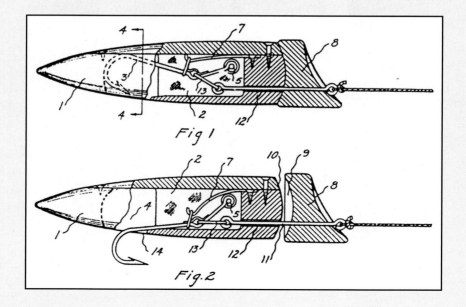

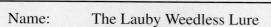

Name:	The Lauby Weedless Lure
Patented:	April 2, 1935, patent #1,996,477, September 24, 1940, patent #2,215,908, and January 8, 1946, patent #2,392,677 by Anton J. Lauby
Origin:	Marshfield, Wisconsin
Size:	2" – 6" long
Material:	Wooden lures and metal spoons
Value:	$50.00 – 200.00

The Lauby Weedless Lure and Weedless Metal Spoons came in a variety of sizes and finishes. The wooden lure shown here is 3½" long and has the 1935 patent number stamped into the copper bar between the eyes.

From patent text: "…a single hook, the barbed end of which, under normal conditions, is concealed in the body of the plug."

The Lauby Weedless Lure.

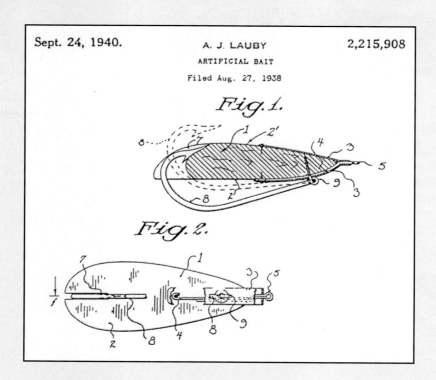

Name:	Darby Spin Head Weedless
Patented:	April 13, 1937, patent #2,077,311 by Tony Darby
Origin:	Michigan City, Indiana
Size:	4" long
Material:	Wood, brass, steel, and spring-steel
Value:	$500.00+ when found in excellent condition.

From patent text: "…the head to rotate as the body is drawn through the water, hooks slidably and rotatably mounted in the body…with spring means acting on the hooks to turn the hooks outwardly of the body when free."

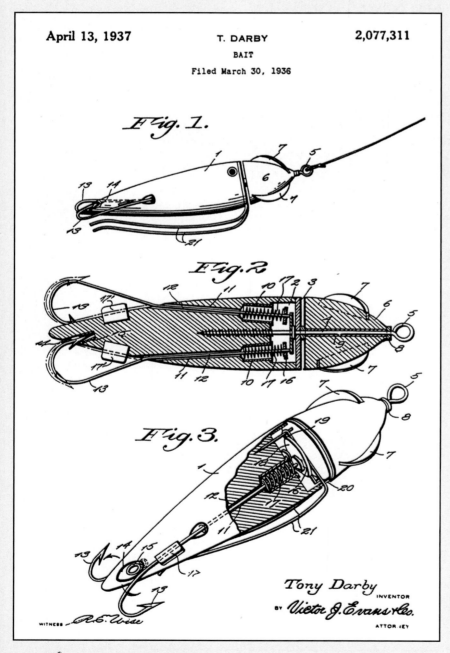

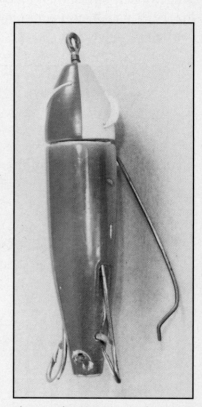

The Darby Spin Head Weedless Lure in the set position.

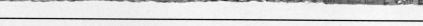

Name:	Kettring Spring Lure
Patented:	May 4, 1937, patent #2,079,509 by Chauncey B. Kettring
Origin:	Grand Lakes of St. Mary's near Montezuma, Ohio
Size:	3½" to 5" in length
Material:	Wood, steel, spring-steel with some having attached buck tail
Value:	$1,500.00+

This lure was made in a variety of color schemes.

From patent text: "…the hooks which are normally held concealed, are released for action when a fish strikes…and fear of the hooks becoming entangled in grass…is eliminated."

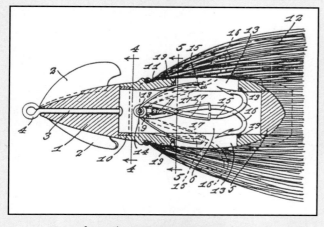

View from the Kettring patent of 1937.

Chauncy Kettring (with pipe) and 7 lb. bass caught with one of his lures from Grand Lakes of St. Mary's, where it was made to be used by family and freinds.

Three different styles of the Kettring Spring Lure.

Name:	The Steger Jawlocker
Patented:	July 19, 1938, patent #2,124,378 by Werner H. Steger
Origin:	Chicago, Illinois
Size:	3" long
Material:	Steel and spring-steel
Value:	$50.00+

From patent text: "...a bait which in plan view assumes the appearance of a frog, while when arranged in open position with the legs in juxtaposition it assumes the appearance of a small fish."

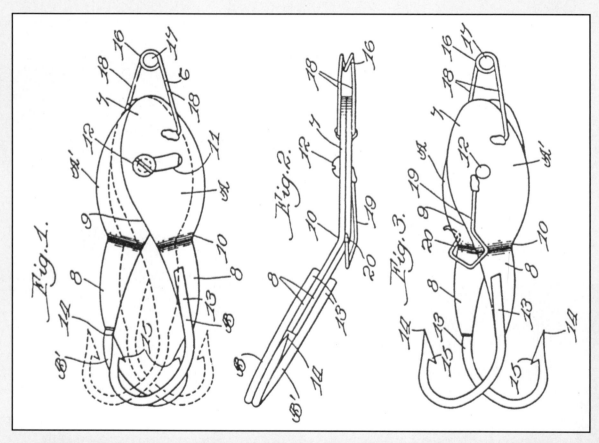

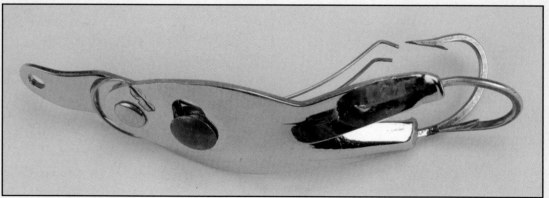

The Steger Jawlocker.

Name:	Reese Land-Em Lure
Patented:	November 1, 1938, patent #2,134,841 by Walter Reese
Origin:	Invented in Gary, Minnesota and manufactured in Emmetsburg, Iowa
Size:	4½" long
Material:	Plastic, steel and spring-steel
Value:	$150.00 – 200.00

This lure came in red, white, or red and white and has Land-Em Lure and the patent date molded into the plastic body.

From patent text: "...a simple and efficient artificial fishing bait or lure, the hook of which will automatically grip into the jaws of the fish as soon as the fish trips the baited hook."

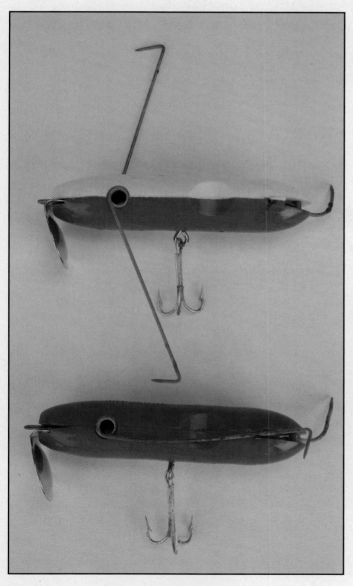

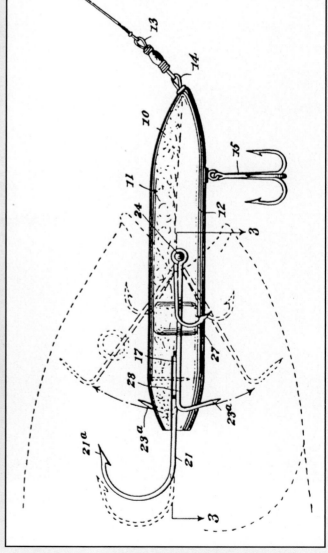

The Reese "Land-Em Lure" shown in the sprung and set positions.

Inventor Walter Reese with a large catfish.

Name:	Marvelure
Patented:	June 20, 1939, patent #2,163,378 by Alexander Horvath
Origin:	Chicago, Illinois
Size:	1⅜", 2¾", and 3" long
Material:	Steel and spring steel
Value:	$20.00 each, $40.00 when found in nice cardboard tube or cardboard box.

From patent text: "…a fishing lure….which resembles a minnow….and will move wigglingly as it is drawn through the water…with the piercing end of the fishhook concealed."

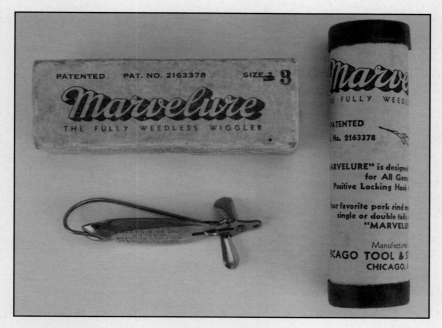

The Marvelure, along with a cardboard tube and a cardboard box.

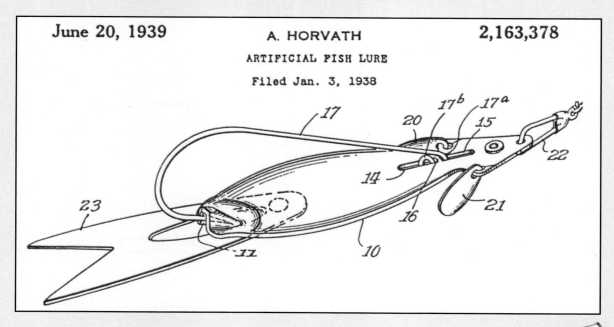

Name:	Felix Hartung Fishing Spoon
Patented:	August 8, 1939, patent #2,168,476 by Felix C. Hartung
Origin:	Chicago, Illinois
Size:	2¾" long
Material:	Steel and spring-steel
Value:	$40.00+

From patent text: "…when the spoon is drawn through the water various currents therearound and therethrough interfere and create a disturbance area effectively concealing the hooks."

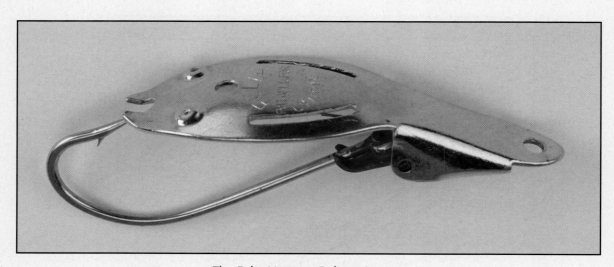

The Felix Hartung Fishing Spoon.

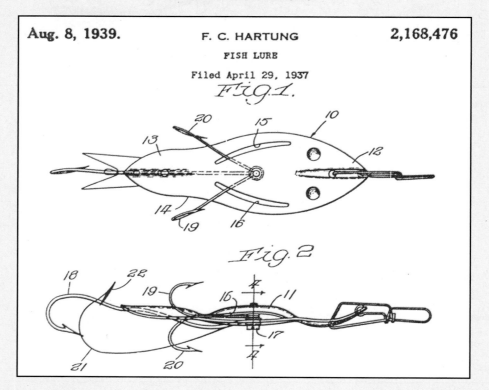

Name:	Hargrett's Cat's Paw
Patented:	May 14, 1940, patent #2,200,670 by Wilson W. Hargrett
Origin:	Wyandotte, Michigan
Size:	3¾" long
Material:	Wood, steel, and spring-steel
Value:	$50.00 – 75.00

The Cat's Paw was produced in at least seven color variations: red and white, frog pattern in light green and dark green, orange with red spots, black with yellow spots, black with orange spots, and can also be rarely found in black with red spots and no painted eyes.

From patent text: "…a fishing plug wherein a trigger plate is provided so that when the latter is pressed toward the plug, as would occur if a fish tried to bite the plug, the hooks swing outward and project laterally beyond the plug."

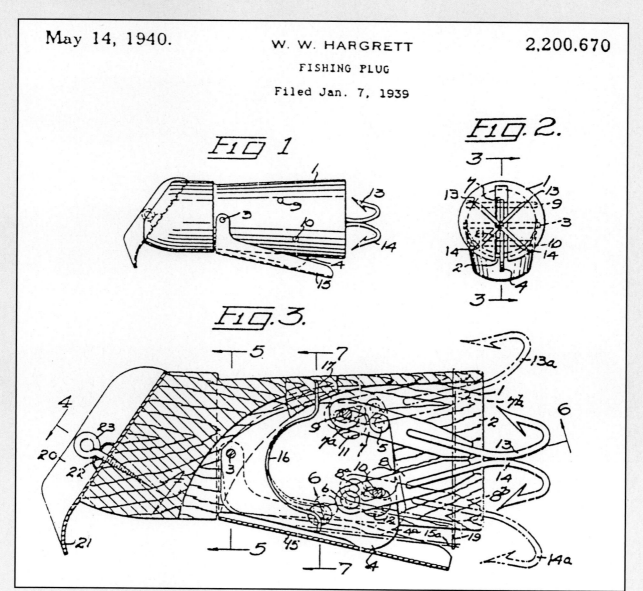

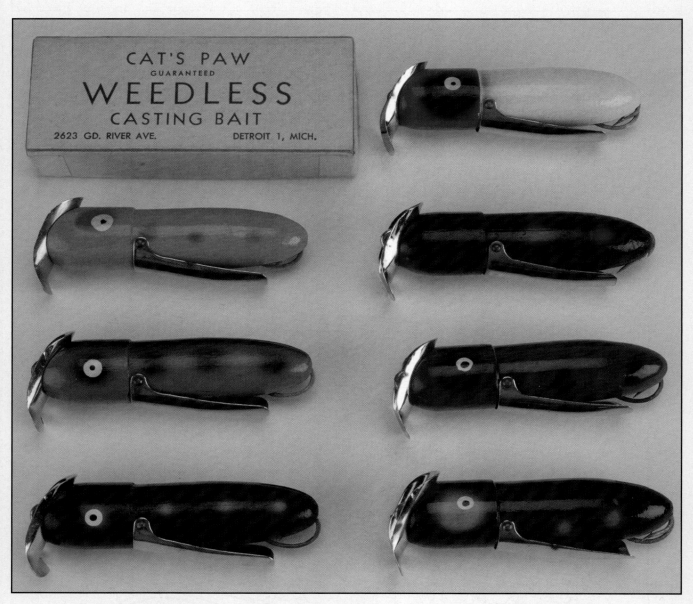

Seven Hargrett's Cat's Paws, showing the colors they can be found in, and a cardboard box.

Name:	Kridler Fish Lure
Patented:	September 12, 1944, patent #2,358,079 by Phillip W. Kridler
Origin:	Detroit, Michigan
Size:	3" long
Material:	Wood, steel, and spring-steel
Value:	$1,500.00+

From patent text: "...a lure which will attract fish by reason of its size, shape and general appearance and which, upon being struck by a fish will release a plurality of hooks out of its contour."

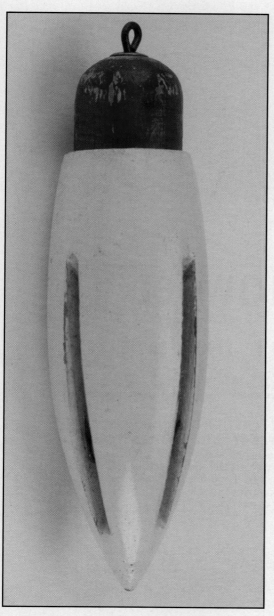

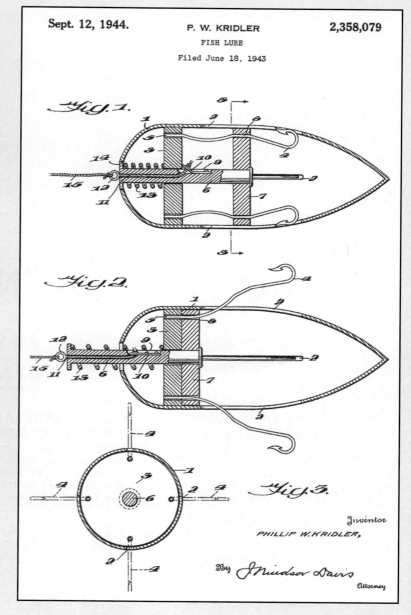

The Kridler Fish Lure. When the fish pulls on the lure, four hooks come out of the body.

Name:	Noweed Spoon
Patented:	Unknown, but probably. 1946 ad states "Pat. Pending."
Origin:	Manufactured by the Noweed Bait Company of Detroit, Michigan
Size:	3⅝" long, 1¼" across
Material:	Nickel or copper with spring-steel. May or may not have upper side painted red and white.
Value:	$400.00+

From advertisement: "Supreme in casting or trolling for bass — pike — walleyes and muskies. …No snags — as hooks are not exposed — till fish strikes."

Noweed Spoon and an advertisement that appeared in the July 1946 issue of Field & Stream magazine.

Spring-loaded Fishing Lures

Name:	The Weeder
Patented:	April 22, 1947, patent #2,419,295 by Phillip Slough
Origin:	Invented in Detroit, Michigan, and manufactured in Chicago, Illinois
Size:	3" long
Material:	First model has wooden body with steel and spring-steel, second model has plastic body.
Value:	First model, $50.00 – 75.00; second model, $25.00 – 50.00; metal spoon, $20.00 – 30.00

The wooden first model is known to have come in the following colors, with others possible:

XR1 — red head-white body
R1 — white head-red body
R2 — all red with white eyes with black center
R4 — red with small white dots
R5 — red with big white dots with black centers
R6 — red with big white dots with green centers
RW7 — one side red, one side white
Y8 — black top, yellow bottom
B8 — black body with yellow spots
S10 — all silver
G11 — all gold
O12 — orange with red stripes with green centers
FR-5 — frog pattern, green with big white spots with black centers
R13 — red body with big yellow dots with four small green dots within each yellow dot

The plastic second model was advertised in nine color combinations; but a clear plastic, an all red, and an all white are known to exist.

No. 1-RH — red head-white body
No. 2-RS — red and white stripe
No. 3-OD — orange dot

No. 4-FF — frog finish
No. 5-PF — pike finish
No. 6-YS — yellow scale
No. 7-PS — perch scale
No. 8-AS — aluminum scale
No. 9-BLS — black scale

Ideel Fish Lures, the company that made the Weeder, also made a metal spoon using the same mechanism, and called it the Ideel Weedless Spoon, which was advertised in three color combinations:

No. 1 ARS — red and white stripe
No. 2 BSF — silver finish
No. 3 CCF — copper finish

From patent text: "One of the hooks remains in fixed position at all times with reference to the body, whereas the other hook is movable to expose the points and the barbs of both hooks."

April 22, 1947.   P. SLOUGH   2,419,295

FISH LURE

Filed Aug. 13, 1945

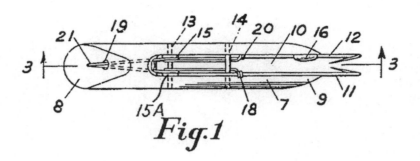

Fig.1

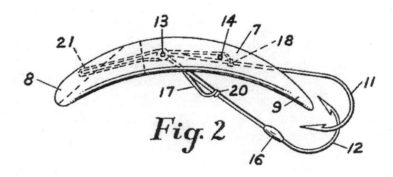

Fig. 2

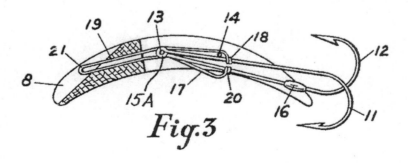

Fig.3

The Phillip Slough patent that shows the wooden version of the Weeder lure.

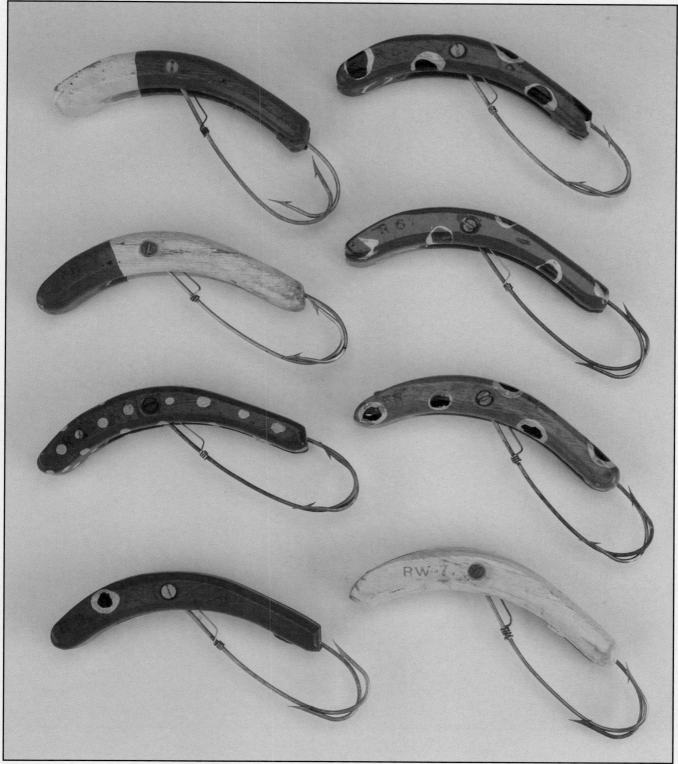

Eight different color combinations of the wooden Weeder.

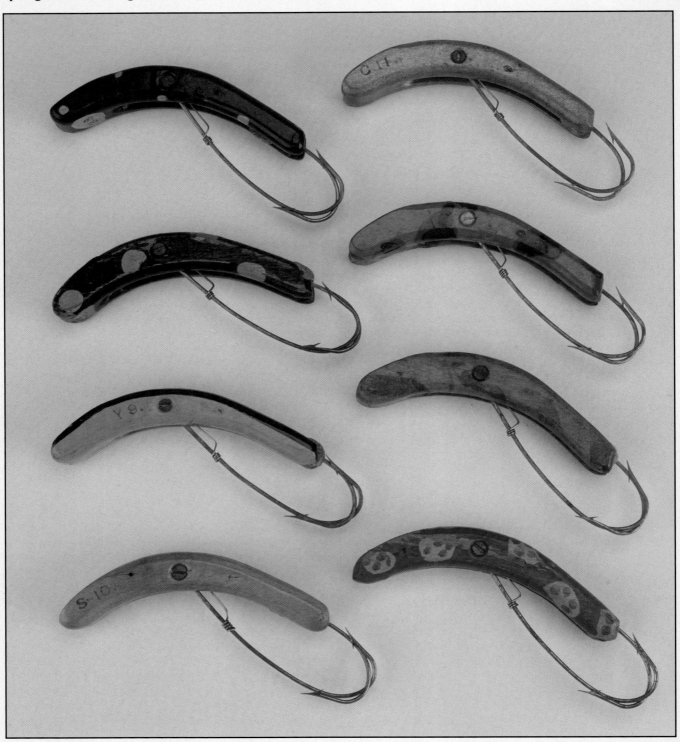

Eight different color combinations of the wooden Weeder.

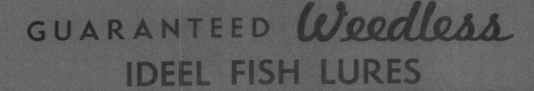

GUARANTEED *Weedless*
IDEEL FISH LURES

NEW! Revolutionary positive WEEDLESS LURES, terrific in their vicious action...they get the big ones in thick weeds, lily pads or around logs. Special PATENTED SPRING HOOK guards the main hook and positively prevents weeds or snags from catching. But when a fish strikes...bingo ...the guard hook flashes up and it's 2 hooks to 1 — he's hooked for the kill.

THE WEEDER
NEW! WEEDLESS! SENSATIONAL! VICIOUS ACTION!

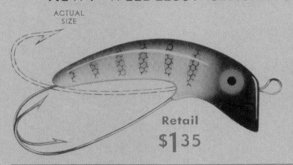

ACTUAL SIZE

Retail $1 35

Made of plastic. Rust proof hooks are moulded in lure . . . can't pull out. Patented weedless construction. Wt. ⅝ oz. Put up in flashy box with cellophane top. Nationally advertised. 9 attractive color combinations.

No. 1-RH	Red Head	No. 6-YS	Yellow Scale
No. 2-RS	Red & White Stripe	No. 7-PS	Perch Scale
No. 3-OD	Orange Dot	No. 8-AS	Aluminum Scale
No. 4-FF	Frog Finish	No. 9-BLS	Black Scale
No. 5-PF	Pike Finish		Retail Price $1.35

IDEEL WEEDLESS SPOON
Guaranteed NOT to Foul in Weeds, Snags, Lily Pads

Chrome plated, has wicked darting action, runs deep, rust proof hooks, patented weedless construction. Wt. ⅝ oz. Put up in flashy box with cellophane top. Nationally advertised.

No. 1ARS—Red & White Stripe
No. 2BSF—Silver Finish
No. 3CCF—Copper Finish
Retail Price $1.25

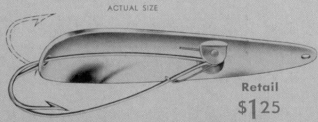

ACTUAL SIZE

Retail $1 25

IDEEL FISH LURES • 6934 South Stewart • Chicago 21, Illinois

Advertisement for the plastic version of the Weeder lure.

Boxes for the Weeder and the Ideel Spoon.

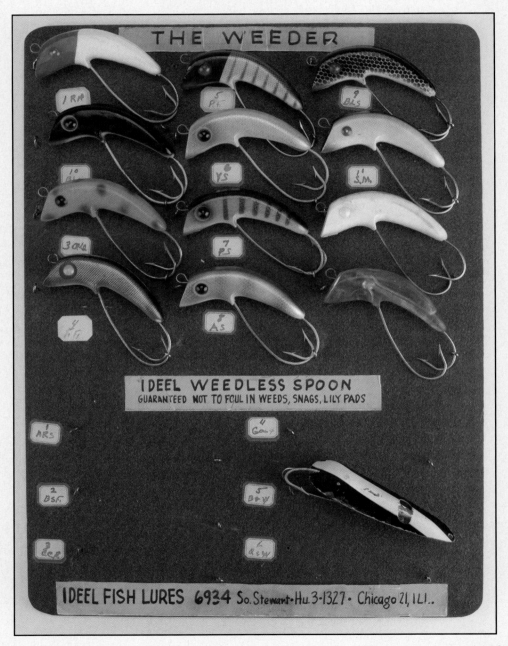

Counter display board that the plastic Weeder and the Ideel Weedless Spoon were sold from.

Name:	The Darto
Patented:	July 15, 1947, patent #2,424,096 by Francis Janchan
Origin:	Milwaukee, Wisconsin
Size:	3¼" long
Material:	Wood, steel and spring-steel
Value:	$30.00 – 50.00

This lure is known to have come with a red head and white body or all in black.

From patent text: "...a hook whose barbed hooked end is releasably held in retracted position within a recess provided in the underside of the tail end of the bait body...and a spring is provided to swing the hook upwardly...when released."

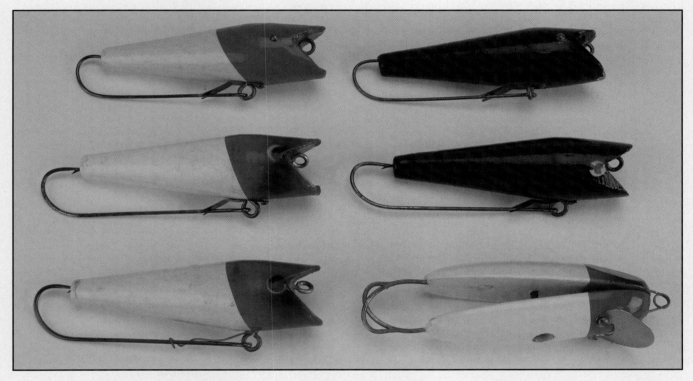

Five varieties of the Darto lure and a Weedo lure, bottom right. Both these lures were manufactured, very briefly, by the Johnson Brothers Co., Delta, Wisconsin.

Name:	The Weedo
Patented:	Unknown, but probably. Manufactured by the Johnson Brothers about 1947.
Origin:	Delta, Wisconsin
Size:	4" long
Material:	Wood, steel, and spring-steel
Value:	$40.00 – 60.00

This lure only came in red and white.

Name:	The Trigger Fish
Patented:	Unknown, but probably. Manufactured by the Davis Tackle Manufacturing Company about 1947.
Origin:	Detroit, Michigan
Size:	4" long when set, 5½" long when sprung
Material:	Plastic, aluminum, steel, and spring-steel
Value:	$100.00 – 200.00 each, when not broken. Add $100.00 when it is found with a nice box.

The Trigger Fish, a shooting lure, came in six color combinations, all of which are pictured on the box and numbered as such:

No. 10 — red body, white head and shield
No. 20 — white body, red head and shield
No. 30 — white body, black head and shield
No. 40 — black body, white head and shield
No. 50 — black body, red head and shield
No. 60 — red body, black head and shield, with the two red and white combinations being the most common. This lure is usually found broken.

From paper advertisement in box: "It is scientifically engineered and manufactured to close production tolerances heretofore unheard of in the fishing lure field."

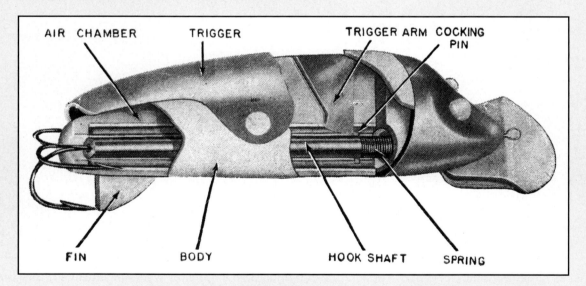

Illustration of the working parts of the Trigger Fish.

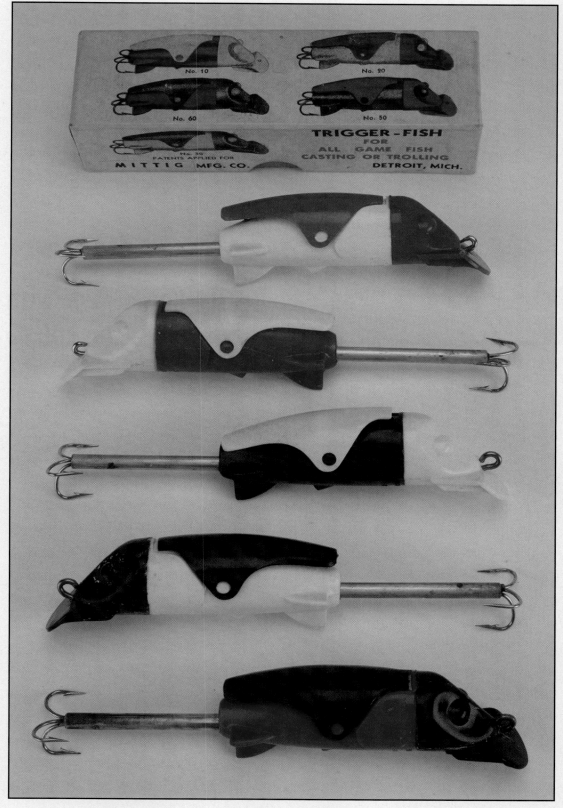

Five different color combinations of the Trigger Fish and an original box.

Name:	The Weed King
Patented:	Unknown, but probably. Manufactured by Sevdy Enterprises about 1950
Origin:	Worthington, Minnesota
Size:	5" long when set, 6¼" long when sprung
Material:	Wood, steel, and spring-steel
Value:	$100.00; double this when it is found in nice picture box.

This shooting lure was advertised in the paperwork in the box as "the greatest bait ever made for bass."

Illustration from the brochure that was included with the box.

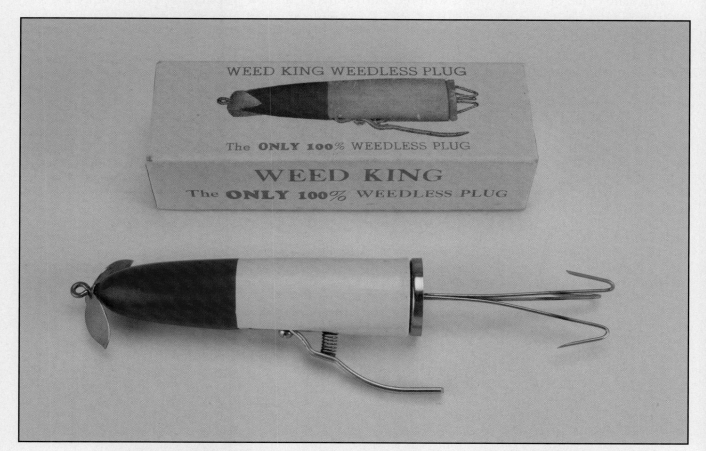

The Weed King lure and the box it came in. The lure is shown in the sprung position.

Name:	The Trip Lure
Patented:	June 13, 1950, patent #2,511,223 by William Sturcke
Origin:	West Englewood, New Jersey
Size:	4¼" long
Material:	Bakelite and brass with glass eyes
Value:	$100.00 – 200.00

Trip Lure came in several colors, with red and white being the most common. "TRIP-LURE" is stamped or painted on each lure.

From patent text: "…fish lure having a plurality of external hooks that may be set or cocked in a closed nested position without requiring the employment of especially designed weed guards or other unnecessary or disadvantageous locking means."

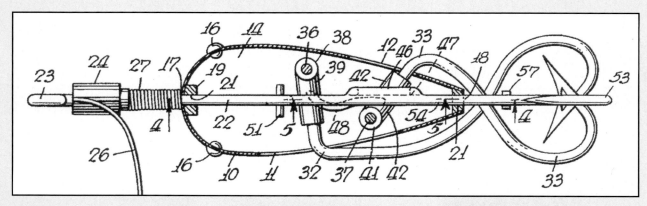

Illustration from the William Sturcke patent granted in 1950.

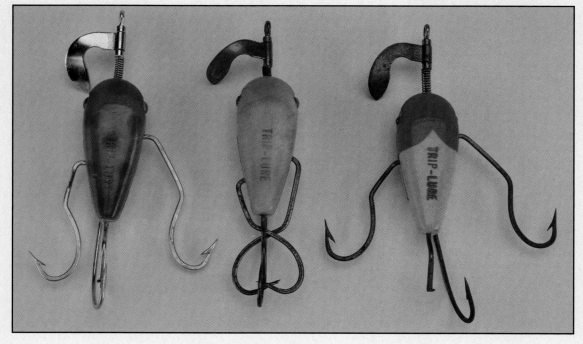

Three different color combinations of the Trip Lure.

Name:	Amspaugh Fish Lure
Patented:	August 1, 1950, patent #2,517,458 by Clarence A. Amspaugh
Origin:	Willoughby, Ohio
Size:	3½" set, 5¼" wide when sprung
Material:	Steel and spring-steel
Value:	$50.00

From patent text: "…weedless, safely transportable fish lure which is provided with expandable, spring type pointed arms."

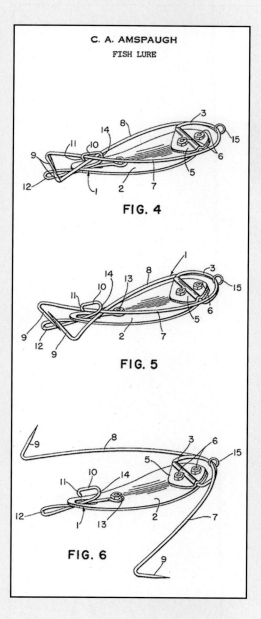

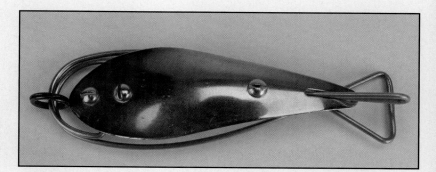

Amspaugh lure in the set position.

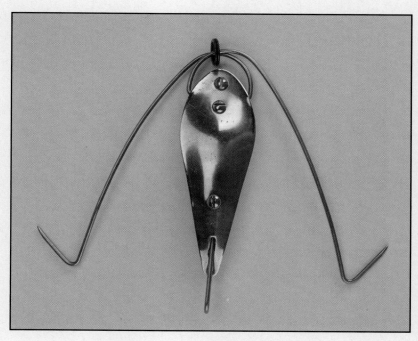

Amspaugh lure in the sprung position.

Name:	Peterson Spring Lure
Patented:	April 24, 1951, patent #2,550,376 by Erick B. J. Peterson
Origin:	Minneapolis, Minnesota
Size:	5" long when set, 7" when sprung
Material:	Steel and spring-steel
Value:	$300.00+

From patent text: "Once the fish mouths the hook sufficiently to unseat the arms from the frame the hooks will automatically be thrown out-wardly with considerable rapidity and force, thus making it impossible for the fish to shake loose."

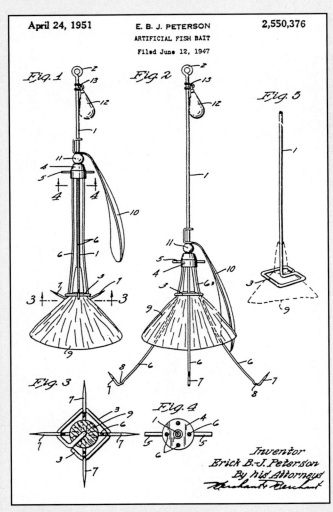

Peterson Spring Lure in sprung position.

Name:	Prentice Weedless Shooting Lure
Patented:	May 8, 1951, patent #2,552,113 by Thomas G. Prentice
Origin:	Detroit, Michigan
Size:	2¼" long wooden body
Material:	Wood, steel, and spring-steel
Value:	$1,000.00+; double this when it is found in a nice box.

From patent text: "a series of projections for ready engagement by the mouth of the fish in taking the bait so that the pull of the fish on the lure will quickly effect… to unlatch the extremity… on which the body is mounted."

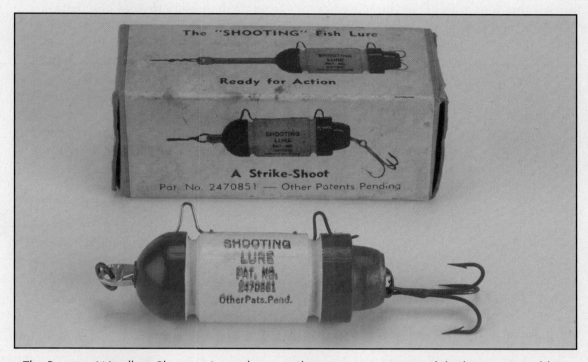

The Prentice Weedless Shooting Lure, shown in the sprung position, and the box it was sold in.

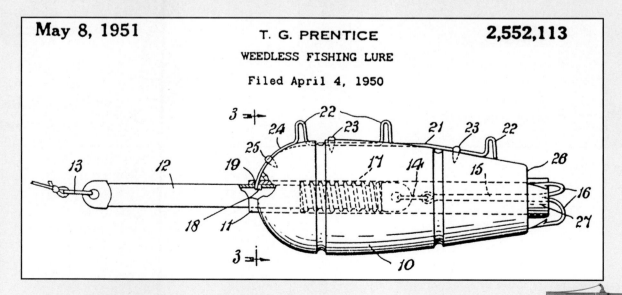

Name:	Anderson Minnow
Patented:	September 11, 1951, patent #2,567,310 by Carl R. Anderson
Origin:	Chicago, Illinois
Size:	4¼" long
Material:	Plastic, steel, and spring-steel
Value:	$75.00 – 100.00

The parchment advertisement that was included in the box for this lure stated that it was available in three color schemes, red-head, perch, and frog. It also states that this lure was illegal in Minnesota, Missouri, and Pennsylvania.

From patent text: "…having a spring actuated hook, which upon being released, by contact of the striking fish, is projected forcibly outward from the bait body to hook the fish."

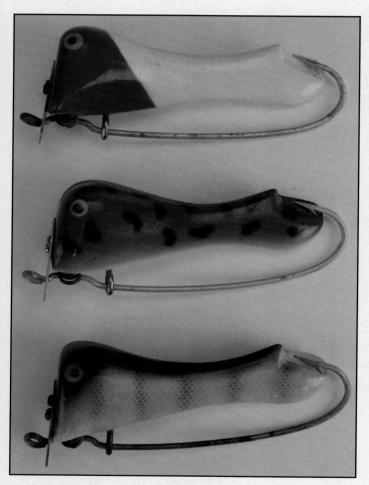

Three different color combinations of the Anderson Minnow.

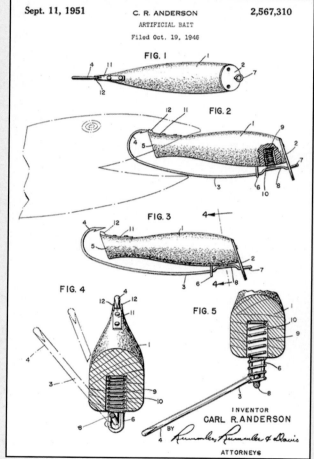

Name:	Acme Weedless Minnow
Patented:	September 25, 1951, patent #2,569,119 by Olaf Tallaksen
Origin:	Chicago, Illinois
Size:	3" long
Material:	Steel and spring-steel
Value:	$20.00

From patent text: "…a spoon with a rigid fish-hook which extends upwardly and is positioned between a pair of downwardly positioned spring actuated fishhooks."

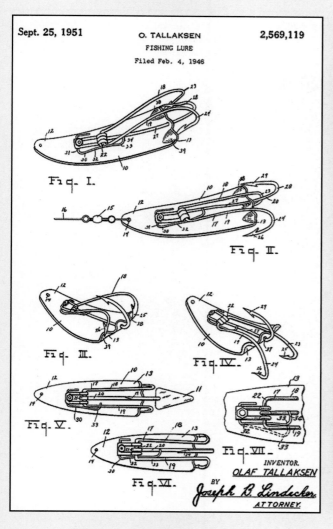

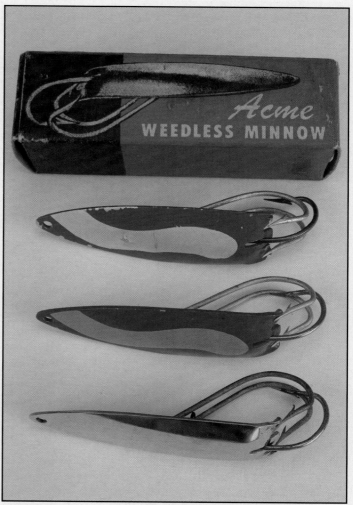

Three different Acme Weedless Minnows and the box a lure was sold in.

Name:	Borgen Weedless Casting Spoon
Patented:	April 20, 1954, patent #2,675,639 by Leif I. Borgen
Origin:	Chicago, Illinois
Size:	2¾" long
Material:	Steel and spring-steel
Value:	$20.00 – 30.00

From patent text: "…to be projected into engagement with the fish's jaws when the fish takes the lure in its mouth."

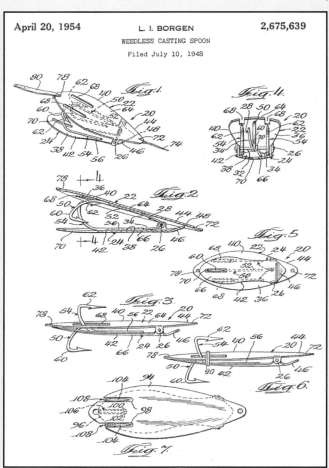

Three Borgen Weedless Casting Spoons and the plastic box a lure was sold in.

Name:	Babcock's Weedless Twin Lure
Patented:	Unknown, but probably. Manufactured by Babcock Manufacturing Company, about 1950s.
Origin:	Oak Harbor, Ohio
Size:	3½" long
Material:	Steel and spring-steel
Value:	$15.00 – 20.00; double this when it is found in a nice box.

Babcock's Weedless Twin Lure and the box it was sold in. The directions pictured below were included in the box.

YOU ARE NOW THE OWNER OF A
NEW *Babcock* WEEDLESS TWIN

FOLLOW THESE SIMPLE INSTRUCTIONS TO
GET MAXIMUM SATISFACTION AND SERVICE

Examine closely your lure as delivered in this package. Do not reverse the position of the hooks, as the lure will not function freely if you reverse their present position.

Do not retrieve too fast or too steady! Reel in slowly. Then stop for a split second, then repeat, etc.

Follow these directions when casting into the thickest of weeds. You'll land the grand-daddies—the ones you've tried for many times in the past—but instead lost your lure.

Babcock MANUFACTURING COMPANY
OAK HARBOR, OHIO

#111A-1-47   PRINTED IN U.S.A.

Name:	Winters Chippewa
Patented:	August 27, 1957, patent #2,803,916 by Emil O. Winter
Origin:	Milwaukee, Wisconsin
Size:	Three sizes, 2½", 2¾", and 3¼"
Material:	Nickel-plated or copper-plated steel and spring-steel
Value:	$20.00 – 30.00

From patent text: "…the movable hook moves upwardly through the body of the lure when the lure is struck by a fish."

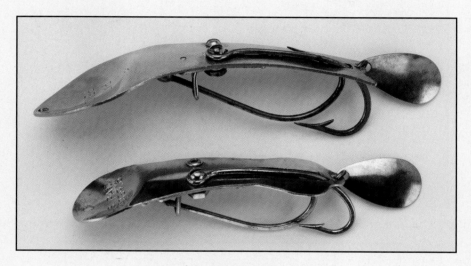

Two sizes of the Winters Chippewa Lure.

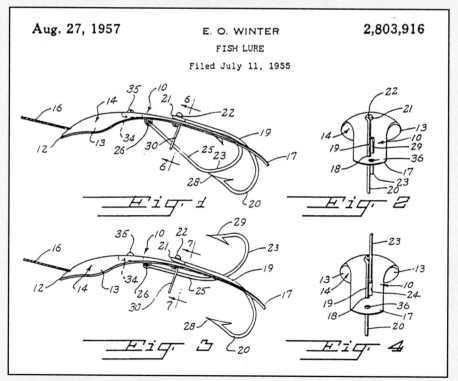

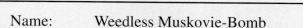

Name:	Weedless Muskovie-Bomb
Patented:	October 7, 1958, patent #2,854,778 by Samuel Polki
Origin:	Invented in Forest Park, Illinois; manufactured in Chicago, Illinois
Size:	4½" long
Material:	Plastic, steel and spring-steel
Value:	$75.00+, add $50.00 if in nice original box.

This lure came in three colors, black, yellow, or red.

From patent text: "...with dual trigger fins, positively retracting and extending hook means, and a molded trigger and hook-camming means which can be set or cocked."

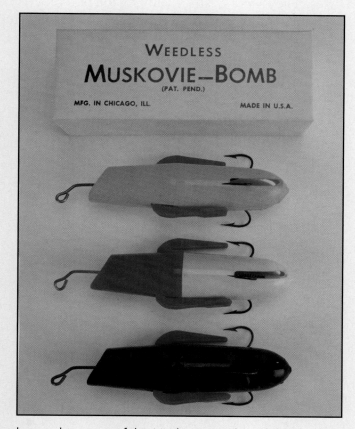

The three color combinations of the Muskovie-Bomb and the box the lure came in.

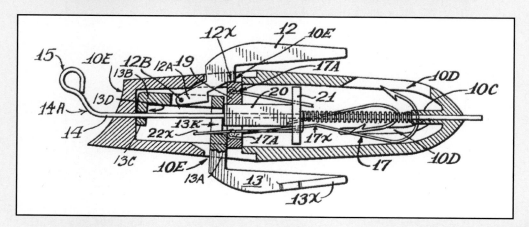

Name:	Got'cha! Also called the STA-KOT.
Patented:	February 28, 1961, patent #2,972,830 by Carl R. Sarnow
Origin:	Bakersfield, California
Size:	3" long and 4" long
Material:	Aluminum and steel
Value:	$10.00 – 20.00

The lure was originally called the STA-KOT and was stamped "Bakersfield, CAL." It was later sold as the Got'cha! and stamped "Reno, NV."

This lure came in two sizes. They were available in four colors: silver, gold, red, and blue. Any color other than silver is uncommon and will be worth much more.

From patent text: "This invention relates to a fishing spoon having gripping hooks which are normally enclosed in its body and are operated only by the pull of a fish on a trailing hook to grip opposite sides of the fish."

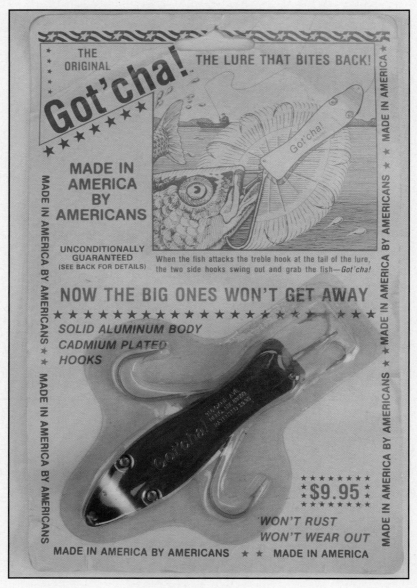

Got'cha! lure on card.

Name:	Weedless Wonder
Patented:	January 30, 1962, patent #3,018,582 by Martin T. Anderson
Origin:	Hope Valley, Rhode Island
Size:	3½" long in the set position; 4½" long when sprung
Material:	Wood, steel, and spring-steel
Value:	$50.00 – 75.00

This type of lure is referred to as a shooting lure, as it forcibly "shoots" the hooks down into the fish's throat.

The Weedless Wonder came in a variety of colors, and some lures had painted eyes and some did not.

From patent text: "…a trigger mechanism upon which the fish will initially bite to release the hooks quickly and to embed the hooks into the mouth of the fish."

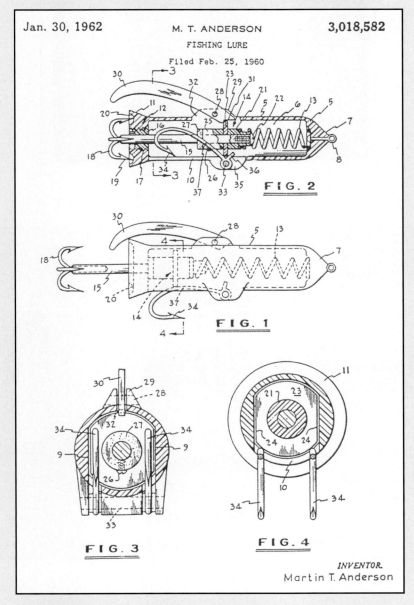

Weedless Wonder on an original card.

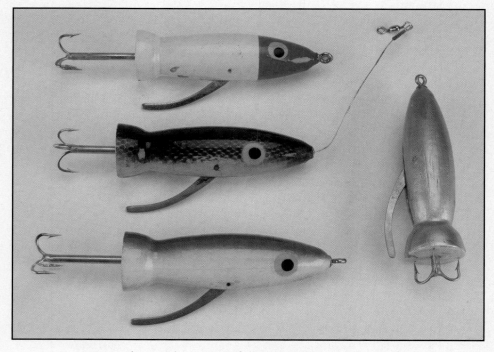

Four color combinations of the Weedless Wonder lure.

Name:	Ike Walton's Weedless Lure
Patented:	Unknown, but patent applied for in early 1960s by Leslie O. Walton
Origin:	Minneapolis, Minnesota
Size:	2½" to 6" long
Material:	Wood or metal bodies with brass, steel and spring-steel
Value:	$300.00+ each for spring-loaded folk art styles; common plastic version on green card about $50.00

These lures were hand-painted by Leslie Walton in a variety of various elaborately detailed patterns.

The inventor was a test pilot for experimental aircraft between 1940 and 1960, and after losing a leg in a 1940 crash, referred to himself as a "one-legged pilot."

These lures were never commercially marketed.

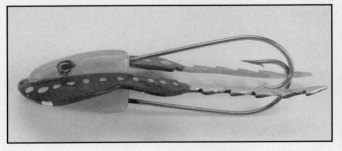
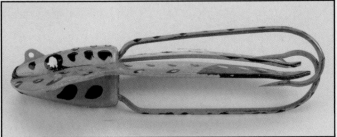

Five different Ike Walton Weedless Lures.

Name:	Myron Leffel Spring Lure
Patented:	September 21, 1976, patent #3,981,094 by Myron J. Leffel
Origin:	Marshfield, Wisconsin
Size:	7" long when set, 9" long when sprung
Material:	Wood, copper, steel, and spring-steel
Value:	$75.00 – 100.00

The lure was made in a variety of colors and color combinations, but in only one size, which would have to be considered musky size.

From patent text: "An artificial fishing bait having a body on which a jaw engaging hook is pivotally mounted for movement through substantially a 180 degree angle between a position adjacent the body and a position extending beyond a bait hook attached to the body."

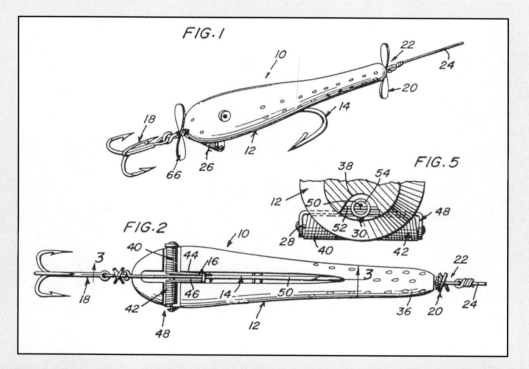

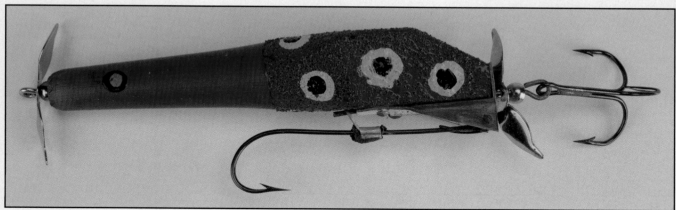

The Myron Leffel Spring Lure, which was named the "Go-Fur."

Glossary

Coil spring — A spring, formed from any gauge of spring-wire, that has a coil formed into it to create an eye. A coil spring can have either one or more loops, or revolutions, to it. An example of a coil spring with one loop would be a common safety pin. An example of a coil spring with multiple loops would be the spring found on a common mousetrap.

Contractile helical spring — A spring whose power is derived from its contracting. An example of this would be the spring found on a common screen door.

Dog — From *Merrian-Webster's Pocket Dictionary*: "a mechanical device for holding something." When used in reference to a trap, as in this book, a dog is the piece of the trap that is by various means inserted into a notch or catch or slot, serving to prevent the release of the tension on the spring or springs and thus setting the trap. When a dog becomes disengaged from its notch or catch or slot, the spring tension is released and the trap is sprung. Dogs can go by other names, such as latches, catches, triggers, tongues or clickets.

Dogless — A trap that does not require a dog in order to be set.

Expansive helical spring — A spring whose power is derived from its expandability. An example of this would be the spring found in a common ballpoint pen.

Flat spring — A spring in the shape of a flat bar. An example of this would be the common leaf springs on a car.

Japanned — When used as an adjective, describes any item that has undergone the japanning process.

Japanning — The process by which surfaces of metal, wood, or glass have applied to them a durable, lustrous finish of several layers of varnish. The varnishes used to obtain a black japan consist of asphaltum with some amount of gum anim dissolved in linseed oil and thinned with turpentine. These layers of varnish are baked on by the use of smoke in heated ovens. This process is intermediate between painting and enameling and produces a surface that is durable and not easily affected by moisture, heat, or other influences.

Killer trap — A trap that is designed to pierce or grasp its victim by the head, neck, or body and kill it. While death may not be instantaneous, most victims die within a comparatively short period of time.

Line-actuated — A fish trap designed so that it is sprung when pressure is applied at the line-tie.

Line-tie — The point at which the line holding the hook or trap is tied.

Striking hook — Also referred to as a striking arm, gaff arm, striking jaw, or grab hook. An auxiliary piece of metal, designed to strike the fish after he pulls on the bait hook. This piece can have more than one point to it, may be barbed or barbless, and may work in conjunction with other striking hooks.

Index

COLLECTOR BOOKS
informing today's collector

www.collectorbooks.com

For over two decades we have been keeping collectors informed on trends and values
in all fields of antiques and collectibles.

FISHING LURES, GUNS & KNIVES

6469	Big Book of **Pocket Knives**, 2nd Ed., Stewart & Ritchie	.19.95
6225	Captain John's **Fishing Tackle** Price Guide, Kolbeck & Lewis	.19.95
5355	**Cattaraugus** Cutlery Co., Stewart & Ritchie	.19.95
5906	Collector's Encyclopedia of **Creek Chub Lures** & Collectibles, 2nd Ed., Smith	.29.95
5929	Commercial **Fish Decoys**, Baron	.29.95
5683	**Fishing Lure** Collectibles, Vol. 1, Murphy/Edmisten	.29.95
6141	**Fishing Lure** Collectibles, Vol. 2, Murphy	.29.95
5912	The **Heddon** Legacy – A Century of Classic Lures, Roberts/Pavey	.29.95
6028	**Modern Fishing Lure** Collectibles, Vol. 1, Lewis	.24.95
6131	**Modern Fishing Lure** Collectibles Vol. 2, Lewis	.24.95
6132	**Modern Guns**, 14th Ed., Quertermous	.14.95
5603	19th Century **Fishing Lures**, Carter	.29.95
5166	Std. Gde. to **Razors**, 2nd Ed., Ritchie/Stewart	.9.95
6031	Standard **Knife** Collector's Guide, 4th Ed., Ritchie/Stewart	.14.95

ARTIFACTS, TOOLS & PRIMITIVES

1868	**Antique Tools**, Our American Heritage, McNerney	.9.95
1426	**Arrowheads & Projectile Points**, Hothem	.7.95
6021	**Arrowheads** of the Central Great Plains, Fox	.19.95
5362	Collector's Guide to **Keen Kutter Cutlery Tools**, Heuring	.19.95
4943	Field Gde. to **Flint Arrowheads & Knives** of N. Amer. Indian, Tully	.9.95
1668	**Flint Blades & Projectile Points**, Tully	.24.95
2279	**Indian Artifacts** of the Midwest, Book I, Hothem	.14.95
3885	**Indian Artifacts** of the Midwest, Book II, Hothem	.16.95
4870	**Indian Artifacts** of the Midwest, Book III, Hothem	.18.95
5685	**Indian Artifacts** of the Midwest, Book IV, Hothem	.19.95
6130	**Indian Trade Relics**, Hothem	.29.95
2164	**Primitives**, Our American Heritage, McNerney	.9.95
1759	**Primitives**, Our American Heritage, Series II, McNerney	.14.95

TOYS & CHARACTER COLLECTIBLES

2333	Antique & Collectible **Marbles**, 3rd Ed., Grist	.9.95
5900	Collector's Guide to **Battery Toys**, 2nd Ed., Hultzman	.24.95
5150	**Cartoon Toys** & Collectibles, Longest	.19.95
5038	Collector's Guide to **Diecast Toys** & Scale Models, 2nd Ed., Johnson	.19.95

5169	Collector's Guide to **T.V. Toys** & Memorabilia, 1960s & 1970s, 2nd Ed., Davis/Morgan	.24.95
6471	Collector's Guide to **Tootsietoys**, 3rd Ed., Richter	.24.95
4945	**G-Men & FBI Toys** & Collectibles, Whitworth	.18.95
5593	Grist's Big Book of **Marbles**, 2nd Ed.	.24.95
3970	Grist's Machine-Made & Contemporary **Marbles**, 2nd Ed.	.9.95
6633	**Hot Wheels**, the Ultimate Redline Guide, 2nd Ed., Clark/Wicker	29.95
6230	**Hot Wheels**, the Ultimate Redline Guide, Vol. 2, Clark/Wicker	.24.95
4950	**Lone Ranger** Collector's Reference & Value Guide, Felbinger.	18.95
6466	**Matchbox Toys**, 1947 – 1998, 4th Ed., Johnson	.24.95
5830	**McDonald's** Collectibles, 2nd Ed., Henriques/DuVall	.24.95
1540	**Modern Toys**, 1930 – 1980, Baker	.19.95
5619	**Roy Rogers and Dale Evans** Toys & Memorabilia, Coyle	.24.95
6237	**Rubber Toy Vehicles**, Leopard	.19.95
6340	Schroeder's Collectible **Toys**, Antique to Modern Price Guide, 9th Ed.	.17.95
6239	**Star Wars** Super Collector's Wish Book, 2nd Ed., Carlton	.29.95
5908	**Toy Car** Collector's Guide, Johnson	.19.95

FURNITURE

3716	American **Oak** Furniture, Book II, McNerney	.12.95
6012	**Antique Furniture** — A Basic Primer on Furniture	.12.95
1118	Antique **Oak** Furniture, Hill	.7.95
3720	Collector's Encyclopedia of **American** Furniture, Vol. III, 18th & 19th Century Furniture, Swedberg	.24.95
6474	Collector's Guide to **Wallace Nutting** Furniture, Ivankovich	.19.95
5359	Early **American Furniture**, A Practical Guide for Collectors, Obbard	.12.95
3906	**Heywood-Wakefield** Modern Furniture, Rouland	.18.95
6338	**Roycroft** Furniture & Collectibles, Koon	.24.95
6343	**Stickley Brothers** Furniture, Koon	.24.95
1885	**Victorian** Furniture, Our American Heritage, McNerney	.9.95
3829	**Victorian** Furniture, Our American Heritage, Book II, McNerney	.9.95

PAPER COLLECTIBLES & BOOKS

5902	**Boys' & Girls' Book Series**, Jones	.19.95
5153	Collector's Guide to **Children's Books**, Vol. II, Jones	.19.95
1441	Collector's Guide to **Post Cards**, Wood	.9.95
5031	Collector's Guide to **Early 20th Century American Prints**, Ivankovich	.19.95

4864	Collector's Guide to **Wallace Nutting** Pictures, Ivankovich	.18.95
2081	Guide to Collecting **Cookbooks**, Allen	.14.95
6234	**Old Magazines**, Clear	.19.95
2080	Price Guide to **Cookbooks** & Recipe Leaflets, Dickinson	.9.95
3973	**Sheet Music** Reference & Price Gde., 2nd Ed., Guiheen/Pafik	.19.95
6041	**Vintage Postcards** for the Holidays, Reed	.24.95

OTHER COLLECTIBLES

5916	**Advertising Paperweights**, Holiner/Kammerman	.24.95
5838	**Advertising Thermometers**, Merritt	.16.95
5814	Antique **Brass & Copper**, Gaston	.24.95
5898	Antique & Contemporary **Advertising Memorabilia**, 2nd Edition, Summers	.24.95
1880	Antique **Iron**, McNerney	.9.95
3872	Antique **Tins**, Dodge	.24.95
5030	Antique **Tins**, Book II, Dodge	.29.95
5251	Antique **Tins**, Book III, Dodge	.29.95
4845	Ant. **Typewriters** & Office Collectibles, Rehr	.19.95
4935	W.F. Cody – **Buffalo Bill** Collector's Guide, Wojtowicz	.24.95
6345	**Business & Tax Guide** for Antiques & Collectibles, Kelly	.14.95
5151	**Celluloid**, Collector's Ref. & Val. Gde., Lauer/Robinson	.24.95
5152	**Celluloid Treasures** of the Vict. Era, VanPatten/Williams	.24.95
3718	Collectible **Aluminum**, Grist	.16.95
6342	Collectible **Soda Pop** Memorabilia, Summers	.24.95
5060	Collectible **Souvenir Spoons**, Book I, Bednersh	.19.95
5676	Collectible **Souvenir Spoons**, Book II, Bednersh	.29.95
5666	Collector's Encyclopedia of **Granite Ware**, Book 2, Greguire	.29.95
6468	Collector's Ency. of **Pendant & Pocket Watches**, Bell	.24.95
5836	Collector's Gde. to **Antique Radios**, 5th Ed., Slusser/Radio Daze	.19.95
4857	Collector's Guide to **Art Deco**, 2nd Ed., Gaston	.17.95
5820	Collector's Guide to **Glass Banks**, Reynolds	.24.95
4736	Collector's Guide to **Electric Fans**, Witt	.16.95
3966	Collector's Guide to **Inkwells**, Badders	.18.95
4947	Collector's Guide to **Inkwells**, Book II, Badders	.19.95

5681	Collector's Guide to **Lunchboxes**, White	.19.95
5836	Collector's Guide to Antique **Radios**, 5th Ed., Slusser	.19.95
5278	Collector's Guide to Vintage **Televisions**, Durbal/Bubenheimer	.15.95
6475	Complete Price Guide to **Watches**, No. 24, Shugert/Engle/Gilbert	.29.95
5145	Encyclopedia of **Advertising Tins**, Vol. II, Zimmerman	.24.95
6328	**Flea Market Trader**, 14th Edition, Huxford	.12.95
5918	Florence's Big Book of **Salt & Pepper** Shakers	.24.95
6458	**Fountain Pens**, Past & Present, 2nd Ed., Erano	.24.95
6459	**Garage Sale** & Flea Market Annual, 12th Edition, Huxford	.19.95
3819	**General Store Collectibles**, Wilson	.24.95
5044	**General Store Collectibles**, Vol. II, Wilson	.24.95
2216	**Kitchen Antiques**, 1790 – 1940, McNerney	.14.95
5991	**Lighting Devices** and Accessories of the 17th – 19th Centuries, Hamper	.9.95
2109	Personal **Antique** Record Book	.4.95
1301	Personal **Doll** Inventory	.4.95
6104	**Quilt Art** 2004 Engagement Calendar	.9.95
5835	**Racing Collectibles**, Racing Collector's Price Guide	.19.95
2026	**Railroad** Collectibles, 4th Ed., Baker	.14.95
3443	**Salt & Pepper Shakers** IV, Guarnaccia	.18.95
6339	**Schroeder's Antiques** Price Guide, 22nd Edition	.14.95
5007	**Silverplated Flatware**, Revised 4th Ed., Hagan	.18.95
6138	Standard **Antique Clock** Value Guide, Wescot	.19.95
5058	Std. Encyclopedia of **American Silverplate**, Bones/Fisher	.24.95
6139	Summers' Gde. to **Coca-Cola**, 4th Ed	.24.95
6324	Summers' Pocket Gde. to **Coca-Cola**, 4th Ed.	.12.95
5057	Treasury of **Scottie Dog** Collectibles, Vol. I, Davis/Baugh	.19.95
5369	Treasury of **Scottie Dog** Collectibles, Vol. II, Davis/Baugh	.19.95
5837	Treasury of **Scottie Dog** Collectibles, Vol. III, Davis/Baugh	.24.95
5144	Value Guide to **Advertising Memorabilia**, 2nd Ed., Summers	.19.95
3977	Value Guide. to **Gas Station** Memorabilia, Summers/Priddy	.24.95
4877	**Vintage Bar Ware**, Visakay	.24.95
5999	**Wilderness Survivor's Guide**, Hamper	.12.95

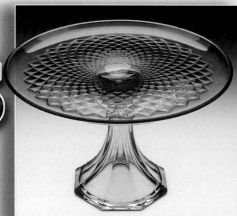
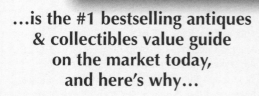